The Origins
of Mathematical
Knowledge
in Childhood

Catherine Sophian
University of Hawaii

LEA Lawrence Erlbaum Associates
Taylor & Francis Group

New York   London

STUDIES IN MATHEMATICAL THINKING AND LEARNING
Alan H. Schoenfeld, Series Editor

For additional information on titles in the Studies in Mathematical Thinking and Learning series visit www.routledge.com

Cover design by Kathryn Houghtaling Lacey.

Cover art: Photo © Bert Myers 2000. Photograph courtesy of Bert Myers, B. Myers Fine Art Photography, www.bymyersphoto.com

Lawrence Erlbaum Associates
Taylor & Francis Group
270 Madison Avenue
New York, NY 10016

Lawrence Erlbaum Associates
Taylor & Francis Group
2 Park Square
Milton Park, Abingdon
Oxon OX14 4RN

© 2007 by Catherine Sophian
Lawrence Erlbaum Associates is an imprint of Taylor & Francis Group, an Informa business

Printed in the United States of America on acid-free paper
10 9 8 7 6 5 4 3 2 1

International Standard Book Number-13: 978-0-8058-5758-0 (Hardcover)

Library of Congress Cataloging-in-Publication Data

The origins of mathematical knowledge in the childhood / Catherine Sophian.
    p. cm. -- (Studies in mathematical thinking and learning)
  Includes bibliographical references and index.
  ISBN 978-0-8058-5758-0 -- 0-8058-5758-3 (cloth : alk. paper)
  ISBN 978-1-4106-1648-7 -- 1-4106-1648-7 (e book)
  1. Mathmatics--Study and teaching (Elementary). 2. Arithmetic--Study and teaching (Early childhood). 3. Cognitive learning theory. 4. Concept learning. I. Title.

QA135.6.S628 2007
372.701'9--dc22
                        2006023683

Visit the Taylor & Francis Web site at
http://www.taylorandfrancis.com

July 31, 2007

To the children of the first Measure Up cohort,
with gratitude for all I learned from them:

Courtney,
Elim,
Jackie,
Jensen,
Kevala,
Macy,
Makenzie,
Michael,
Reed,
and
Richard.

Contents

Preface

Writing this book has been an exciting undertaking for me, as it gave me the opportunity to fully develop and articulate a perspective on mathematics development and learning that I arrived at piecemeal, over many years, in thinking about specific research topics such as the development of children's counting, how children come to understand many-to-one correspondences, and the persisting confusions students have about fraction magnitudes. I am grateful to Henry Wellman for first suggesting that I present my research and my ideas in book form, and for the serendipitous confluence of that suggestion with a series of informal conversions with Chris Donlan that helped me to realize that I did have something important to say.

It is my greatest hope that this book will bring about a shift in perspective in both the developmental psychology of mathematical cognition and the field of mathematics education, a shift that brings the two fields into greater confluence with one another. Developmental psychology has contributed a rich body of knowledge about young children's thinking about quantities and the beginnings of counting, but it is largely silent about all the developments that follow the child's entry to elementary school. It is as if we believe that school learning replaces development, so that once schooling has begun there is nothing more to learn about development. Mathematics education, on the other hand, has contributed rich analyses of what is entailed in learning and understanding school topics such as arithmetic word problems, place value notation, and rational numbers, but it makes less reference than I believe it profitably could to the knowledge developmental psychology is garnering about children's cognition and how it develops—in part because the theoretical perspectives that have been most prominent in developmental work are not as informative about instructional issues as the alternative perspective that I articulate in this book.

An important historical antecedent for the kind of confluence between developmental psychology and mathematics education that I envision is the work of a small group of Russian psychologists and educators several decades ago that resulted in a curriculum known today as the El'konin-Davydov curriculum. My own work owes a substantial intellectual debt to theirs. I particularly acknowledge the strong impact on my thinking of a seminal paper by Gal'perin and Georgiev on the concept of unit, and of a series of papers by V. V. Davydov that represent the thinking behind the El'konin-Davydov curriculum. The most fundamental idea I have derived from those papers is the idea that mathematical thinking begins, not with counting, but with comparisons between quantities, in particular the identification of equality and inequality relationships. The assumption that mathematical thinking begins with counting pervades both developmental theorizing and early instructional practices, but has seldom been systematically juxtaposed with other possibilities.

The alternative view that comparisons between quantities are the starting point for mathematical thinking has far-reaching implications both for developmental theorizing and for a variety of instructional issues. Although my ideas are very much compatible with the Russian work, the particular claims I make about the ramifications for developmental theory of tracing the origins of mathematical thinking to comparisons between quantities rather than to counting, and also about instructional ramifications of recognizing the importance of the concept of unit, are mostly my own, shaped, of course, by the ideas and research findings of many others.

An important influence on the development of my thinking about both developmental and instructional issues related to mathematics learning was the opportunity to interact closely with Barbara Dougherty and her colleagues at the Curriculum Research and Development Group at the University of Hawaii as they began their work on an innovative elementary mathematics curriculum called Measure Up. Although not a direct translation of the El'konin-Davydov curriculum, the Measure Up curriculum does adhere closely to the conceptual progression that characterizes that curriculum. I am extremely fortunate that, through my contact with this project, I had the opportunity to become much more closely acquainted with the Russian writings than previously, to learn about the current state of that work in Russia, and most importantly, to observe the first cohort of children learning first-grade mathematics in the Measure Up program. That experience was invaluable for enriching my understanding of young children's mathematical thinking. I am deeply grateful to the children who participated in those classes, and also to the teachers and staff who made me welcome there. I am also grateful to Barbara Dougherty for including me more broadly in staff meetings, professional conferences, and working groups through which I was able to gain a much more thorough understanding of the El'konin-Davydov curriculum and the ideas behind it.

One other individual whose contributions I'd particularly like to acknowledge is Dan Berch. Dan patiently and thoroughly read each and every chapter as I completed it, giving me a sense of an audience that sustained me through the long-term writing effort. In addition, he often brought to my attention additional research papers that enriched my treatment of a number of topics, and he always offered kind and at the same time penetrating thoughts about the ideas I presented and the way I expressed them. If any lack of clarity, errors, and omissions remain, they are, of course, solely my responsibility.

Chapter 1

Cognitive Development
and Mathematics Learning

Questions about the origins of mathematical knowledge and how that knowledge changes over childhood are central to both the field of cognitive development and that of mathematics education. Developmental psychologists have long been interested in questions about the origins of mathematical knowledge and its relation to other aspects of cognitive development. Nevertheless, they have seldom investigated children's knowledge about the mathematical topics taught in school, other than simple addition and subtraction. Mathematics education researchers, conversely, have given a great deal of attention to school topics and to alternative methods of instruction in those topics, but have seldom considered their relation to the kinds of mathematical thinking children engage in prior to receiving any formal schooling. A basic premise of this book is that theoretical and empirical progress in both fields will benefit greatly from integration and synthesis of their respective findings and analytic perspectives.

The centrality of research on children's mathematical thinking to theoretical accounts of cognitive development dates back to the work of Piaget (e.g., 1970), who used the term *logico-mathematical knowledge* to encompass a wide range of conceptual knowledge, including knowledge about conservation, class inclusion, seriating, transitivity, and spatial perspective-taking. Piaget held that, notwithstanding the apparent diversity of these concepts, they are linked developmentally in that all of them depend on the construction of a new kind of logical reasoning—concrete operational thought—that allows children to coordinate different aspects of a situation or event so as to understand the relations between them. Likewise, a further logical advance occurs several years later—the emergence of formal operational thought—bringing

1

with it such cognitive abilities as combinatorial reasoning, counterfactual inference, and an understanding of proportionality.

Contemporary discussions of cognitive development diverge from Piaget's in that knowledge acquisition processes are thought to be, to a large degree, domain-specific (cf. Hirschfeld & Gelman, 1994; Kail, 2004), and hence to differ across different kinds of content. Nevertheless, the logico-mathematical tasks that figured prominently in Piaget's work remain of great interest today as researchers endeavor to characterize the conceptual knowledge of very young children (e.g., R. Gelman, 1982) and the nature of developmental change (e.g., Siegler, 1995; cf. Sophian, 1997). Moreover, within accounts of domain-specific development, knowledge about numbers has been posited to be one of the "core" domains of cognitive development (R. Gelman, 1991). Children's counting, a form of mathematical knowledge that Piaget did not study in depth, has been of particular interest from this perspective as an indication that children possess substantial mathematical knowledge even in the first years of life.

A consequence of the tendency of developmental researchers to focus almost entirely on aspects of mathematical knowledge that are acquired before children begin to participate in formal schooling is that issues surrounding the teaching and learning of mathematics in school are seldom examined from a developmental perspective. An important exception to this generalization, however, is the work of the Russian psychologist and educator, V. V. Davydov (e.g., 1975a), who drew together developmental, instructional, and mathematical analyses as the foundation for the development of mathematics curricula. Although Davydov's ideas remain important today, his work is now several decades old, and research on children's mathematical thinking and learning has expanded greatly in the meantime. Unfortunately, advances within both developmental psychology and mathematics education are once again proceeding largely without regard to those in the other field, so that the need for integration is again great.

A major goal of this book is to examine issues concerning the teaching and learning of mathematics (traditionally the purview of the field of mathematics education) from a developmental perspective. In doing so, my major concern is with the issue of how the knowledge children acquire early in childhood affects their ability to grasp the mathematical material to which they are introduced later. In short, I believe that the integration of a developmental perspective into research on mathematics education can add a valuable long-term perspective that is often absent because instructional research tends to focus on knowledge acquisition within a single school year (or less).

At the same time, I hope this book will also demonstrate to developmentalists that they have much to learn from research in mathematics education. Developmental psychology is fundamentally concerned with how knowledge develops, and in addressing that point, it cannot ignore the ways in which instructional practices may affect children's knowledge.

TWO PERSPECTIVES ON THE DEVELOPMENT OF MATHEMATICAL KNOWLEDGE IN CHILDHOOD

Most developmental research on children's mathematical thinking begins with the premise that counting, or some form of determining the numerical values of discrete quantities, is the foundation for much of children's developing knowledge about mathematics. Several theoretical accounts (e.g., R. Gelman, 1991, 1998; Wynn, 1992a) have posited an innate counting mechanism that enables infants to detect the numerical properties of collections of pictures or objects. Others (e.g., Klahr & Wallace, 1976) have held that infants initially have only a very limited, perceptually based mechanism for distinguishing among sets of one, two, or three, but this mechanism has still been construed as foundational to the development of numerical concepts.

A contrasting position holds that what is most fundamental for mathematical development is not counting or other mechanisms for apprehending numerosity, but rather basic ideas about relations between quantities—in particular the ideas of *equality*, *less than*, and *greater than* (Davydov, 1975a). These ideas apply to continuous quantities as much as to numerical (discrete) ones; thus this perspective holds that the acquisition of numerical concepts has important foundations in prenumerical forms of thinking about quantities. As we will see, this alternative view leads to very different ideas about how best to structure instruction in mathematics.

In order to clarify the contrast between these two perspectives, the concept of *number* needs to be differentiated from that of *quantity*. In the senses most pertinent to the present discussion, *Webster's New World Dictionary* (Neufeldt & Guralnik, 1994) defines number as "a symbol or word, or a group of either of these, showing how many or which one in a series"; and quantity as "an amount" or, more informatively, "that property of anything which can be determined by measurement." A critical point of contrast in these definitions is ontological; numbers exist only as symbols whereas quantities are properties of things that exist in the physical world. Thus, in counting, we start with a physical quantity, normally a discrete one, and we assign a series of numbers to its elements to arrive at a number that represents the quantity in its entirety. Numbers, then, are not physically present in collections of objects but rather are a product of our mental representations of those collections. This point becomes clear when we consider collections of things that can be counted in alternative ways. For instance, a collection of socks might be counted as six individual socks or as three pairs of socks. Clearly, which numerical value we get is a function of how we represent the physical materials.

What makes the distinction between numbers (symbolic entities) and quantities (physical entities) difficult is that we often use the label *number* for the physical property that we measure by counting; thus we say a bouquet consists of a number of flowers. More technically, however, the numerical properties of collections are termed *numerosities* and distinguishing that term from number in its symbolic sense will help to keep the relation between numbers and quantities clear. In brief, *quantities* are physical properties of things that we can measure; and numbers are symbols used to represent the measured values of quantities. Note, though, that measurement does not have to involve the use of number; it can be as simple as inserting a stick into two holes in order to decide which one is deeper (Bryant & Kopytynska, 1976). Therefore, while counting (other than "rote counting," or the recitation of counting words without relating them to objects) presupposes a quantity (specifically, a numerosity) that will be represented by the number obtained by counting, quantity comparison does not presuppose number.

The Position That Counting is Foundational

The counting-based position is most explicit in theories that posit some kind of innate counting mechanism as the starting point for development (R. Gelman, 1991, 1998; Wynn, 1992c), but it is not restricted to those theories. For instance, some theories that do not posit an innate counting mechanism instead attribute an important role to *subitizing* (Klahr & Wallace, 1976; Cooper, 1984)—a perceptual process in which small numerosities (up to about three) are apprehended holistically and concurrently. Although these theories differ in important ways from theories that postulate innate counting, they converge with those theories in seeing the identification of small numerical quantities as the starting point for children's mathematical development.

The most well articulated version of the innate counting theory (Gallistel & Gelman, 1992) posits a mechanism called the *accumulator*, which carries out a nonverbal form of counting. Figure 1.1 illustrates the essential components of this mechanism. An impulse generator emits impulses at regular intervals; these impulses must pass through a gate to reach the accumulator, which stores the impulses. When the gate is closed, the impulses cannot get to the accumulator. Because the gate opens briefly each time a to-be-counted item is encountered, the contents of the accumulator increase as more items are counted. Thus, the final state of the accumulator is indicative of how many to-be-counted items were encountered. The number of impulses that pass through the gate is not precisely the same each time it opens, and therefore the end states of the accumulator are somewhat imprecise representations of numerosity; but they are ordered because the contents of the accumulator always increase as more items are counted.

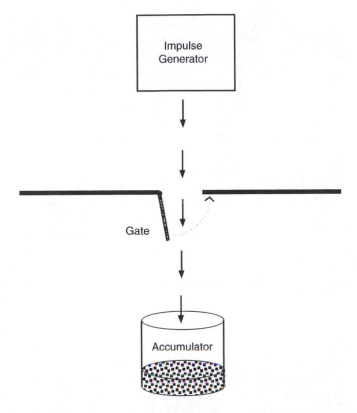

Figure 1.1.   A diagrammatic representation of the accumulator mechanism for nonverbal counting.

The importance of the accumulator mechanism, within the counting-first theories, is that it embodies important principles that any counting procedure must honor, and to which children's verbal counting in particular must conform, if it is to provide valid numerical information. For instance, the gate opens just once for each item being counted, and the states of the accumulator occur in a fixed order (from less full to more full) each time a series of items is counted. The nonverbal counting mechanism thus contains implicit knowledge about how counting works. It is hypothesized that children build on that knowledge as they learn to count verbally, because they expect the verbal counting system to work on the same principles as the nonverbal system. In addition, the knowledge implicit first in nonverbal and then in verbal counting eventually becomes more explicit, so that, for example, children can use the relation between number and one-to-one correspondence that is embodied in counting to reason about number conservation (R. Gelman, 1982).

A rather different developmental account, but one that still views numerical processing as the foundation for the development of mathematical knowledge, holds that the ability to identify absolute numerosities, even for a few small quantities, provides a reference point for discovering the significance of other kinds of quantitative information. According to this view, what is crucial is not the process by which quantities are initially enumerated but the information about numerical quantities that results from the process. Even a very limited subitizing process provides a basis for working out the relations among different small numerosities (e.g., that two is less than three) because it gives children a means of observing that when an object is removed from a collection with a numerosity of three, that numerosity changes to two, and conversely when an object is added to a collection with a numerosity of two, that numerosity changes to three (Cooper, 1984). In addition, by counting or constructing correspondences between sets whose numerosities they can discern by subitizing, children gain an appreciation of the numerical significance of these other processes that they can then use to extend their numerical processing beyond the limits of subitizing (Klahr & Wallace, 1976).

Clearly, accounts of numerical development that differ in whether they consider counting or subitizing to be the child's first method of enumeration correspondingly take very different positions as to the origins of important mathematical concepts such as one-to-one correspondence. Nevertheless, they share the fundamental (and largely unexamined) assumption that numerical information about collections of events of objects, whether that information is generated by counting or by subitizing, is encoded very early in life and that the mechanisms that allow infants to detect numerosity are the foundation for further development.

The Comparison-of-Quantities Position

Notwithstanding the intuitive appeal of the idea that numbers, in particular counting numbers, are the foundation for mathematics, Russian psychologist and educator V. V. Davydov (1975a) presented a persuasive argument that this idea is not correct. The motivation for his analysis was to determine how best to teach mathematics. Working from the assumption that instruction should begin with the concepts that are most fundamental to mathematics, Davydov critically examined the idea that number is fundamental. He pointed out that numerical systems are defined on the basis of a chain of other concepts—among them the concepts of *set*, *equivalence*, and *power*—and argued that those concepts are therefore more fundamental than number. Sets are not merely physical collections, just as a piece of string is not in itself a "length." A collection of objects becomes a set, just as the string becomes a length, only when it is considered as a quantity to be evaluated in relation to other quantities via the concepts of *equivalence*, *greater than*, and *less than*. When we assign a numerical value to a set, we establish that that set is a member of an equivalence class that contains all sets that have that particular numerosity, and that it stands in a greater-than or less-than relation to sets that differ from it in numerosity.

The numerosity of a set, moreover, like the numerical measure of a continuous quantity, is not a function of its physical composition alone. When we count a collection of items, just as when we measure a continuous quantity, we must first decide what counts as "one" and then iterate that unit across the set (Drabkina, 1962; cited in Davydov, 1975b). If our unit is individual items, we get one count result; but if it is pairs, we get a smaller result; if it is parts (say, buttons on shirts), a larger result. In exactly the same way that different measurements are obtained for a length of string depending on whether inches or centimeters are adopted as the unit of measure, the numerical result we get by counting depends on our choice of unit.

Thus the concept of *unit* is another conceptual prerequisite for an understanding of number. Moreover, although in children's earliest counting, discrete objects characteristically function as the counting unit, Gal'perin and Georgiev (1969) argued that equating units with objects is profoundly inadequate conceptually. In order to understand units of measurement, and particularly how variations in unit size affect numerical outcomes, children need to differentiate the mathematical concept of unit from the everyday notion of an object.

Although the observations made by Davydov (1975a, 1975b) and his colleagues about the dependence of the concept of number on more fundamental concepts, such as set, equivalence, and unit, are mathematical rather than cognitive in character, they have profound cognitive-developmental ramifications. They suggest that the origins of children's mathematical thinking, and even their numerical knowledge specifically, may lie neither in the activity of counting nor in the perceptual apprehension of numerical information through subitizing, but rather in the quantitative comparisons on which an understanding of numbers depends. The importance of quantitative comparisons is particularly clear with respect to the formation of the concept of unit, which is comparative in two fundamental ways. First, as Gal'perin and Georgiev (1969) noted, a fundamental aspect of the notion of unit is the idea of equivalence between units. And second, the observation that different units can be applied to the same quantities leads to the recognition that numerical values are essentially representations of the relation between the quantity they represent and a chosen unit.

The thesis that comparisons between unenumerated quantities may be developmentally prior to any form of numerical representation accords nicely with recent research indicating that results that for many years have been accepted as evidence of numerical knowledge in infancy may instead be a function of nonnumerical discriminations based on continuous properties of the stimuli, such as contour length (Mix, Huttenlocher, & Levine, 2002). This line of research is discussed in detail in chapter 2. Although young children's detection of relations among continuous amounts has received relatively little study in its own right, there is some evidence that this ability is already present, at least in rudimentary form, very early in development. For instance, 2-year-old children can identify the circle that matches a sample from a pair of circles that differ by 1 inch in diameter, with circle sizes ranging from 4 versus 5 to 8 versus 9 inches (Sera & Smith, 1987); and 5-month-old infants can discriminate between a container that is one fourth filled with a colored liquid and an identical container that is three fourths filled (Gao, Levine, & Huttenlocher, 2000). The research findings concerning children's knowledge about continuous quantities are reviewed in chapter 3. Neither the findings concerning infant numerical discriminations nor those concerning discriminations among continuous quantities can be taken as anything like decisive refutations of the counting-first position. Nevertheless, they do indicate the potential fruitfulness of considering the alternative thesis that counting, and numerical knowledge in general, build on more basic ways of thinking about quantities.

NATURE, NURTURE, AND DOMAINS OF DEVELOPMENT

The oldest debate in developmental psychology is the nature/nurture debate between those who believe that knowledge is principally an outcome of learning (nurture) and those who believe it is primarily a product of our biological heritage (nature). Even the classic advocates of the opposing positions in this debate, however, acknowledged that both nature and nurture are essential for development. John Locke (1894), for instance, who famously characterized knowledge as deriving entirely from experience, nevertheless described the power to think as a faculty deriving from nature:

> Nature never makes excellent things for mean or no uses: and it is hardly to be conceived that our infinitely wise Creator should make so admirable a faculty, as the power of thinking ... to be so idly and uselessly employed ... as to think ... without remembering ... without doing any good to itself or others. (p. 135)

Locke thus implicitly makes a distinction between knowledge, which he maintains is acquired through experience, and the capacity to think, which he attributes to nature (or to a divine Creator). Furthermore, he views the capacity to think as playing quite an active role in the formation of ideas; for instance, he attributes ideas about mental activities such as thinking, doubting, and willing to the mind "reflect[ing] on its own operations about the ideas got by sensation, and thereby stor[ing] itself with a new set of ideas ..." (p. 141), and ideas of number to the act of "repeating this idea [of unity] in our minds, and adding the repetitions together ..." (p. 270). In thus indicating not only the importance of experience but also the contributions that the mind itself makes, Locke anticipates the contemporary position that the contributions of nature and nurture cannot be separated inasmuch as the impact of experience always depends on biological characteristics of the organism (Cole, 1992; Tomasello, 1999) and the phenotype is not simply an "expression" of the genotype but rather the result of a dynamic process to which both genetic and environmental factors contribute (Lickliter & Honeycutt, 2003). What is new today is an effort to specify exactly how genes interact with experience to generate a developing phenotype (Johnston & Edwards, 2002).

Chomsky (1959) initiated a profound shift in theorizing about nature and nurture by postulating that the structures of language are not acquired through general learning mechanisms but rather through the operation of mental processes that are specialized for the complex task of language learning. Although considered a prototypical nativist position, Chomsky's claim introduced a profoundly new way of thinking about learning as well. It pointed out that learning need not be a general process that operates in the same way on all inputs but could instead be a product of highly specialized mechanisms that apply only to specific types of input and support learning only within a specific domain. This idea has since been extended to domains other than language, including theory of mind (Charman & Baron-Cohen; 1995; Leslie, 1994) and mathematics (Butterworth, 1999; Dehaene, 1997; R. Gelman, 1991), and elaborated into the theoretical position that the cognitive system is intrinsically modular (Fodor, 1983; Spelke & Tsivkin, 2001). However, as Johnston and Edwards (2002) noted, genes do not directly specify behavior or even a plan or blueprint for behavior; what they specify is the polypeptide sequences of proteins that are involved in brain structure and function. The path from genotype to behavior is a complex one in which genetic activity affects (and is affected by) protein synthesis and intracellular biochemistry, which in turn affect (and are affected by) neural growth, which affects neural activity, which, along with sensory stimulation and other physical influences, affect behavior. The complexity and bidirectionality of this pathway makes it clear that although modules may be thought of as in some sense genetically determined, they cannot be attributed exclusively to nature as opposed to nurture any more than any other aspect of the phenotype can be.

A very different theoretical perspective on domain specificity comes from the influential work of Lev Vygotsky (1978) on the cultural context of development. Vygotsky's main concern was with the ways in which cultural practices and associated tools and symbol systems mediate the development of particular kinds of knowledge. This perspective suggests that cognitive domains are shaped at least in part by domains of cultural activity, building on the particular forms of activity (together with the tools and symbol systems to support them) that a culture has developed for coping with different facets of life. Knowledge acquisition processes, in this view, vary across content areas in ways that reflect cultural practices.

Although the perspectives of Chomsky and Vygotsky converge in the view that cognitive-developmental processes are to a large degree domain-specific, they differ profoundly in their views as to the origins of that domain specificity. Indeed, the contrast between them reflects the reframing of the nature/nurture debate, not as a debate about which contributes more to development, but as one concerning which controls the way in which cognition is carved into domains. The "situated rationalist" (Resnick, 1994) and "rational constructivist" (R. Gelman, 1991, 1993) positions are clear instantiations of contemporary nativism, in that both characterize mathematical development as beginning with innate domain-specific structures that guide early learning about numbers. Tomasello's (1999) cultural learning position, on the other hand, is more of a nurture position, notwithstanding its recognition of the importance of biological evolution in providing the necessary structures to support cultural learning. Although clearly recognizing the contribution of biology to human development and especially to the ways in which humans learn from one another, for the most part Tomasello (1999) does not posit the existence of multiple, innately given, cognitive domains within which development takes place. (Excepted from this generalization are domains that are relatively old evolutionarily and not specific to primates, such as spatial orientation.) Rather, he sees cultural learning in all its varieties as stemming from a common cognitive adaptation—the ability of humans to recognize each other's intentions and to use that knowledge in learning from one another. The cultural learning perspective of Vygotsky on domain specificity is nicely instantiated in Gal'perin and Georgiev's (1969) discussion of the need to distinguish between everyday objects and mathematical units. In suggesting that instruction plays a crucial role in the construction of a mathematical concept of unit, they are clearly giving cultural learning processes a fundamental role in the emergence of ways of thinking that are specifically mathematical.

SENSE MAKING AND THE DISTINCTION BETWEEN A MATHEMATICS OF QUANTITIES AND A MATHEMATICS OF SYMBOLS

Independent of the issue of whether numbers or unenumerated quantitative comparisons are more fundamental—either in mathematics itself or in mathematical development—it is important to distinguish between numerical knowledge and quantitative knowledge. *Numeracy* refers to knowledge about numbers (which may or may not be used to represent physical quantities); it includes knowledge of the count sequence, knowledge that two is less than three, knowledge of number facts like $2 + 3 = 5$ and $7 \times 6 = 42$, and all kinds of knowledge about how the numerical symbol system works. *Quantitative knowledge* refers to knowledge about physical quantities and relations between them (which may or may not be represented numerically); it includes knowledge that the amount of water we have does not change when we pour it from one container to another (unless we spill!), knowledge that a whole cookie is more to eat than just a piece of that cookie, and much more. Of course, some knowledge is both numerical and quantitative, for example, knowing that if two collections initially contain the same number of objects, then moving a single object from one collection to the other will result in the collection from which the object was taken having two fewer objects than the other.

Mathematical knowledge embraces both numerical knowledge and knowledge about quantities, and more. Thus, for example, knowledge of algebraic formulae, such as how to factor binomial equations, is neither strictly numerical nor directly concerned with physical quantities and the relations between them. Resnick (1992) characterized this kind of knowledge as a "mathematics of operators." Although it is clearly a legitimate part of mathematical knowledge, a detailed examination of it is beyond the scope of this book inasmuch as the focus here is on the origins of mathematics knowledge and the mathematics of operators is a later development. Nevertheless, it is important to keep in mind its existence, as a satisfactory account of early mathematics development must be consistent with the eventual attainment of a mathematics of symbols, if not universally at least by some individuals.

In characterizing the marked differences between Brazilian children's intelligent and flexible mathematical problem solving in the context of practical problems related to selling produce in the marketplace and their much poorer performance on school-type rote problems involving identical computational content, Carraher, Carraher, and Schliemann (1987) drew a distinction between "manipulation of quantities" and "manipulation of symbols." The latter, they argue, is much more prone to error because it is not grounded in children's familiarity with real-life quantities that helps them make sense of the marketplace problems. What Carraher et al. characterize as manipulation of symbols resembles what Resnick (1992) terms a "mathematics of numbers" (the antecedent to a mathematics of operators, in her analysis) in that the operations conducted on numbers are no longer tied to imagined or real actions on physical quantities. But there is a vital distinction to be made. Insofar as the symbol manipulations Carraher et al. describe are not constrained by the mathematical meanings of the symbols, they arguably do not comprise any kind of mathematics at all. Symbolic forms of mathematics do not need to be, and should not be, collections of arbitrary and unconstrained procedures. Indeed, symbolic representations can be powerful tools for generalizing mathematical ideas (Schliemann & Carraher, 2002) and developing them further (Arcavi, 1995). Symbolic problem solving becomes error prone and illogical only when children (or adults, for that matter) adopt symbol manipulation procedures without understanding the mathematical logic behind them, logic that has its roots in thinking about physical quantities but need not remain tied to them.

COMING ATTRACTIONS

Most of the existing research on children's early mathematical knowledge was originally framed in relation to the counting-first position. Many of the accumulated research findings take on new meaning when considered from the alternative perspective of the comparison-of-quantities position, although the studies were not designed to contrast the two positions. The goal of this book is to examine the compatibility of the comparison-of-quantities position with the available research, and then to consider the developmental and instructional ramifications of the conclusions that emerge from that undertaking.

Research on children's early counting knowledge has made a profound contribution to our understanding of early mathematical development by showing that that development begins long before children learn the conventional counting sequence and also that verbal counting is far more than a rote performance. Chapter 2 reviews this research, giving particular attention to the major claims about early counting that have been made from the counting-first perspective and critically reexamining the evidence adduced in support of those claims. Aspects of early mathematical knowledge other than counting are also important to consider, however, in particular, knowledge about continuous quantities and about equivalence and ordinal relations between quantities. Chapter 3 pulls together what is known about these aspects of children's quantitative reasoning, drawing both upon research that was originally carried out to address issues concerning children's counting and also upon a smaller body of research on children's ideas about length, area, and spatial forms of proportionality.

The next three chapters of the book examine the implications of the comparison-of-quantities position perspective for several important aspects of children's developing mathematical knowledge. A major contribution of the comparison-of-quantities position is to highlight the importance of an understanding of mathematical units, which is the focus of chapter 4.

According to the counting-first position, children's counting is from the beginning informed by a "what to count" principle, which essentially indicates that there are no restrictions on the sorts of things that can be counted. However, findings from both Russian (e.g., Gal'perin & Georgiev, 1969) and U.S. research (Shipley & Shepperson, 1990; Sophian & Kailihiwa, 1998) indicate that young children have substantial difficulty adopting items other than discrete objects as units of counting.

Chapter 5 then examines children's learning of whole-number arithmetic. Evidence that children often use counting-based strategies to add and subtract suggests a close link between counting knowledge and knowledge of addition and subtraction. Instruction that treats multiplication as repeated addition and division as repeated subtraction in effect extends the link between counting and arithmetic to multiplication and division. The comparison-of-quantities perspective offers a deeper conceptual analysis of arithmetic knowledge, however, one that emphasizes the differences between addition and subtraction, on one hand, and multiplication and division, on the other, in the ways in which units are used to obtain numerical representations of quantities.

The focus of chapter 6 is on children's understanding of fractions and the difficulties that often arise in fraction learning. Whereas the counting-first perspective views fractions as inherently problematic in that they do not fit the ways of thinking about numbers that guided children in learning to count and in making sense of whole-number arithmetic, the comparison-of-quantities perspective suggests that the main difference between whole numbers and fractions is that fractions entail using units in a new way. This perspective leads to the recommendation that fraction instruction build on a measurement perspective, within which the reasoning underlying the use of fractional units is made explicit.

The final two chapters of the book consider, in turn, the developmental and educational ramifications of the research discussed in earlier chapters and of the new perspectives on that research developed in those chapters. The primary developmental conclusion, advanced in chapter 7, is that, although mathematics learning surely has some biological foundation, the acquisition of mathematical knowledge is not based on innate domain-specific mechanisms. Correspondingly, the developmental course children follow in acquiring mathematical knowledge is not heavily canalized; rather, it is strongly influenced by social interactions and cultural practices, including schooling. This conclusion, of course, means that the study of mathematics development cannot be separated from the study of mathematics instruction and its impact on learning. Chapter 8 examines the ramifications of the comparison-of-quantities perspective developed in earlier chapters for three fundamental instructional issues: (a) the formulation of instructional objectives, (b) the integration of conceptual and computational aspects of instruction, and (c) the conceptual integration of arithmetic instruction with instruction with other aspects of mathematics, especially measurement, geometry, and data analysis. Three important recommendations for mathematics education emerge from this analysis. The first recommendation is that the formulation of instructional objectives for a given level of instruction be guided by a long-term perspective. Educators should consider what students will be expected to learn in the future, and what conceptual knowledge they will need in order to be able to learn it effectively, in designing curricula for early childhood mathematics. The second and third recommendations are instantiations of this one. They hold that instruction in arithmetic should be grounded in quantity comparisons and specifically in an understanding of numerical representations as representations of the relation between a unit and a total quantity; and that mathematics instruction should aim from the outset for generality in students' understanding of mathematical concepts and principles.

Chapter 2

Children's Counting

A landmark event in the study of children's mathematical development was the publication of R. Gelman and Gallistel's (1978) book, *The Child's Understanding of Number*. In this book, R. Gelman and Gallistel undertook to remedy the perceived failure of Piaget's (1952) account of logico-mathematical development, with its emphasis on the limitations of preoperational thought, to adequately characterize the knowledge that very young children do have about mathematics. To this end, they called attention to the richness of children's counting knowledge. They made the ground-breaking observation that there is a high degree of systematicity in even very young children's counting, which they argued belies the Piagetian idea that counting is initially merely a rote process without conceptual substance. R. Gelman and Gallistel maintained instead that the systematicities in children's early counting reflect knowledge about the logical requirements of counting—characteristics a count must have if it is to provide valid information about numerosity. They claimed that, although young children cannot articulate the principles of counting explicitly, their adherence to them shows that they know principles in much the same way as speakers of a language give evidence of knowing its grammatical rules by adhering to them in their speech even though they seldom can state the grammatical rules explicitly.

R. Gelman and Gallistel (1978) identified three principles that are essential if the outcome of a count is to accurately represent the number of objects in the set being counted, and they asserted that even children's early counting efforts conform with these principles. These "how to count principles" are: (a) the *one-to-one principle*, which specifies that each item in the collection to be counted must be assigned one and only one count tag; (b) the *stable-order principle*, which specifies that the tags must be used in a fixed order;

and (c) the *cardinal principle*, which specifies that the final count term serves not only as a tag for a specific item but as a representation of the cardinality of the whole collection. In addition, R. Gelman and Gallistel claimed that children's counting honors two "permission" principles: the *order-irrelevance principle*, which indicates that the items being counted may be tagged in any order; and the *abstraction principle*, which indicates that all kinds of things can be counted (e.g., the collection need not be homogeneous). Although there is some disagreement around several of these principles, particularly as characterizations of children's earliest counting (cf. regarding the cardinal principle, Fuson, 1988; Fuson, Pergament, Lyons, & Hall, 1985; Sophian, 1987; regarding the order-irrelevance principle, Baroody, 1984; Briars & Siegler, 1984; Cowan, Dowker, Christakis, & Bailey, 1996; and regarding the what-to-count principle, Shipley & Shepperson, 1990), there is no question but that R. Gelman and Gallistel opened a whole new way of thinking about children's counting, and consequently about early conceptual development, with their intriguing analyses of the regularities in children's early counting.

The notion of implicit knowledge of fundamental principles is the cornerstone of R. Gelman's (1991, 1993) rational-constructivist account of the development of numerical knowledge. This account views the principles of counting as a skeletal structure that guides children as they learn to count. Its fundamental claim, therefore, is that the principles are present even before children have learned to count; rather than being some sort of distillation of what children have learned, they provide a foundation for that learning. Three important sets of research have been inspired, at least in part, by this position: (a) research on the numerical knowledge of preverbal infants; (b) research on young children's counting and their understanding of what it means; and (c) research on children's understanding of aspects of mathematics that do not fit well with the hypothesized principles, in particular, fractions. In this chapter, the focus is on the first two of these. The research on children's understanding of fractions is presented in chapter 6.

NUMERICAL KNOWLEDGE IN INFANCY

The question of what numerical knowledge, if any, infants have before they have learned to count verbally has stimulated a substantial body of research, but it is a complex one in which several controversial issues persist. These issues range from disputes as to the validity of findings of small-number discrimination in infants to debates about how infants represent numerical information. It is useful to organize a discussion of the issues and the evidence in terms of a hierarchical series of questions. The first question, of course, is simply whether infants respond to numerical properties of arrays of objects and sequences of events. This was the starting point for research on numerical knowledge in infancy. But, given evidence for such responsiveness, a series of questions arise about the basis for it. Because number implies the existence of countable units of some kind, an important question is whether infants' responses are in fact based on the processing of the items within an array or sequence as separate units, or on some aggregate property of the collection as a whole, such as surface area, contour length, or cumulative duration. Insofar as evidence for processing of individual items can be adduced, another question arises: Are infants only attending to the individual objects, or are they detecting the numerical value of the collection composed of all the individuals taken together? Finally, if infants engage in truly numerical processing in the latter sense, it becomes important to identify the kinds of processes and representations they use to do so. Because the principles-first position postulates that children have important knowledge about the structure of counting before they have learned the verbal counting sequence, researchers working within that theoretical framework have postulated that infants have a nonverbal counting mechanism that incorporates the fundamental principles of counting. Before that hypothesis can be effectively evaluated, however, more fundamental issues about what infants are responding to when they display seemingly numerical behavior need to be addressed.

Are Infant Discriminations Based on Continuous Properties Rather Than Number?

The study of infant numerical abilities originated with the adaptation of methods based on visual preferences to the study of infant numerical discriminations. On the premise that if infants prefer one array to another, they must see them as different, visual preferences were used for many years to investigate infants' perceptual abilities (e.g., Fantz, 1958). Furthermore, because infants generally look more at visual arrays that differ from previously presented arrays than at arrays like those they have already seen (Fantz, 1964), researchers could test for discrimination between arrays that differed in particular ways by familiarizing infants with one type of array and then testing for preferences for a different type of array. If infants detect the difference, they should look preferentially at the array that is different from the ones they have been seeing. Applying this logic to numerical discrimination, researchers showed infants a series of arrays that all had the same numerosity, and then tested whether they would look more at an array with a different numerosity than at another array with the familiar numerosity. Evidence that a change in numerosity, with other characteristics of the arrays controlled, elicited increased looking would indicate that infants discriminated the new numerosity from the old one. In fact, in early studies, that result was obtained when both the familiar and novel numerosities were quite small (e.g., 2 vs. 3) but not when they were larger (e.g., 4 vs. 6; Starkey & Cooper, 1980; Strauss & Curtis, 1981).

Arrays that differ in numerosity, however, will generally differ in a variety of continuous properties as well, such as total surface area and contour length. Even the first researchers to investigate infant number discrimination were aware of this potential confound and tried to address it. Strauss and Curtis (1981), for instance, varied the size and positions of the items in the familiarization arrays from trial to trial. Because nothing but numerosity was constant from one habituation trial to the next, they reasoned that if habituation occurred (and it did), it had to be based on numerosity, and consequently that dishabituation to a stimulus that had a different numerosity could be unambiguously attributed to the change in number. Several considerations, however, make this reasoning less compelling than it initially seemed.

A methodological assumption of the initial research on infant numerosity discrimination was that as long as factors other than numerosity vary across successive habituation trials, those factors cannot account for evidence of habituation or of preferential looking at test arrays that differ in numerosity from the habituation arrays. However, it is possible that infants habituate to the central tendency of varying properties of the familiarization arrays, and then discriminate between test arrays on the basis of their similarity or dissimilarity to that central tendency. Studies of category formation in infancy have provided evidence for just that sort of habituation and differentiation (Sherman, 1985; Strauss, 1979). In numerosity discrimination studies, arrays composed of different numbers of items inevitably do differ on average in surface area and contour length (unless a systematic difference in item size across arrays of different numerosities is introduced), and so the central tendency of a set of familiarization arrays is likely to differ more in such properties from a test array with a different numerosity than from a test array that has the same numerosity. Accordingly, randomly varying item sizes within a series of familiarization trials does not adequately control for discrimination based on continuous properties that covary with numerosity.

The viability of accounts of infant numerosity discrimination that are based on continuous rather than numerical properties of the arrays is strengthened by the fact that significant results generally consist of only small differences in looking time in the aggregate data of a fairly large group of infants. Because the data are aggregated across different test stimuli, an overall positive result need not mean that reliable discrimination occurred for all subgroups of infants in a counterbalanced design. It might be that the effect actually stemmed only from the behavior of those subgroups for whom the numerically novel test array did differ appreciably from the central tendency of the familiarization arrays and thus for whom a continuous-quantity interpretation is most viable.

To evaluate the role of continuous quantitative properties of numerical arrays in findings of infant small-number discriminations, Clearfield and Mix (1999) pitted changes in number from habituation to test arrays against changes in contour length. Their experimental design is illustrated in Figure 2.1. Infants were habituated to arrays that always consisted of a fixed number of squares—two or three—of fixed size. Thus, both number and contour length (as well as other continuous properties, such as total stimulus area) were constant across the habituation arrays, which varied only in the positions of the squares. After habituation, infants were shown two types of test arrays. One consisted of two squares that were larger than those in the habituation arrays, so that their combined contour length was the same as that of the habituation arrays that contained three squares. The other consisted of three squares that were smaller than the squares in the habituation arrays, so that their combined contour length matched that of the habituation arrays that contained two squares. Thus, regardless of whether infants were habituated to two-item or three-item arrays, one of the two test arrays always matched the habituation arrays in numerosity but not in combined contour length, whereas the other matched the habituation ar-

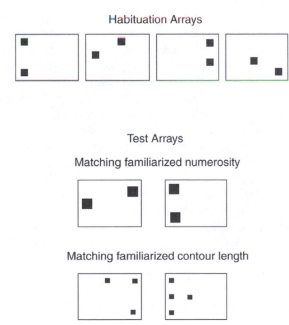

Figure 2.1.   Design used by Clearfield and Mix (1999) to differentiate between infant discrimination based on numerosity versus total contour length.

rays in contour length but not in numerosity. Clearfield and Mix found that infants dishabituated, that is, they showed renewed looking, to the change in contour length, with number unchanged, but not to the change in number, with contour length held constant. That result was replicated in studies by Clearfield and Mix (2001) and by Feigenson, Carey, and Spelke (2002, Experiment 2).

Across infants, Clearfield and Mix's (1999) design nicely controls for possible effects of the size of individual items while contrasting effects of contour length and numerosity, because item size is the same in all the habituation arrays, and test arrays composed of a particular size of square serve equally often as the numerosity match and the contour-length match, depending on the numerosity to which infants were previously habituated. It is not straightforward, however, to extend the findings obtained with fixed-size familiarization trials to the interpretation of the results of other number discrimination studies, in which item size and, therefore, contour length and other continuous properties of the arrays vary across habituation trials. Evidence that infants habituate to contour length and not to number when both are constant across a series of habituation arrays by no means establishes that they do the same when the number is constant but contour length and other continuous properties are varying from trial to trial.

At least two studies have obtained evidence that young infants can, under some circumstances, discriminate between visual arrays differing in number even when continuous properties of the arrays, such as contour length or surface area, have been carefully controlled (e.g., Feigenson, 2005, with one- vs. two-item arrays composed of objects varying in color, pattern, and texture; Wynn, Bloom, & Chiang, 2002, with two- vs. four-item arrays in which the items are collections of dots that move together). It should be noted, however, that even with item size controlled, it is still possible to account for these results on the basis of continuous properties of the arrays. The problem is that test trials that match the familiarization trials in total contour length or surface area differ from them in the size of individual items, whereas trials that match the familiarization trials in item size differ from them in these aggregate properties. It may seem more parsimonious to assume that infant discriminations are based on the same feature, that is, numerosity, on both subsets of trials, but we must remember that infants are simply looking at what interests them. There is no reason why both changes in item size and changes in aggregate amount might not elicit interest.

Object Files and Numerical Collections

A different concern about small-number discriminations is that they may be based on infants' processing of the individual objects within an array rather than on processing of the numerosity of the array as a whole. This is a subtle but potentially important distinction. Because number presupposes the identification of separate units to be enumerated, infants clearly must individuate the elements of an array in order to represent it numerically. The object-file theory (Carey, 2001; Simon, 1997) holds that that is all they do. Thus, they encode a two-object array, for example, as "this thing and that thing," and therefore distinguish it from an array that consists of "just this thing" (one object), or "this, that, and the other" (three objects). This account, like contemporary accounts of subitizing (the preattentive apprehension of small numbers of items; Trick & Pylyshyn, 1994) in adults, builds on theories of visual perception that posit an early stage of processing in which a small number of objects are identified by spatial location, without initially processing their features (Kahneman, Treisman, & Gibbs, 1992). Because this perceptual processing is believed to be restricted to a small number of items, object-file accounts of infant numerical perception account well for experimental results in which infant numerical discriminations have been limited to small set sizes (e.g., Strauss & Curtis, 1981), but they are not a viable basis for recent findings of large-number discrimination by infants (e.g., Xu & Spelke, 2000).

Simon (1997) characterized the object-file account of infant number discriminations as "nonnumerical" on the grounds that the processes it invokes are not specific to numerical processing. In contrast, Carey (2001), although acknowledging that it only implicitly represents number, nevertheless argued that object-file representations are numerical in that they represent sets of objects and number-relevant transformations on those sets, such as addition, and in that object-file models can be compared via a one-to-one correspondence process to determine equivalence or greater-than/less-than relations.

In my view, both of these interpretations miss the central mathematical issue, which may be clarified by comparing a (mental) object-file model to a (physical) set of tallies. In both cases, objects are individuated and represented one by one, and the resulting representation can be used to make numerical inferences about collections of objects. But what is critical about a tally is that it is recognized as a cumulative totality; we make the marks in order to represent numerical information and, accordingly, are interested in the aggregate of all the tally marks rather than in each individual one and its correspondence to a particular item being tallied. In contrast, object files, even if they preserve no featured information about the individual objects they are representing, nevertheless are first and foremost representations of those objects considered one at a time. If we, as adults, could see the object files in an infant's mind, we might treat them like a tally and focus on the cumulative number of them rather than on how they map onto particular objects. But are infants treating them that way?

In short, the distinction between numerical and nonnumerical accounts of the role of object files in infant numerical discrimination turns on whether infants are using object files only to represent particular objects (even if those objects are identified only by their location rather than by features intrinsic to the objects), or whether they are in some manner considering the aggregate of the object files, and thus of the objects to which they correspond. The two alternatives are not easy to distinguish empirically, in part because object files and numerical representations are not mutually exclusive; rather, the individuation of the objects within an array is a necessary but not sufficient condition for enumerating the array. The issue, therefore, is not whether or not infants represent the individual objects but whether they also form a representation of the numerosity of the array as a whole.

An important source of evidence bearing on this issue is research on infants' discrimination not simply between different small numerosities but between pairs of arrays characterized by the relations of equality and inequality or less than and greater than. The latter sort of discrimination is important evidence for the formation of numerical representations because equality and inequality are not relations between the individual items in two arrays being compared but between the numerosities of the whole arrays.

The first empirical research on infants' detection of equal and unequal relationships between numerical collections was reported by Cooper (1984). In a clever adaptation of the habituation procedure, he familiarized infants not with single visual arrays but with pairs of them presented successively. The first array was presented for a fixed, brief interval and then immediately followed by another, which might have the same numerosity or a different numerosity. Across the habituation trials, the numbers of items in the arrays varied, but the relation between the first and second arrays was always the same. At test, sequences that diverged from that relation were introduced, for example, if infants had been familiarized with sequences in which the first and second arrays always had the same numerosity, at test they saw a sequence in which the second array differed in numerosity from the first.

Cooper's (1984) intriguing finding was that 10- to 12-month-old infants distinguished between the familiarized relation and the new one when the shift was from sequences in which both of the successively presented arrays had the same numerosity to sequences in which the numerosity changed, or vice versa, but they acted as if no change had occurred when the shift was from sequences in which the first array was smaller in numerosity than the second to sequences in which it was larger, or vice versa. In other words, the infants discriminated "same numerosity" from "different numerosity" but not "greater than" from "less than." The latter discrimination, however, was found to occur among slightly older infants, 14- to 16-month-olds.

An intriguing possibility is that the transition from distinguishing only between same-numerosity and different-numerosity pairs of arrays to also distinguishing between pairs in which the second array is less than versus greater than the first corresponds to the emergence of genuinely numerical representations. After all, *ordinality* is what distinguishes quantitative inequality from nonquantitative difference. Red and green are different colors, but we cannot say that one is greater than another unless we compare them on a quantitative dimension such as wavelength. Cooper (1984) suggested that infants discover the ordinal relations between small numerosities by observing how actions of putting another object in a collection or taking one away affect its numerosity, as determined by subitizing. This hypothesis is consistent with the interpretation of his findings as indicating the emergence of representations of numerosity if we interpret subitizing as a process that generates object-file representations but not representations of numerosity itself.

A recent study by Brannon (2002) replicated the developmental lag between discriminations of equality from inequality and discriminations of less-than from greater-than reported by Cooper (1984)—but Brannon reported evidence of the latter type of discrimination several months earlier than it was obtained in Cooper's work. Specifically, Brannon found that 11-month-old infants, but not 9-month-olds, discriminated between three-item numerical sequences presented in ascending versus descending order, while both age groups discriminated between sequences in which numerosity remained constant and sequences in which it changed. Both Cooper's and Brannon's results, in indicating that infants for a time do not distinguish between less-than and greater-than relations although they do distinguish between relations of numerical equality versus inequality, are inconsistent with the view that infant number discriminations reflect the operation of an innate counting mechanism, because any form of counting would be expected to provide ordinal as well as equality/inequality information; but they are compatible with the possibility that a mechanism like counting that provides both cardinal and ordinal information may become available well before children begin to engage in verbal counting. The unexplained discrepancy between Cooper's and Brannon's findings concerning the age at which discrimination is made (not until 14 to 16 months of age in Cooper's study, versus as early as 11 months in Brannon's), however, indicates the need for further research on this important topic.

Forms of Numerical Representation

A long-standing debate concerns the nature of numerical representations in infancy. One view is that small-number discrimination is based on subitizing, a perceptual process that allows viewers to apprehend several items at once and know how many there are, without having to go through them one by one, as in counting (e.g., Cooper, 1984; Shipley & Shepperson, 1990). A contrasting view postulates a nonverbal counting mechanism called the *accumulator* (Gallistel & Gelman, 1992). The accumulator collects impulses that can reach it only when a gate is open, and the gate opens for a brief interval as each successive item or event is "counted." Thus, after a series of items have been encountered, a readout of the contents of the accumulator provides an indication of how many times the gate opened, and thus of how many items there were.

Because the subitizing process is thought to operate holistically rather than sequentially, it fits well with the evidence that infants are not initially sensitive to the ordinal relations between numerosities but only to whether two numerosities are the same or different (Cooper, 1984). On the other hand, however, because subitizing is thought to be limited to very small numerosities even in adults (e.g., Mandler & Shebo, 1982; Trick & Pylyshyn, 1994), it cannot account for recent evidence that infants can discriminate between numerosities as large as 8 versus 16 (e.g., Lipton & Spelke, 2003; Xu & Spelke, 2000).

The accumulator model, on the other hand, fits nicely with evidence that infants can discriminate between large numbers, provided that the ratio contrast between them is large, because the main limitation on counting with the accumulator is the increasing variability of the readings from the accumulator as numerosity increases, and a large contrast between numerosities would allow for successful discrimination even in the face of high variability. But it is not clear how the operation of an accumulator-type mechanism can be reconciled with evidence that young infants are not sensitive to ordinal relations between small numerosities that they can discriminate (Brannon, 2002; Cooper, 1984).

Theoretically, the accumulator model offers an appealing account of how counting principles might exist prior to the acquisition of verbal counting and somehow guide children as they learn to count verbally. The basic idea is just that the operation of the accumulator mechanism embodies the counting principles and, on the basis of their experience with it, children come to expect verbal counting to follow those principles as well. In particular, (a) each occurrence of the gate opening is paired in a one-to-one manner with an item in the collection being counted (the one-one principle); (b) the successive states of the accumulator always occur in the same order (the stable order principle); and (c) the final state of the accumulator represents the cardinal value of the set (the cardinal principle). And of course, that state is the same regardless of the order in which items are counted or of what sorts of items they are (the order-irrelevance and abstraction principles).

An influential argument against the subitizing position has been that subitizing is too low-level a mechanism to account for the richness of infants' numerical abilities. Two important lines of research were inspired by this reasoning: research on infants' ability to detect cross-modal numerical matches, and research on infants' understanding of the numerical effects of addition and subtraction transformations.

The assumption driving investigations of infants' ability to detect cross-modal correspondences in numerosities was that such an ability would reflect abstract numerical knowledge rather than merely perceptual information derived from a subitizing mechanism (Starkey, Spelke, & Gelman, 1990). To test for the ability to detect cross-modal numerical correspondences, Starkey et al. examined infants' looking times to two simultaneously presented visual arrays, one of which contained two items while the other contained three, that were presented concurrently with an auditory stimulus consisting of sequences of either two or three drum beats. Starkey et al. found that infants looked preferentially at the visual array that matched the numerosity of the drum beats. Oddly, however, other investigators have found visual preferences in the opposite direction, that is, greater looking at the visual array that did not match the concurrent auditory stimulus (Mix, Levine, & Huttenlocher, 1997; Moore, Benenson, Reznick, Peterson, & Kagan, 1987). It is difficult to know how to interpret such divergent effects. On the one hand, significant differences in either direction constitute evidence that infants distinguish between the two arrays. On the other hand, Mix et al. argue that the fact that the findings go in opposite directions may indicate that they either reached significance only by chance or, following Moore et al., that they reflect the impact of arousal-related factors on infants' looking preferences rather than numerical processing specifically. Patterns of looking determined by infants' levels of arousal could vary across studies because of seemingly minor differences in the stimuli that have ramifications for infants' arousal levels. Additionally, the arousal hypothesis is attractive because it offers an explanation of why the sound sequence infants hear would have any impact on which visual array they look at. After all, because the visual arrays are static, neither one can have any temporal or causal relation to the auditory stimulus, and so it is not clear what cognitive purpose would be served by looking more (or less) at the one that happens to match the auditory stimulus in numerosity.

Another line of research evaluating the richness of early numerical knowledge investigated infants' expectations about the outcomes of numerical transformations. The idea that infants' knowledge about small numerosities is initially unordered suggests that, at least early in infancy, they should not be able to anticipate the result of adding or removing an object from a small numerical collection while it is out of view. On the other hand, because the accumulator mechanism lends itself easily to computing addition and subtraction results, the accumulator model suggests that infants may have arithmetic knowledge from a very early age. To investigate addition and subtraction abilities in young infants, Wynn (1992a) measured how long 5-month-old infants looked at arrays that were revealed when a screen was removed after the completion of a small-number addition or subtraction transformation. Figure 2.2 schematically represents the procedure. The infants were shown one or two objects that were then screened from view; then, within the infants' view, either another object was placed behind the screen along with an object that was originally by itself, or one of two objects originally behind the screen was taken away. The screen was then removed, revealing either the appropriate number of objects (e.g., example, two, if a second object was added to one that was hidden) or some other number of objects (either a single object or three objects after presentation of the 1 + 1 hiding sequence). Infants looked longer when the removal of the screen revealed a different number of objects than the arithmetic operation should have produced than they did when the arithmetically appropriate number of objects was revealed. Thus, Wynn (1992a) inferred that they were surprised by the anomalous result.

Similar studies conducted by other investigators have replicated Wynn's (1992a) results (Koechlin, Dehaene, & Mehler, 1997; Simon, Hespos, & Rochat, 1995; Uller, Carey, Huntley-Fenner, & Klatt, 1999) and even extended them to large-number arrays (McCrink & Wynn, 2004). However, the concerns about continuous-quantity confounds raised with respect to

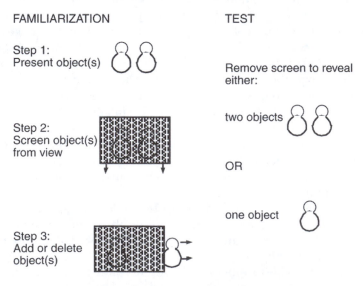

Figure 2.2. Procedure used by Wynn (1992a) to study infants' understanding of numerical transformations.

the basic small-number discrimination studies are also applicable to these studies. Consistent with a continuous-quantity interpretation, Feigenson, Carey, and Spelke (2002) found that infants looked more when the outcome array had the to-be-expected number but an unexpected aggregate amount (i.e., one small object when one large one was expected, or two small objects when two large ones were expected) than when it had an unexpected numerosity but the to-be-expected aggregate amount (i.e., two small objects when one large one was expected, or one large object when two small ones were expected). McCrink and Wynn, however, took care to control for aggregate amount in their study of large-number addition and subtraction.

A more troubling concern is the possibility that what appear to be responses to anomalous arithmetic results may in fact reflect a combination of more mundane influences on infants' looking, in particular, greater looking at more complex (i.e., larger numerosity) arrays and familiarity preferences (Clearfield & Westfahl, in press; Cohen & Marks, 2002). In support of this interpretation, Cohen and Marks (Experiment 3) reported preferential looking at the familiar rather than the novel numerosity in the absence of an arithmetic transformation. However, as that result is itself at odds with other number discrimination studies in which novelty preferences are typically observed, it is difficult to determine how applicable their conclusions are to other studies. At a minimum, however, their work does highlight a methodological weakness of virtually all the other infant arithmetic studies, which is that the anomalous outcomes have nearly always been the numerosity that was present prior to the arithmetic transformation. Under these circumstances, any differential looking that occurs might reflect (a) differentiation between possible versus impossible arithmetic results, (b) differentiation between the original numerical value versus a changed value, or (c) novelty or familiarity preferences. Clearly, in light of these alternative interpretations, no result can be taken as strong support for the conclusion that arithmetic computation occurred. Cohen and Marks's data is much more informative simply because they provide a wider range of test stimuli (0, 1, 2, or 3, regardless of the problem presented).

Large-Number Discrimination in Infancy

Several recent studies have demonstrated that infants as young as 6 months of age can discriminate between arrays or event sequences involving quite large numerosities, albeit only when the two numerical values differ substantially. The findings are remarkably consistent across studies. Since the first published report of large-numerosity discrimination (Xu & Spelke, 2000), there have been at least six additional research reports (Brannon, Abbott, & Lutz, 2004; Lipton & Spelke, 2003; Wood & Spelke, 2005a,

2005b; Xu, 2003; Xu, Spelke, & Goddard, 2005), all corroborating the basic result that 5- to 6-month-old infants can discriminate large numerosities provided there is a ratio of 2.0 between the numbers. For example, in Xu and Spelke's (2000) research, 6-month-old infants were successful in discriminating between arrays of 8 versus 16 items but not between arrays of 8 versus 12 items. Brannon et al. (2004) and Wood and Spelke (2005a) likewise obtained successful discriminations between sets as large as 8 versus 16. Similar evidence for large-numerosity discriminations has been obtained in studies in which the stimuli were sequences of events rather than simultaneously presented visual arrays (Lipton & Spelke, 2003; Wood & Spelke, 2005b).

Clearly, large-numerosity discriminations are not based on processing each individual object separately, because the numerosities involved far exceed the limitations of the object-tracking system (Trick & Pylyshyn, 1994). Moreover, the temporal characteristics of large-numerosity discrimination appear to be independent of the number of objects. Wood and Spelke (2005a) manipulated the length of time that successive large-numerosity arrays were exposed in order to determine how much time infants needed to extract numerical information from them. They established that 6-month-old infants could discriminate 4-item arrays from 8-item arrays under conditions in which a new array appears every 2 seconds, but they failed to make that discrimination when the presentation rate was increased so that a new array appeared every 1.5 seconds. Furthermore, 6-month-olds were also able to discriminate 8-item arrays from 16-item arrays presented at the 2-second rate, suggesting that it does not take any longer to process a greater number of items. Nine-month-old infants succeeded in discriminating 4-item arrays from 8-item arrays presented at the 1.5-second rate, which had been too fast for the 6-month-olds, indicating an increase with age in processing speed.

There also appear to be improvements between 6 and 9 months of age in the precision with which infants discriminate between different large numerosities. Wood and Spelke (2005b) found 9-month-olds able to successfully discriminate 4 from 6, and Lipton and Spelke (2003) found them able to discriminate 8 from 12, whereas parallel studies with 6-month-olds yielded evidence of discrimination only with the more extreme contrasts 4 versus 8 and 8 versus 16.

Surprisingly, several investigators have found that infants fail to discriminate between small numerosities that are in the same ratio relation as larger numerosities that they can discriminate. Thus, Xu (2003), Lipton and Spelke (2004), and Wood and Spelke (2005b) all found that 6-month-old infants failed to discriminate between 2 and 4 items although they were successful in discriminating 4 from 8 items. Similarly, Lipton and Spelke (2004) found that 9-month-olds who could discriminate 4 from 6 items failed on 2 versus 3 items. Xu (2003) interpreted his results as support for the thesis that distinct representational systems underlie small- versus large-number discrimination, an interpretation that is consonant with the distinction between exact and approximate numerical systems that other researchers have made on the basis of findings of dissociable neuropsychological deficits (Dehaene & Cohen, 1991) and of distinct patterns of brain activation in neuroimaging experiments (Dehaene, Spelke, Pinel, Stanescu, & Tsivkin, 1999). Lipton and Spelke (2004) suggested that findings that infants do not discriminate between small numerosities "strengthen the hypothesis that approximate number representations are not computed for small numbers" (p. 289). This perspective appears to be shared by Xu (2003), who suggests that infants fail to discriminate 2 from 4 items because these numerosities are encoded in different systems—the small- and large-number systems, respectively. It is not clear, however, why the approximate system should be unable to represent small numerosities approximately, in the same way it represents larger ones. A concern is that, if approximate processing really is restricted to numerosities greater than 2 or 3 items, that may be because it depends upon distributional properties that cannot be observed in arrays of only a very few items, properties that are not truly numerical such as the proximities between neighboring items, compared with the spatial magnitude of the array as a whole; or the emergence of clusters of items that are in very close proximity. Whether or not these kinds of factors in fact account for infants' or adults' ability to make large-numerosity comparisons is clearly an issue that can only be resolved with further research. Another issue that needs to be addressed is how comparisons between very small numerosities and much larger numerosities are done, comparisons such as 2 versus 12 items. Although this type of comparison has not been tested with infants, it seems clear that older children and adults could easily identify an array of 12 dots as more numerous than an array of 2, even without determining the exact number of dots in the array of 12. If infants can discriminate numerosities like these, clearly the two-system explanation for their failure to discriminate 2 from 4 items needs to be reevaluated. And if they cannot, then an important question is how the functioning of the exact and/or the approximate system changes developmentally so that the juxtaposition of a small and a large numerosity ceases to be problematic.

Interpretive Issues Surrounding Infancy Research

Clearly, the question of what infants know about number has inspired a sustained and multifaceted research effort. Although this effort is still very much a work in progress, the basic conclusion that infants can, at least under some circumstances, make some numerical discriminations now seems well established. The scope of their numerical abilities, however, continues to be hotly debated. Findings such as cross-modal numerical matching (Starkey et al., 1990) and discrimination of correct from incorrect arithmetic results (Wynn, 1992a), which are often cited in support of the thesis that rich numerical abilities are present within the first 6 months of life, have turned out to be difficult to replicate (e.g., Mix et al., 1997; Feigenson, Carey, & Spelke, 2002) and even more difficult to interpret (Clearfield & Westfahl, 2006; Cohen & Marks, 2002; Haith, 1998). On the other hand, although there is considerable support for the idea that infants discriminate between arrays on the basis of continuous quantitative dimensions more readily than they do on the basis of number (Clearfield & Mix, 1999, 2001; Feigenson et al., 2002), the conclusion that infants do not use number at all in discriminating between small sets (Mix, Huttenlocher, & Levine, 2002) does not appear to be tenable in light of recent studies in which discrimination between small sets differing in numerosity has been obtained even with strict controls for continuous properties (Feigenson, 2005; Wynn et al., 2002).

The divergent conclusions in the literature on infant numerical knowledge are a good illustration of a problem that Haith (1998) identified in an insightful discussion of interpretive issues that pervade research on infant cognition. Haith pointed out that considerable confusion results from the use of terms such as *representation* and *inference* without careful differentiation among different gradations of these phenomena, and criticized the "[use of] evidence of fragments for a concept as evidence for the whole" (p. 175). He argued that this practice obscures developmental changes by treating the first indications of an emerging ability as if they were equivalent to the mature form of that ability.

Consistent with Haith's (1998) analysis, the research on infant numerical abilities has been heavily driven by yes/no questions such as "Do infants form numerical representations?", "Do infants count?", and "Do infants add and subtract?" Much of the disagreement about the answers stems from differences in how researchers define these abilities and how they test for them, including the age of the infants they study, the experimental task(s) they use, and many details of procedure. Because there is no single correct definition nor any single true indicator of the presence or absence of any ability, however well defined, theoretical progress is likely to be limited so long as researchers rely on empirical tests of yes/no questions to address the controversies in the field.

An obvious way in which to begin moving beyond yes/no questions is to incorporate developmental comparisons more systematically in studies of infant numerical abilities. Surprisingly few investigations have included more than one age group of infants, and the age groups selected for study are often a function of the testing methods being used rather than of the kinds of abilities being examined. As a result, although we have a good deal of evidence about how infants of various ages respond in a range of experimental settings, we have very little information about developmental progressions in their numerical abilities.

In the meantime, although the intensive investigation that infant numerical abilities have received has been useful in clarifying methodological issues and in establishing that some numerical abilities are present in the first year of life, it has not taken us far in resolving the theoretical issues that motivated so much of the research. Given the inconsistencies across studies, it is not possible to draw firm conclusions at this time. Oddly, the clearest results are for large-number discriminations, an area of research that does not have strong ramifications for or against the position that infants are capable of nonverbal counting. It is more difficult to draw conclusions about how and when infants represent small numerosities, in part because of the relatively large number of inconsistencies across different studies in this area. On one hand, it appears that at least some findings from infancy research are not compatible with the strong conclusion that infants initially respond only to continuous properties such as contour length and not to the numerosities of small collections. At the same time, however, the findings as a whole are consistent with the suggestion that continuous quantitative properties may be at least as central as numerical ones to the ways infants perceive events and make quantitative comparisons.

Furthermore, even when infants do respond to changes in numerosity, it is not necessarily the case that they are representing the numerical values of the quantities they are comparing. Alternatively, they might be detecting correspondence relations between the quantities without determining the numerical value of either one. Just as we might, from watching a carousel on which only some of the horses were occupied (and there was never more than one child to a horse), conclude that there were more horses than children without knowing how many of either there were, infant numerical discriminations may be based on some kind of matching process that does not entail arriving at numerical values (precise or imprecise) for the sets.

Although it is not clear at present how such a matching process might work, especially for large-number comparisons, that hypothesis is as consistent with the available infant data as is the postulation of an innate counting mechanism. We only have evidence that infants detect numerical relations between sets, not that they assign numerical values to those sets.

More importantly, the units that infants use to make numerical comparisons (whether on the basis of numerical values generated through a counting process or on the basis of correspondence relations) are likely to be perceptually defined entities, items that are segmented one from another on the basis of spatial or temporal discontinuities such as gaps between the edges of items in a spatial array or marked changes in rate, magnitude, and/or direction of motion. Certainly, there is no evidence that infants can arrive at different numerical conclusions about a given quantity as a result of adopting different counting units (analogous to counting individual shoes vs. pairs of shoes). Thus, in infants' numerical reasoning, units are conflated with everyday objects in exactly the manner which Gal'perin and Georgiev (1969) discussed. Their analysis of the mathematical inadequacy of this way of thinking about units thus suggests that infant numerical discriminations do not constitute evidence for a conceptual understanding of number.

COUNTING AND CARDINALITY

With the acquisition of language, children begin to learn the words for small numerosities, and over the preschool period their counting abilities grow rapidly. Alternative accounts of development in this period are generally in agreement about children's how-to-count knowledge but diverge in their views as to the relation between that procedural knowledge and developing conceptual knowledge, specifically, the knowledge that counting provides information about the cardinal value of a set.

Of all the counting principles identified by R. Gelman and Gallistel (1978), the most central theoretically and the most challenging to document empirically is the cardinal principle, which recognizes the special significance of the last term in a count as a representation of the cardinal value of the whole set. The other how-to-count principles—the one-to-one principle and the stable-order principle—are meaningful only in conjunction with the cardinal principle because the cardinal principle establishes the goal of counting, a goal that can only be attained by adhering to all three principles. In other words, it is only because we want our counts to result in a number that accurately characterizes the cardinality of a set that it is crucial not to mix up the order of the count tags or deviate from a one-to-one mapping between tags and items to be counted. Yet it is on this point—the cardinal significance of the final term in a count—that observations of children's counting provide the least compelling evidence of principled knowledge.

R. Gelman and Gallistel (1978) cited, as evidence of knowledge of the cardinal principle, the observation that, at the end of a count, children commonly either repeat the last count term or at least state it with special intonation and emphasis, as if to signify, "this is the answer." However, like other regularities in children's counting, the intonation and emphasis given to the last word in a count could be just a reproduction of features of the counts children have seen others perform. It may not even be specific to counting; similar intonation patterns characterize the final word in other recitations. For instance, in the children's game "Duck, Duck, Goose," a child circles around a ring of his or her playmates, tapping each one in turn and saying "duck" until he or she chooses instead to say "goose"—at which point the child so tagged gets up and chases the first child around the circle. Clearly, the word "goose" in this activity has no cardinal significance, but like the final tag in a count, it is typically pronounced with extra emphasis and at a higher pitch than the preceding "duck" utterances. Similarly, in unpublished work, I found that when 2-year-old children were asked to name the colors of a series of objects, they often used greater emphasis and a higher pitch in stating the color of the last item in the series than they did for the earlier items. The special intonation given to the final word in a count, then, may not signal cardinality specifically, but something more general—perhaps the accomplishment of a feat (similar to the expression, "ta-da!"). Even repeating the last count term might be just an indication that the child recognizes that term as the "result" generated by the count, without any accompanying knowledge of the cardinal meaning of that result.

Understanding That Counting Yields a Cardinal Value

Because an understanding of cardinality entails realizing that the last term in a count represents the quantity of the whole set, it should be possible to evaluate children's understanding of cardinality by looking at their ability to use the results of a count to answer questions about that quantity. Several lines of evidence bear on this point. Fuson et al. (1985) studied how young children responded when asked about the number of objects in a set they had just counted. If children realize that the last number in their count represents the entire set, they might be expected to answer such questions by simply restating that last number rather than by recounting all the items. In fact, 3- and 4-year-old children very often respond in just this way, but 2-year-olds rarely do. Because the younger children are not very accurate in their counting, it might be thought that their tendency to recount reflects some insecurity about their counts. However, this idea did not fit well with the effects of set size in the study. Children's counting was significantly more accurate when the sets were small (two to four items) than when they were larger (five to seven items), but the likelihood that children would respond to the "How many?" question without recounting did not vary with numerosity. In fact, most children responded in the same way to all or nearly all of the problems.

Le Corre, Van de Walle, Brannon, and Carey (2006) addressed the relation between children's learning of the counting sequence and their understanding of cardinality by comparing the performance of 2- to 4-year-old children across small-numerosity (one to three items) and larger-numerosity (four to eight items) arrays on several numerical tasks, including the "give-a-number" task (Wynn, 1990; see also Sophian, 1987), the WOC, or

"What's on this card?" task (R. Gelman, 1993), and the "counting puppet" task (Briars & Siegler, 1984; Gelman & Meck, 1983), in which children are asked to judge whether a puppet counts correctly. Varying levels of success across tasks supported the conjecture that the difficulties children have with the give-a-number task are due at least in part to task-specific performance demands, such as the need to remember the target number while counting out items (Frye, Braisby, Love, Maroudas, & Nicholls, 1989; Sophian, 1987). At the same time, however, the highest numerical value at which individual children demonstrated understanding of the relation between counting and cardinality was very often the same, or very close, across tasks. Thus, Le Corre et al. suggest that children acquire an understanding of the cardinal meanings of the first few number words one by one, often long after they have incorporated that word in their counting. This interpretation, of course, is directly contrary to R. Gelman and Gallistel's (1978) thesis that knowledge of counting principles, including cardinality, precedes and guides the learning of the counting procedure.

If young children, when they are first learning to count, do not understand that counting provides information about the cardinal value of a collection, what do they think it is about? Sophian (1987) suggested that children first learn to count as a kind of recitation game (similar to the "This little piggy went to market ..." rhyme that people recite while wiggling a child's toes one by one) and only later come to appreciate the quantitative meaning of what they are doing—first as a way of obtaining the numerical value of a single set and later as a way of determining the relation between two sets. Wynn (1990) drew a very similar conclusion based on her own studies of children's performance on a range of counting-related tasks. Both investigators hypothesized that, before counting has acquired quantitative significance, children's decisions about whether to count are controlled by situational cues, such as the presence of a collection of discrete items, and the adult prompt, "How many?" or "Count them" (presumably because adults respond positively when children do count in these contexts).

Two kinds of evidence provide empirical support for that hypothesis. Fuson (1988) showed that children who correctly answered a "How many?" question about a set they had just counted often were unable to indicate what the number they gave as an answer referred to (i.e., by making a gesture that encompassed all the objects). Even more strikingly, Wynn (1990) found that young children sometimes altered the sequence of counting terms so as to make the results of a count conform to the number they wanted. For example, a child who put out three objects in response to a request that he put out five, responded to a request that he count the objects by pointing to each in turn and saying, "one, two, five." Wagner and Walters (1982) observed the same kind of adjustments to the counting sequence in their longitudinal study of young children's numerical concepts.

Counting and Comparisons Between Sets

Mathematically, a particularly important aspect of understanding the cardinal significance of a count is understanding that the outcome of a count does not only establish the numerical value of the counted set but also provides information about its numerical relation to other sets whose cardinal value is known. Sophian (1987, Experiment 1) examined children's understanding of this aspect of cardinality by asking children questions about the numerical relation between two sets (e.g., "If we give the balloons to the clowns, can each clown have a balloon?") and observing whether or not they counted the collections as a way of determining the answers. Of particular interest was their performance in a condition in which the collections were separated spatially and arranged in different configurations, as illustrated in Figure 2.3, so that visual inspection was not an effective way of ascertaining the relation between the collections. For the most part, preschool children did not count under these circumstances, and correspondingly were not very accurate in evaluating the numerical relations between the collections. Importantly, however, the children had little trouble answering the same sorts of questions about collections that were presented in a manner that facilitated visual comparison (i.e., with items from the two collections in one-to-one correspondence except for the extra item in the larger collection, if the two collections were numerically unequal). Thus, the children's tendency not to count in the spatially separated condition was not due to a lack of understanding of the relational questions that were posed.

In a subsequent study, Sophian (1988) tested preschool children's understanding of counting as a basis for numerical comparison in another way. In order to rule out performance factors such as lack of confidence in

Figure 2.3. Configuration of a separated-sets array in Sophian's (1987) research. The child is asked whether there is a balloon for every clown, but she or he cannot visually evaluate the correspondence between the sets because they are spatially separated and arranged in different configurations.

their counting accuracy, the children in this study were not asked to determine the relation between two numerical collections themselves but rather to evaluate the way a puppet counted. The array presented to the puppet always consisted of two types of objects, grouped separately from one another, for example, a group of big horses and a group of little horses. On different trials, the experimenter asked the puppet either to evaluate the relation between two subsets ("Is there a big horse for every little horse?") or to determine the numerosity of the two subsets combined ("How many horses are there?"). On half the trials of each type, the puppet counted all the items together and on half the puppet counted each subset separately. The experimenter then asked the child, "Was that a good way for the puppet to find out?" The results were very clear. Regardless of the question the puppet had been asked, the children overwhelmingly approved counts that included all the objects, whereas their responses to counts of the two subsets separately were mixed.

Other evidence that preschool children do not understand the connection between counting outcomes and relations between sets comes from research examining children's understanding of one-to-one correspondence. In a study of children's understanding of sharing, Frydman and Bryant (1988) found that 4-year-old children readily divided a collection of discrete items into equal shares by distributing items to each recipient in turn in a one-to-one fashion (a form of sharing also observed by Miller, 1984). After the shares had been created, however, Frydman and Bryant went on to ask the children how many items were in each share. Children readily counted to determine the numerosity of the first share about which they were questioned. Interestingly, however, they did not simply use the result of that count to answer a subsequent question about a second share. Instead, they undertook to count that share as well. Moreover, when the experimenter prevented them from doing so (screening the objects from view), only 10 of 24 children were able to give the correct answer, that is, the number they had just gotten by counting an equivalent share.

Sophian, Wood, and Vong (1995) further examined children's understanding of the idea that a count of one set could provide information about the numerical value of a second corresponding set by comparing children's performance in two conditions. The first was quite similar to Frydman and Bryant's (1988) task, in that children observed the construction of two sets through a one-to-one allocation process, then were instructed to count one of those sets, and finally were asked how many objects were in the other set, which was screened from view. Although the 3-year-olds in this study were not very successful in identifying the numerosity of the hidden set even when they were explicitly told to count the corresponding visible set (mean percentage correct = 52%), 4- and 5-year-olds performed fairly well in that condition. However, the performance of the 4-year-olds (but not that of the

5-year-olds) dropped substantially in a second condition, which differed from the first only in that the children were not explicitly told to count the visible set of objects but only to move them from one location to another on the table in front of them. The patterns of performance of 4-year-olds and 5-year-olds across the two conditions are shown graphically in Figure 2.4. In the move condition, although the objects that the children had moved remained visible and the children could have counted them, 4-year-olds were substantially less likely to use them to determine the numerosity of the corresponding screened set than they were when they had been explicitly told to count the visible set.

Which Comes First: Principles or Performance?

Sophian's (1987) conclusion that an understanding of the cardinal significance of counting emerges only in the latter part of the preschool period diverges from the rational-constructivist thesis (R. Gelman, 1991, 1993) that counting principles are already in place as children are learning to count and guide them in that learning. If children initially learn counting as a kind of recitation game and only later come to appreciate its quantitative significance, then the kind of principled knowledge R. Gelman de-

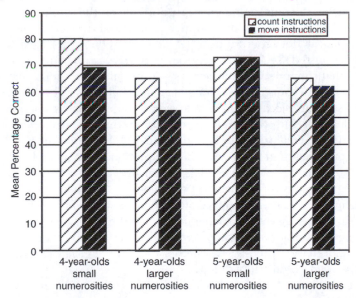

Figure 2.4. Percentages of problems on which the 4- and 5-year-olds in Experiment 2 of Sophian, Wood, and Vong (1995) correctly identified the numerosity of a hidden collection on the basis of a one-to-one correspondence relation between its elements and the elements of a visible set that they had either been instructed to count or just to move from one location to another.

scribes must be a result of learning to count rather than a "skeletal structure" that supports the learning process. Conversely, if the principles are present as children begin learning to count, then a lack of understanding of the quantitative significance of counting cannot be the explanation for the limitations Sophian (1987) and others (e.g., Saxe, 1977; Schaeffer, Eggleston, & Scott, 1974) observed in the ways young children do and do not use counting.

The incorrect but principled counts observed by R. Gelman and Gallistel (1978) support the idea that children know the principles first, and gradually graft their culture's conventional counting sequence onto them as they learn to count. However, as Siegler (1979) noted, the strength of this evidence as support for the view that principles precede counting developmentally is qualified by the small number of occurrences of incorrect but principled counts.

Another line of evidence for the principles-first position comes from the study of children's ability to detect errors in counts they observe. R. Gelman and Meck (1983) reasoned that an error-detection task was more likely to reveal the full extent of children's knowledge than their own counting, because it places fewer performance demands on the children that could interfere with the demonstration of their competence. Accordingly, in two experiments (one on the one-to-one principle and one on the stable-order principle), they had children watch a puppet counting and asked them to judge whether "it was OK to count the way he did or not OK" (p. 347). Nearly all of the children tested (3-, 4-, and 5-year-olds) judged correct counts OK, including ones that contained "pseudoerrors"—unusual but not incorrect ways of counting, such as counting the arrays in an unusual order. They were slightly less consistent in rejecting counts that violated the principles of one-to-one and stable order, but still did so far more often than not. In a third experiment on the cardinal principle, 3- and 4-year-old children again watched as a puppet counted, but in this case at the completion of the count he was again asked, "How many?" On some trials, he answered correctly; on others, he gave one of three types of incorrect responses: (a) answering with the next number in the counting sequence after the one with which the count had ended, (b) answering with an earlier number in the counting sequence, or (c) answering with a nonnumerical property of the last-counted item such as its color. Children were then asked whether the puppet gave the right answer, which they had no difficulty doing.

The most compelling aspect of these results is that children were able to distinguish between correct but unusual counts and incorrect ones. Because presumably children had rarely if ever seen others count in either of these ways, the fact that they were able to identify which ones were correct and which were not cannot be explained by modeling and thus provides strong support for the notion that they had principled knowledge. Inasmuch as R.

Gelman and Meck (1983) did not assess the children's procedural knowledge, however, the result does not establish that the principled knowledge was developmentally prior to the corresponding procedural knowledge. It is not unusual for 3-year-old children, particularly middle-class children, to have learned to count at least small sets accurately (as R. Gelman & Meck themselves show in a fourth experiment), and it could be in that process that they gained knowledge of the counting principles.

Two subsequent research projects (Briars & Siegler, 1984; Frye et al., 1989) provided a direct test of the relation between counting ability and the ability to identify counting errors, by collecting independent measures of the two and examining patterns of success and failure. In both studies, children's error detection performance was substantially lower than R. Gelman and Meck (1983) had reported, particularly on problems that required either the identification of correct but nonstandard counts as correct or the rejection of incorrect counts. Furthermore, both studies obtained evidence that success on the error-detection task was a later rather than an earlier achievement than successful counting itself. For instance, in Briars and Siegler's Experiment 2, nine 3-year-olds met a 75% correct criterion for accurate counting but failed to correctly reject 75% of incorrect counts in the error-detection task, whereas no children showed the opposite pattern of failing to meet the criterion for accurate counting yet correcting rejecting 75% of counting errors in the error-detection task. Similarly, Frye et al. (Experiment 2) reported evidence from a Guttman scalogram analysis examining patterns of success and failure across counting versus error-detection tasks with small (4- or 5-item) or large (12- or 14-item) sets (using a criterion of 75% correct to define success on each task). The results of this analysis indicated that both successful counting with small sets and successful counting with large sets preceded successful error detection with either set size (although within each task, success with small sets preceded success with large ones).

WHERE DO WE GO FROM HERE?

The ideas about young children's counting that R. Gelman and Gallistel (1978) introduced more than 25 years ago have clearly been scientifically productive, in that they essentially gave birth to a field of inquiry that is still growing today. The fruitfulness of that inquiry is apparent both in the methodological innovations that have emerged from it and in the expanding scope of the research in terms of the range of numerical abilities and the range of age groups that have been addressed. Yet investigators remain divided as to the most promising interpretations of the accumulated research findings, and it does not seem likely that a consensus will emerge any time soon.

Despite the continuing theoretical controversy, progress is evident in the articulation of new and promising perspectives on the developmental origins of numerical knowledge. To my mind, a particularly interesting advance in thinking about numerical development was the introduction of the idea that early number-related behavior may arise from object-file representations rather than from representations of number (Simon, 1997). This idea is not merely an alternative explanation for findings initially thought to reflect substantial numerical abilities in infancy. By distinguishing between the representation of individual objects and the representation of number, it helps us to think more clearly about what it means to represent number, and it points to a potentially important link between early numerical cognition and the fundamental ability to parse the world into separate objects (Spelke, Breinlinger, & Macomber, 1992). The potential developmental ramifications of this link are intriguing, specifically the possibility that numerical processing may grow out of the processes by which very young infants individuate objects (Sophian, 1997). In the remainder of this book, I develop a related theoretical perspective about numerical development and about mathematical development more generally—a perspective that questions the widely held assumption that the detection of numerical properties of collections of objects or events is the initial kernel from which the bulk of children's mathematical development proceeds. That assumption is shared, at least implicitly, by all of the theoretical perspectives on early numerical knowledge that I have discussed in this chapter. But what foundation is there for it? As noted in chapter 1, it is not consistent with Davydov's (1975a) analysis of the relations between the concept of number and other mathematical concepts, such as equality, less than and greater than, and unit. And as the work on small-number discrimination reviewed earlier in this chapter shows (e.g., Clearfield & Mix, 1999, 2001; Feigenson, Carey, & Spelke, 2002), it is not particularly consistent with patterns that discriminative-looking infants show when numerical differences are pitted against differences in area or contour length. It does appear to accord reasonably well with the behavior of preschool children, who, for instance, approach the task of creating equal shares of a continuous quantity by first breaking it up into smaller pieces and then distributing those pieces in such a way as to create numerically equal collections (Miller, 1984). But such results need not mean that counting is at the forefront from the beginning of development; they are equally compatible with the idea that number becomes an important tool for quantitative thinking as children gain proficiency in counting.

An important corollary of the idea that counting may not be conceptually or developmentally primary is the recognition that number is just one dimension of magnitude, and counting is just one way of describing and comparing quantities. The development of children's counting and whole-number knowledge, then, is inseparable from the development of other kinds of mathematical knowledge, including knowledge about other quantitative dimensions (length, area, volume, mass) and knowledge about other kinds of numbers (especially rational numbers).

Chapter 3

Quantitative Comparison Without Numbers

Numerosity is just one dimension along which quantities can be compared. Others are length, area, volume, and mass. Similarly, counting is just one of a class of procedures for comparing quantities. Indeed, both discrete and continuous quantities can be compared without any reference to number. For example, two collections of discrete objects can be precisely compared by putting elements of the two collections into one-to-one correspondence until all the elements of one collection have been exhausted and then determining whether any elements of the other remain unpaired. Two lengths can be precisely compared by placing them side by side in order to determine whether either one extends past the end of the other, or by using an intermediary such as a stick, and comparing how far along the stick each of the lengths extends. Volumes can be compared by placing two quantities into identical containers (or placing each volume in succession in the same container) and observing whether they rise to the same height.

Whereas the *counting-first view* holds that counting is the foundation for children's developing quantitative reasoning, the *comparison-of-quantities view* suggests that nonnumerical forms of comparison may be developmentally and conceptually antecedent to numerical ones. To complement chapter 2's discussion of research on children's counting, in this chapter I review what is known about young children's use of forms of quantitative comparison that are nonnumerical in the sense that they do not involve assigning numerical values (exact or approximate) to the quantities being compared.

I begin by examining what is known about children's use of correspondence relations to compare numerical quantities without counting. Two developmental insights emerge from the available studies. First, the differentiation of number from continuous quantitative dimensions is an important developmental achievement, one that appears to be attained only gradually over the years of early childhood. And second, children make numerical comparisons on the basis of correspondence relations between two collections before they do so by counting.

Next, I examine what is known about how children make comparisons between two kinds of continuous quantities—lengths and areas. The process of comparing lengths by aligning them and checking whether one extends beyond the end of the other appears to be a very basic skill, one that has mostly been presupposed in studies of other issues rather than investigated in its own right. However, the errors young children make on length conservation tasks support the conclusion drawn from studies of numerical comparison that different quantitative dimensions are not clearly differentiated in early childhood. Likewise, differentiation among dimensions is again an issue in the comparison of areas, in that young children often judge the taller of two rectangles to be greater in area even if it is much narrower than the other rectangle. However, if the alternatives can be superimposed, young children show considerable facility in comparing them on that basis.

Finally, I consider research on children's reasoning about proportional relations among unenumerated quantities. In contrast to numerical forms of proportional reasoning, which are characteristically difficult for young children, the spatial proportionality problems used in this research are solved correctly by children as young as 4 years of age.

I conclude with a discussion of the idea that although children begin making quantitative comparisons very early in development, they only gradually make clear distinctions among different quantitative dimensions. Noting that there is not good empirical evidence on the basis of which to differentiate between this interpretation of developmental changes and interpretations based on the idea that children learn to choose among comparison strategies, I nevertheless offer my own reasons for considering the gradual-differentiation hypothesis promising, and I discuss its instructional ramifications.

COMPARING NUMERICAL QUANTITIES WITHOUT NUMBERS

For clarity, it is important to distinguish two senses in which children might compare numerical quantities without numbers. The first is related to the issue raised in infancy research as to whether infants' numerosity discriminations may be based on continuous properties of the arrays presented to them rather than on number (cf. chap. 2). Insofar as collections of items are compared on the basis of continuous properties like those considered in the infancy research, those comparisons are not, in fact, numerical ones. The quantities may be characterized as numerical in that they are composed of discrete items, and the comparison may even have been elicited by a numerical question, but the comparison itself is nonnumerical inasmuch as it is based on continuous rather than discrete properties of the quantities to be compared. The second sense in which numerical comparison may be done without numbers is quite different, in that the comparison is in fact based on the numerical properties of the quantities to be compared, even though the comparison is made without determining the numerical value of either quantity. Instead, spatial or temporal correspondence relations between quantities are used to determine whether they are numerically equal or not.

Differentiating Number From Other Quantitative Dimensions

The potential for children to confuse numerical relations between sets with other kinds of quantitative relations first came to researchers' attention in the context of Piagetian research on number conservation. Piaget (1952) observed that young children who have judged two rows of counters equal in number when they were placed side by side often maintain that one row has more when the counters are displaced so that one row becomes much longer than the other. Although there has been intense debate as to the reasons for this error and its developmental ramifications (e.g., Bryant, 1972; R. Gelman, 1982; McGarrigle & Donaldson, 1975), there is no doubt that it does occur.

A common assumption is that it reflects children's reliance on length as a cue to number (e.g., Bryant, 1972; Siegler, 1995). This interpretation presupposes that children know what sort of judgments they are being asked to make, but rely on inadequate strategies to make them. An important alternative, however, is that children are not clear as to the distinction between different sorts of quantitative comparison—in this case, between numerical comparison and length comparison. In this view, it is not that children take row length as an indicator of number, but rather that they respond on the basis of a global impression about the amount in each row without differentiating between alternative dimensions of quantity such as row length versus number.

Bryant's (1972) study of conservation of inequality provides a good illustration of these alternative interpretations. In Bryant's study, a numerical difference between two rows (containing 19 counters vs. 20 counters) was first established by presenting the rows in one-to-one correspondence, with an unpaired item in the more numerous set. The rows were then rearranged so that either the row of 19 became substantially longer than the row of 20, or else the two rows ended up equal in length but with varying spaces between items so that pairings between items were not salient. Bryant found that when the final array consisted of rows differing in length, children chose the longer (but numerically lesser) one, but when the rows were equal in length, they conserved their initial inequality judgment. His interpretation was that the salience of length differences obscured children's knowledge that the initial inequality between the rows would remain unchanged by altering the spacing of the items within rows. Thus, he argued that children do possess conservation knowledge, but may fail to rely on it in the face of conflicting length cues. However, the results are equally interpretable in terms of a global notion of quantity in which length and numerosity are not clearly distinguished. This account differs from Bryant's in that it does not take children's success in the equal-lengths condition as evidence of specifically numerical reasoning. Children are conserving quantity in some sense, in that they rely on the relation between the collections that was established initially to judge the relation between them after the transformation. But that may not mean they are reasoning specifically about the relative numerosities of the rows and expecting that relation to be unchanged by the transformation. Although it is clear to us (adults) that the quantitative relation that was established initially is an inequality in numerosity, the children themselves may have used the correspondence relations in the original array only as an indicator of amount in a more global, undifferentiated sense. Then, when the items are repositioned so that there are no strong cues as to whether the amounts are the same or not, they rely on their initial global impression to answer the question that is posed.

This possibility also suggests an alternative interpretation for training studies in which children have been taught to conserve number (e.g., R. Gelman, 1982; Siegler, 1995) or to use counting as a means of comparing two sets (Michie, 1984). Specifically, the training effects may reflect learning about the distinction between row length and number rather than learning about the reliability of alternative ways of making numerical judgments. For example, R. Gelman (1982) taught 3- and 4-year-old children to conserve number by giving them training trials in which they counted each set and compared the numerical values before the transformation; then, after the transformation, the children were explicitly asked whether the numerical value of each row was still what it had been as well as whether the relation between the two rows was still the same. R. Gelman suggested that this training was effective because it enabled the children to access knowledge about one-to-one correspondence that is implicit in their counting. Alternatively, it may be that what the training accomplished was to clarify for the children the distinction between numerical properties of the collections, which were not affected by the transformation, and the lengths of the rows, which were.

Similarly, Siegler (1995) reported marked improvements in number conservation over four training sessions in which children received feedback on their judgments. Siegler interpreted the progress in terms of strategy choice; children learned that reasoning about whether or not anything was added to or removed from the array was a better basis for solving the problems than reasoning about whether the rows were equal in length after the transformation. This interpretation assumes that children's goal from the outset was to find ways to compare the collections numerically, and over the course of training they learned how best to do it. However, Siegler's results are equally consistent with the idea that training enabled them to understand more clearly what the task was. In this view, they learned to differentiate between number and other quantitative properties of the arrays as they received feedback about their judgments. Interestingly, the children made the most progress when, after being told whether they were correct, they were asked to explain the basis for the experimenter's judgment. It may be that the effort to articulate why the arrays were or were not equal in number, often in the face of conflicting length cues, helped children to make the distinction between number and row length.

One factor that clearly needs to be considered in evaluating alternative interpretations such as the strategy choice hypothesis versus the differentiation hypothesis is the role of language. In particular, insofar as children fail to differentiate appropriately between quantitative dimensions, is it just that they are unable to interpret the question that has been posed or does their lack of differentiation have a more fundamental basis, in a global conceptualization of quantity? The term *more* is notoriously ambiguous (e.g., Gathercole, 1985; Laxon, 1981; Moore & Frye, 1986), and it is plausible that training procedures that provide feedback about children's judgments could help them to arrive at the intended interpretation of these terms. However, conservation errors have been observed even in studies that have replaced explicitly quantitative questions ("Which is more?") with choice tasks ("Which would you rather have?") involving attractive food substances (e.g., S. A. Miller, 1976). Presumably, insofar as children differentiate between different aspects of quantity, their preferences will be based on their judgments of aggregate amount rather than on factors such as row length. Therefore, the occurrence of errors even in this context strongly suggests that the confusion goes deeper than just a linguistic ambiguity. Training procedures that improve performance, then, may not only clarify the question being posed but also help children to appreciate the need to distinguish, at a conceptual level, between different aspects of quantity. This is not to say, however, that children encode only a single global impression of quantity. If they did not at some level take note of the fact that two rows differed in number as well as length, it is not clear how feedback as to the correctness of their judgments about the quantitative relations between the rows could help them to learn to focus on number rather than length. It appears, therefore, that when children see stimuli such as rows of objects, more than one quantitative property of those stimuli is encoded. It is a big step, however, from encoding those properties to realizing that they do not always co-vary and determining which has the greatest relevance for a particular kind of quantitative comparison.

Clear evidence that different quantitative properties are encoded comes from studies that have succeeded in demonstrating differentiation on the basis of a particular quantitative dimension by constructing problems so as to eliminate differences on other potentially salient dimensions. Brannon and Van de Walle's (2001, Experiment 2) study of early numerical discrimination illustrates this idea. In the study, 2- and 3-year-old children were asked to identify the "winner" (the more numerous) of two collections, which were arranged nonlinearly in separate, covered boxes, paired so as to present numerical contrasts ranging from one versus three to four versus five and four versus six. Sticker size was varied so that the collection that was more numerous was sometimes greater in total area and sometimes smaller in total area than the less numerous collection. After the comparison task, the children received two counting tasks that involved identifying the number of items in arrays of two to eight items. Two aspects of the results were quite interesting. First, in the numerical comparison task, the children performed above chance on each of the numerical contrasts that were tested. Performance did not vary significantly across the different numerical contrasts, nor across problems on which the numerical relation between the arrays was congruent versus incongruent with the relation between their aggregate areas. Second, performance did not vary with age but it did vary with children's counting ability. In particular, children who were completely unsuccessful on one or both of the two counting tasks responded at chance, and substantially lower than the rest of the sample, on the comparison task. However, beyond the achievement of minimal counting ability, variations in children's levels of performance on the counting tasks did not predict their performance on the comparison task.

Other studies indicate that preschool children, especially, but older children as well to a degree, have difficulty differentiating between number and other quantitative dimensions. In some studies, number is inappropriately used to make continuous quantity comparisons; in others, continuous quantitative properties are used when a numerical comparison is called for. K. F. Miller's (1984) work on children's dividing up of quantities into equal shares nicely illustrates inappropriate reliance on number to compare overall amounts. Faced with sharing out a continuous quantity, such as a strip of clay "spaghetti," 3- and 5-year-old children often cut the total quantity into pieces in order to distribute them in a turn-taking fashion ("one for you and one for you"). But when the number of pieces a child created was not a perfect multiple of the number of recipients, she or he would run out of pieces in the last round of the distribution. Several children solved this problem by taking one of the pieces that a short-changed recipient already had and cutting it in two to create another piece for him. This strategy, while equating number across shares, clearly does not alter the aggregate amount, in a continuous quantity sense, of the short-changed share. Thus it seems clear that the children's focus was on making the shares numerically equal rather than on equating the aggregate amount of "spaghetti" across shares.

In a subsequent study, K. F. Miller (1989) obtained further evidence of this kind, showing that 3- and 5-year-old children typically judged that two initially identical rows of items were no longer equal in amount after an item from one of the rows was cut in half. At the same time, the children tended to disregard changes in item size that left the numerosities of the rows unaffected, which again is consistent with the idea that they were focusing on number rather than aggregate amount.

Older children—8- and 10-year-olds—performed much better on the problems involving cutting items in half, but the 8-year-olds still gave evidence of having difficulty differentiating between quantitative dimensions on other problems in the study. Specifically, their judgments were quite error-prone on problems in which one of two initially identical arrays was replaced with another that differed in a quantitative dimension that was irrelevant to the type of quantitative comparison they were asked to make. Thus, after watching the experimenter replace one of two initially identical arrays with an array composed of the same number of larger or smaller items, even 8-year-old children often judged that the array composed of the larger items was more numerous. Similar confusions occurred on length-comparison problems, in which one of two initially identical lengths of clay was replaced with one that was wider or narrower (but the same length), and on area comparison problems, in which one of two initially identical squares of clay was replaced with a square that was either thicker or less thick (but the same in area). On the length-comparison problems, children often stated that the wider alternative was longer, and on the area comparison problems, they often stated that the thicker alternative was greater in area.

As the patterns of performance on the K. F. Miller's (1989) substitution problems suggest, confusions between different quantitative dimensions are by no means limited to the use of numerical information in comparing overall amounts. Indeed, number is not always the dominant factor in young children's judgments about aggregate amount. On a comparison task in which children were shown pairs of pictorial arrays that differed orthogonally in number and in aggregate amount, Sophian (2000a) found no evidence that young children, who relied on number to identify the alternative that was greater in aggregate amount, focused on the size of individual pieces rather than on the number of pieces. Examples of the arrays used in this study can be seen in Figure 3.1. The pictured items were described as cookies, and the children were asked which alternative on each problem would give a Cookie Monster toy more to eat. None of the age groups tested—3-, 4-, and 5-year-olds—based their choices primarily on the numerical properties of the arrays. Instead, the 3-year-olds often made the error of basing their judgments on the size of individual items within the array rather than on the aggregate amount. Thus, they tended to perform better on the conflict problems than on the agreement problems because of the salient difference in cookie sizes on those problems. It seems likely that the very large differences in size in this study—often much greater than the 2:1 difference K. F. Miller produced by cutting—led children to focus on item size rather than number in this case.

Taken together, the results of conservation studies and other studies involving quantitative comparison suggest that young children encode a variety of quantitative aspects of the materials presented to them but often fail to select the most appropriate basis of comparison for the problems posed to them. The fact that, across tasks, children are responsive both to number and to continuous dimensions of quantity indicates that they are able to ap-

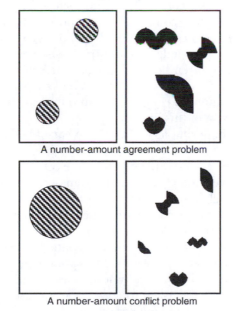

A number-amount agreement problem

A number-amount conflict problem

Figure 3.1.   Examples of the stimuli used by Sophian (2000a). In the upper panel, the array on the right is both more numerous and greater in aggregate area. In the lower panel, the array on the right is more numerous but the one on the left is greater in aggregate area (and in the area of individual items).

prehend both types of quantitative relations. However, difficulties in selecting the most appropriate basis for comparison on different problems
suggest that they have not differentiated clearly between different aspects
of quantity. Instead, the numerical and nonnumerical properties of the
quantities being compared have a strong effect on whether children focus
on numerical or nonnumerical aspects of quantity in making a comparison.
Despite the conflation of continuous-quantity comparisons and numerical
comparisons in young children's judgments, however, they may not be un-
aware that length, for example, is different from number. Instead, they may
not discriminate between different types of quantitative comparisons because they do not realize that a quantity can be greater than another in one
respect but not in another. As a result, they do not appreciate the importance of selecting the appropriate type of quantitative comparison for a
given problem and instead allow whatever quantitative features are
particularly salient to dominate their reasoning.

Using Correspondence Relations to Make Numerical Comparisons

R. Gelman and Gallistel's (1978) analysis of counting noted that sound
counting presupposes the establishment of a one-to-one correspondence
between the items being counted and the terms of a count sequence. It
would thus appear that counting presupposes an understanding of
one-to-one correspondence. However, R. Gelman (e.g., R. Gelman, 1982)
has maintained that knowledge about one-to-one correspondence is initially embedded in children's counting procedures and remains inaccessi-
ble in other contexts for some time. Research examining children's use of
correspondence relations to compare sets and its relation to counting provides an empirical test of this idea.

Sophian (1987, Experiment 1) showed 3-year-old children arrays composed of two types of objects and asked them to judge whether each of one
type of item could be paired with an item of the other type (e.g., "Are there
enough trucks for every man?"). When the items were presented in pairs—a
man beside each truck, with an extra man on some trials—children almost
never counted and yet were correct on a substantial majority of trials, indicating that they used the pair-wise presentation to evaluate the relation between the two sets. Presenting the items in a spatially separated manner—a
group of men and a group of trucks—led to poorer performance than the
paired presentation, and only a modest increase in counting. In a second
experiment, children were asked to create a second set that was equal in
number to the first (e.g., to put out just enough balloons so that every clown
could get one), under conditions that either permitted or precluded pairing each new object with one of the items comprising the original set. (In the

latter case, the experimenter required that the new items be placed in a separate tray, which was shaped differently from the original array so that children could not reproduce the spatial configuration of those items.) When allowed to pair the items, 3-year-old children generally did so and thereby achieved predominantly correct performance even though they rarely counted the items. When pairing was prevented, however, counting increased only slightly and performance dropped markedly. Older preschoolers (4- and $4\frac{1}{2}$-year-olds) likewise did better on problems where the items could be spatially paired than on ones where that was precluded, notwithstanding substantial age-related increases in the use of counting on the latter problems.

These results suggest that very young children are more facile with comparing sets on the basis of one-to-one correspondence relations between their elements than with comparing them via counting, although counting skills develop rapidly over the latter part of the preschool period. A further study in which reasoning based on one-to-one correspondences was directly contrasted with reasoning based on numerical values corroborates this developmental pattern. Sophian, Harley, and Martin (1995, Experiment 1) presented children with a matching-to-sample task in which they were asked to identify the pictures that best matched brief stories about two complementary types of things. The story presented information either about the numerical value of one set (e.g., "Here are four clowns") or about the numerical relation between two sets (e.g., "Every clown wants his own umbrella, and there is an umbrella for each clown"), or both. Of particular interest was performance on conflict problems, in which children had to choose among three pictures: (a) one that matched the numerical value in the story, (b) one that matched the relational information in the story, and (c) one that did not match the story in either respect. Children received a block of these problems at the start of the experiment and then another after a series of no-conflict trials on which they received feedback about numerical and relational matches (in counterbalanced order). Groups of 3-, 4-, and 5-year-old children all performed above chance on the no-conflict feedback trials. However, only the 4- and 5-year-olds were above chance in identifying both numerical and relational matches on the conflict trials (choosing each type of matching picture more often than the nonmatching picture). The 3-year-olds were at chance on the initial block of conflict trials, and after the training they chose the relational match but not the numerical match significantly more often than the nonmatching picture. Thus, the results suggest that children pay more attention to correspondence relations between sets than to specific numerical values in the early part of the preschool period, but the impact of numerical information on children's reasoning increases as the children get older.

COMPARING LENGTHS

Lengths are the simplest of continuous quantities to compare because they involve only one dimension and that dimension is visually accessible (unlike mass). The comparison of lengths by placing items side by side and comparing their endpoints is so fundamental that it is generally taken for granted rather than empirically investigated in research on children's reasoning about length. For instance, studies of length conservation (e.g., McGarrigle & Donaldson, 1975) start with two linear quantities such as pieces of string placed side by side so that the ends match and the question is posed, "Are they the same length?" However, data on these initial judgments are not typically reported; instead the focus is on how the children respond after a transformation of the array that caused the ends no longer to be in alignment. Similarly, in his study of children's ideas about measurement, Bryant (1982) took for granted that children could compare two lengths when they were placed side by side and used that knowledge to demonstrate to the children the validity of comparing objects that are not side by side by using an intermediate measure.

Some direct evidence of facility in comparing lengths as early as 3 years of age comes from K. F. Miller's (1989) research, in which he included a transformation where one of two aligned lengths of spaghetti was replaced with another of a different color, which was again aligned with the remaining length of spaghetti in the original color. Miller reported that 94% of 3-year-olds' responses, and 100% of those of older children, were correct following this transformation. Thus, it is clear that even quite young children are facile in comparing lengths when the lengths are directly aligned with one another. This finding, of course, accords well with the evidence that children rely heavily on row length in number conservation and numerical comparison tasks (e.g., Bryant, 1972; Cowan, 1987; Michie, 1984). Although those results indicate that young children may not differentiate clearly between length and number, they also make it clear that young children easily identify the longer of two rows.

The extensive data showing that young children have difficulty reasoning about continuous quantities on Piagetian tasks like length seriation (Inhelder & Piaget, 1964) and conservation (Piaget, Inhelder, & Szeminska, 1960) may appear inconsistent with this conclusion. However, Piaget's concrete operational tasks were deliberately constructed so as to require children not just to make a single comparison between quantities but also to coordinate that comparison either with another comparison or with some other information (such as information about how an array was modified in a conservation problem). Thus, in length seriation studies, the ability to compare the lengths of two sticks is presupposed; the problem of interest arises when children must determine the proper placement for additional sticks, which are not as long as the longer of the original sticks but longer than the shorter one. What is difficult for the children is to coordinate the two relations—to think of a given stick as simultaneously shorter than one comparison stick and longer than another. If anything, the presupposition in this work that children are able to identify the longer of two sticks is consistent with the idea that young children are facile in comparing two lengths that are spatially aligned with one another.

In length conservation studies, similarly, children's ability to discern the initial equivalence of two lengths is presupposed; the focus is on children's interpretation of transformations that introduce bends in one of the lengths so that the endpoints no longer match. Here the challenge is to recognize that the initial relation between the lengths still holds even after the appearance of the array has been changed. Characteristically, very young children conclude that two lengths that were initially equal are no longer the same after bends have been introduced in one of them (Inhelder, Sinclair, & Bovet, 1974; Light, Buckingham, & Robbins, 1979, Experiment 1; Neilson, Dockrell, & McKechnie, 1983; Piaget et al., 1960). What is noteworthy about this response is that, although it is incorrect in that the total length has not changed, it is consistent with another quantitative property of the stimuli, the distance between endpoints, which does decrease when a bend is introduced. Thus, it may be that nonconservation responses stem from a lack of clear differentiation between different quantitative dimensions, specifically in length conservation problems between the total length of a path versus the as-the-crow-flies distance between its endpoints, rather than from a lack of understanding of how the transformation affects the specific dimension about which the children are queried.

Distinguishing Length From Other Quantitative Properties

Direct evidence of a failure to clearly differentiate length from other quantitative aspects of a situation comes from studies involving lengths made up of a number of distinct sections, so that a numerical dimension is also present. Under these circumstances, children often rely on numerical comparisons to answer questions about relative length. For example, Inhelder et al. (1974) reported that when shown two straight roads with matching endpoints, one made up of five 7-cm matchsticks and the other of seven 5-cm matchsticks, some children indicated that the row composed of a greater number of matchsticks would be "longer to walk." Children are especially likely to rely on number in this way when the "roads" they are comparing are oriented differently so that their endpoints cannot be compared, but numerical comparisons can even take precedence over comparisons between endpoints in some cases.

At the same time, that fact that in number conservation studies, which also pit the dimensions of number and length against one another, young children often base their judgments on row length (a continuous dimension) rather than number (e.g., Bryant, 1972; Siegler, 1995) indicates that number is not necessarily a more salient quantitative dimension than length. Young children make both numerical comparisons and length comparisons, but they have difficulty determining which dimension is the appropriate one to consider in a given problem situation.

The idea that a lack of differentiation between quantitative dimensions, some of which are affected by a transformation while others are not, contributes to young children's errors on length conservation tasks fits nicely with the results of an experiment that compared children's responses to two different types of length questions (K. F. Miller & Baillargeon, 1990, Study 1). In this study, 3- to 6-year-old children were asked to make judgments about the distance between two blocks before and after a screen was interposed between them (without changing their positions). In the Piagetian version of the task, the posttransformation question was whether the blocks were "now nearer together, farther apart, or still the same distance apart" (p. 106). An alternate version of the task asked children to choose a stick that would just fit between the two blocks so as to form a bridge. Here the posttransformation question was simply, "Now which stick will just fit between the blocks?" (p. 106). Children's performance on the bridge-building task reached 100% correct by 5 years of age and was significantly, and substantially, better than their performance on the parallel Piagetian task at each age level. Although children were not above chance in choosing the correct stick before the transformation, they believed the same stick would fit after the screen was introduced as before. The difference between this result and the tendency of children to judge that the blocks were no longer the same distance apart in the Piagetian version of the task appears to reflect the disambiguating effect of posing the question in terms of the functional goal of spanning the end blocks to form a bridge. The need to actually span the distance between the blocks makes it clear that what is at issue is the actual total distance and not the empty space or the appearance of the array.

Measuring Length

Research on children's understanding of measurement as it pertains to length has focused on the fundamental notion of using an intermediary to compare two lengths that cannot be directly juxtaposed. The effective use of an intermediary entails a kind of transitive inference in which the relation of each measured entity to the intermediary provides a basis for inferring their relationship to each other. If we symbolize the lengths to be compared as L1 and L2, and a span on the intermediary corresponding to the length L1 as I, then the possible inferences are:

L1 = I, L2 = I; therefore L1 = L2
L1 = I, L2 < I; therefore L2 < L1; and
L1 = I, L2 > I; therefore L2 > L1

Bryant and Kopytynska (1976) reported several studies indicating that children as young as 5 years of age are capable of making these types of inferences. In a clever experimental task, they asked children to determine whether holes drilled in pairs of blocks were equally deep or which was deeper. Because the bottoms of the holes, which were either 4 or 6 inches deep, were not visible, the comparison could not be made through direct visual inspection. A stick was provided, marked in such a way that both 4-inch and 6-inch lengths corresponded to distinctive points on the stick. Even in the absence of any instructions to use the stick, fully 75% of 5-year-olds used it appropriately on all four trials, and correspondingly answered all the depth-comparison questions correctly.

K. F. Miller (1989, Experiment 2) extended this work to even younger children. He contrasted a "finding" task, in which children had to find an object hidden in one of two holes, with a comparison task in which they were simply to compare the depth of the holes. In his procedure, children were explicitly shown that they could use a stick to compare the depth of the holes, and they were asked to verify that the two holes were equally deep. In the comparison task, the depth of the holes was then varied from trial to trial by hiding a short dowel in one of the holes, thus reducing the depth to which a stick could be inserted into the hole. Children were asked which hole would make a better hiding place for children who wanted to find a hiding place "where you only go in a little bit" (p. 599). In the finding task, the same short dowels were placed in the holes, but they were described as "children" who hid in the holes. Even 3-year-old children were successful on the finding task, although it was not until 4 years of age that children succeeded on the comparison task. K. F. Miller's explanation of children's better performance on the finding task is that measurement procedures are acquired as tools for doing particular kinds of things: "As with real tools, procedures such as measurement may initially be learned to accomplish specific ends and only gradually be adapted for more general purposes" (p. 600). This specificity in the ways in which measurement tools are initially used may well be related to the problems young children have in distinguishing between different quantitative dimensions. When asked which chimney will better serve as a hiding place "where you only go in a little bit," young children may not be as clear that what is at issue is the depth of the chimneys, rather than other quantitative properties such as the highly visible size of their openings. In inserting a stick to probe for a hidden child, the focus is not on any quantitative property of the chimney but on the physical impact of an obstacle (the hidden child) on the act of inserting a stick.

A particularly critical concept for the measurement of length (and other quantitative dimensions) is the notion of *iterating a unit*. Nunes, Light, and Mason (1993, Experiment 1) reported that 6- and 8-year-old children found it "nonproblematic" (p. 44) to use a fixed length of string to compare two lines that could not be directly juxtaposed, provided that one or both of the lines was equal in length to the string. However, the children had more difficulty when the string length corresponded to either half the length of one or both of the lines, or to twice the length of one or both of the lines, so that the children needed to either iterate a unit corresponding to the string's length or subdivide that unit in order to use the string effectively.

Iteration appears to be less problematic when a unit to be iterated is explicitly provided. Thus, for example, Hiebert (1984b) reported high levels of success among first graders who were asked to use Cuisenaire rods to make a straight road that would be the same length, or "just as far to walk," as one that had a bend in it. Children frequently covered the original road with the rods, and then attempted to move the rods as a group to the designated location for the new road. Not infrequently, they were unsuccessful in making the move without disturbing the arrangement of the Cuisenaire rods, but when this happened they realized that all they had to do was put the pieces back together (in any order), thus demonstrating an understanding that it was the sum of the small units that assured that the new road would be equal in length to the original road.

COMPARING AREAS

Comparing areas is much more complex than comparing lengths, for several reasons. First, area is two-dimensional. Some investigators have suggested that young children focus on only one salient dimension in thinking about area (e.g., Bausano & Jeffrey, 1975; Piaget et al., 1960); others suggest that they consider both dimensions but combine them incorrectly (Anderson & Cuneo, 1978; Wilkening, 1979). Furthermore, direct comparison is less straightforward with areas than it is with lengths. When two shapes are fairly similar, an effective way of comparing their sizes is to superimpose them (Yuzawa, Bart, & Yuzawa, 2000), but this strategy breaks down if the shapes differ substantially. For instance, in comparing a square and an isosceles right triangle, there will inevitably be sections of each that extend beyond the edges of the other if the smaller one is greater than half the size of the other. The comparison process then becomes one of evaluating the relative size of the protrusions of each shape beyond the edges of the other, or of imagining ways to rearrange one or both quantities so that their shapes are more comparable.

Most of the research on children's ideas about area has focused on whether, and if so how, they combine length and width information in thinking about area. Studies undertaken from a psycholinguistics' perspective, investigating children's interpretations of the terms *big* and *little*, indicated that 3- to 5-year-old children tend to focus on one dimension, typically height, in comparing the sizes of rectangles (e.g., Hobbs & Bacharach, 1990; Ravn & Gelman, 1984). Although stimulus characteristics that made width more salient could lead children to focus on width instead of height (e.g., Bausano & Jeffrey, 1975; Coley & Gelman, 1989), the majority of young children's judgments remained unidimensional in that they were based on height or width, but not both.

In contrast to this conclusion, however, studies conducted within the framework of functional measurement indicate that as early as 5 years of age, children combine both height and width in making ratings of stimulus size (Anderson & Cuneo, 1978; Wolf, 1995). The difference between these results and those indicating unidimensional judgments is primarily methodological. Whereas the studies of children's interpretation of big and little pit choices based on one dimension against choices based on area, the functional measurement studies assess the impact of each factor independently. Although some cases of unidimensional responding have been observed (e.g., Verge & Bogartz, 1978), the primary focus of these studies has been on the distinction between additive and multiplicative rules for combining the two dimensions. The multiplicative rule is correct, because area is a product of height and width, but in many cases children appear to combine the dimensions additively instead (e.g., Anderson & Cuneo, 1978; Wilkening, 1979). Interestingly, even a brief opportunity to handle the shapes can lead to a shift from additive to multiplicative responding (Wolf, 1995).

Yuzawa et al. (2000) examined 4- to 6-year-old children's strategies for physically comparing geometric shapes that were presented as cardboard cutouts. The most common strategy, occurring on approximately 46% of trials, was to place the stimuli side by side, a procedure that was not particularly effective. However, in about 32% of trials, the children placed the stimuli one on top of the other. This strategy, unlike the side-by-side strategy, was highly correlated with correct size comparison judgments ($r = .67, p < .01$). The pairs of shapes that were used lent themselves well to comparison via superimposition because when the sizes were the same, the shapes were also congruent (specifically, both were triangles with sides of 6, 8, and 10 cm), and when they differed, the shapes differed in only one dimension.

(Specifically, different-sized circles differed in diameter; different-sized rectangles differed only in width; and different-sized triangles differed in either height or length but not both.) Thus, when the sizes were the same, the shapes could be superimposed so that all the edges aligned perfectly, and when they differed, the smaller shape could be positioned so that it fit entirely within the larger.

Consider, in contrast, the relation between the square and the triangle in Figure 3.2. If we try to superimpose them, some part of each will inevitably stick out beyond the perimeter of the other. But it is possible to see that nevertheless they are the same size by imagining cutting each in half—the square along its diagonal, and the triangle along its access of symmetry (as indicated by the dotted lines in the figure). Although the original shapes cannot be cleanly superimposed, half of the square (cut diagonally) is exactly the same as half of the triangle. This example illustrates the close relation between superimposition and measurement. The small triangles that result from cutting each of the shapes in Figure 3.2 in half become a unit by means of which the two shapes can be compared. Because each of the large shapes can be superimposed with two of the small triangles, we know that they are the same size.

Not surprisingly, the notion that a shape can be cut and its pieces rearranged without changing its area is not transparent for young children. Nevertheless, Yuzawa et al. (2000) provided evidence that young children can use a procedure of superimposing units on larger shapes to make area judgments. The same children who participated in the size comparison task just described were subsequently presented with an area choice task in which they were given two identical "standard" rectangles and shown a series of five target shapes varying in size. The task was to identify the target shape that was the same area as the two standard rectangles. Of particular interest is children's performance in a "manipulative judgment" condition, wherein they were allowed to handle the stimuli, on a subset of the problems constructed so that the two standard rectangles could be perfectly su-

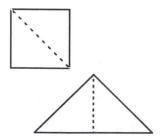

Figure 3.2.   Comparing areas of different shapes. Here, the fact that the area of the square and the large triangle are the same can be made clear by imagining cutting both of them into two smaller triangles.

perimposed on the correct target shape. On these problems, even the younger children (predominantly 4-year-olds) were correct 54% of the time, and the older ones (predominantly 5-year-olds) were correct fully 80% of the time. Performance was far lower on problems in the same condition that did not lend themselves well to comparison via superimposition because neither dimension of the correct target stimuli matched either the length or width of the standard rectangle. On these, the two age groups were correct only 20% and 36% of the time, respectively.

COMPARING SPATIAL PROPORTIONS

Ratios between two continuous quantities play an important role in the perception of objects and the physical interactions between them. As noted in chapter 1, for instance, even infants notice how much of an object is supported by a surface on which it rests, and the infants react differently to perceived support relations when the majority of the object is supported than when the majority overhangs empty space (Baillargeon, Needham, & DeVos, 1992, cited in Baillargeon, Kotovsky, & Needham, 1995). Similarly, ratios between height and width appear to play an important role in the perception of shape, forming the basis for distinctions such as "fat" versus "skinny." One object can look skinnier than another, even if it is wider, if it is also very much taller, and children as young as 4 years of age can identify which of two small rectangles matches a larger sample in this proportional property (Sophian, 2000b, Experiment 2). Thus, although proportional reasoning involving specific numerical values can be very difficult for children and even adults (e.g., Behr, Harel, Post, & Lesh, 1992; Lawton, 1993; C. F. Moore, Dixon, & Haines, 1991), it appears that even young children effectively engage in some nascent forms of proportional reasoning (see also Singer, Kohn, & Resnick, 1997). And there is some evidence that they may be more successful in doing so in reference to continuous quantities rather than discontinuous ones (Spinillo & Bryant, 1999).

A critical element of proportional reasoning even in its most basic forms is that it involves "second-order" reasoning about relations between relations (Piaget & Inhelder, 1975; Spinillo & Bryant, 1991). Thus, for example, since the notion of skinniness is itself relational, comparing the skinniness of different objects involves thinking about how the relation between width and height in one compares to the relation between width and height in the other. An important caveat in testing for proportional reasoning, however, is that in some cases dimensions that are defined relationally can also be perceived in their own right (i.e., nonrelationally). Thus, for example, *density* is defined as the relation between number and length or area, but density can also be perceived directly as the distance between neighbors. Therefore, comparing the density of two arrays does not necessarily involve proportional reasoning. It is less clear whether judgments of "skin-niness" can be understood that way. For some shapes, such as triangles, dif-ferences in skinniness will alter the angles in the figure, so that one triangle can be perceived as skinnier than another, not by comparing height–width relations, but by comparing how sharp the smallest angle is. In rectangles, the angles do not change, but a more subtle configurational property might be the basis for perceiving different degrees of skinniness. Certainly, if we sketch in the diagonals of a rectangle, the angle at which they meet will vary as a function of how skinny it is. If this property is the basis for children's comparative judgments, it would not be valid to interpret their success in comparing rectangle shapes to proportional reasoning.

To more decisively test children's ability to evaluate spatial proportions, Sophian (2000b, Experiment 3) examined their reasoning about another kind of proportional relation—the relative size of two parts of an ani-mal-like figure (a smaller circle representing the head and a larger one rep-resenting the body). In this context, it was possible to introduce differences in configurational properties even between stimuli for which the propor-tional relation was the same, by changing the position of the head in rela-tion to the body. Figure 3.3 illustrates the stimuli. The 4- and 5-year-old children in the study successfully differentiated test stimuli that matched the proportional relation in the sample from ones that did not, and they did so just as accurately when the sample and test stimuli differed in configura-tion as when they were alike in configuration. Thus, the study provides evi-dence that young children can compare spatial proportions even when stimuli that match proportionally do not match in configuration.

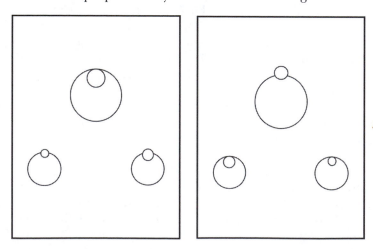

Figure 3.3.   Examples of the stimuli used by Sophian (2000b, Experiment 3). Two problems are shown. In each, the alternative at the bottom right is a propor-tional match to the larger sample figure.

QUANTITY COMPARISON IN DEVELOPMENTAL PERSPECTIVE

In considering the theoretical contrast between a counting-first position and a comparison-of-quantities position, a natural question to ask is whether the evidence supports the view that counting precedes other kinds of quantitative comparison or vice versa. This question, however, is impossible to answer clearly at present, in part because the developmental beginnings of continuous-quantity comparisons have not been examined in any sustained and systematic way and also because the nature of the processes underlying the quantitative discriminations that infants do make remains far from clear. What can be said on this question is only that it would be premature to assume that either type of quantitative reasoning—comparison of quantities or enumeration—has clear precedence over the other.

Beyond indicating the need to refrain from hasty conclusions on this point, the research that has been reviewed on children's early quantitative comparisons is useful in shedding some light on the nature of developmental changes in the ways children think about quantities. Of particular interest is the observation, made in relation to several different kinds of quantity comparisons, that young children often base their comparative judgments on a different quantitative dimension than the task specifies. Asked to compare numerosities, they may compare the lengths of the rows in which the items are placed; yet asked to compare lengths they may compare numerosities! Asked to compare size (areas, in the two-dimensional context in which most of these problems are posed), they may focus only on length along one dimension, and asked to compare aggregate amounts, they may compare the size of a single piece, or they may disregard piece size and base their comparison on the number of pieces. Clearly, it is important to understand the reasons for these shifts in the dimensions along which comparisons are made, what they indicate about children's quantitative reasoning, and how children come, with development, to base their comparisons (for the most part) on the dimensions about which they have been queried.

Two alternative interpretive frameworks have been suggested. According to one, often advanced in discussions of children's errors in reasoning about discrete quantities, the problem children have is in selecting effective ways of making the quantitative judgments that are asked of them. In this view, children base comparisons between discrete quantities on row length because they do not realize that length can be unreliable as a cue to relative numerosity. Thus, an important aspect of development is learning what kinds of information are and what kinds are not reliable indicators of how quantities compare on a designated dimension. A somewhat different perspective holds that children are not just unclear as to the best cues to relative numerosity or other quantitative dimensions; they are unclear about the distinctions among the dimensions themselves, or at least about which dimension is at issue in certain experimental tasks. Thus, on this view, development consists in large part in coming to appreciate the conceptual distinctions between length, numerosity, area, and so on.

The empirical evidence does not provide a strong basis for choosing between these accounts (both may have some degree of validity), because experimental manipulations designed to clarify the reliability of alternative cues also provide information that could clarify the type of quantitative comparison that is being requested. My own leaning, however, is toward the latter account (although not necessarily to the exclusion of the former), for two reasons. The first is simply the pervasiveness of findings that children base their responses on a different quantitative dimension than the one about which they were queried. It is hard to understand why, if children do distinguish clearly between dimensions, they so often base their judgments on a dimension other than the one about which they have been asked. Second, and more compelling, is the way children talk about the comparisons they are making. Reported justifications for quantitative judgments (e.g., Siegler, 1995) never refer explicitly to the idea that one quantitative dimension is a good basis for making decisions about another. Instead, children say one of two kinds of things. They may refer directly to a particular type of quantitative comparison, for example, indicating that one row is longer, or stating the numerical values of each row, as if that relation was what they had been asked to evaluate (even when it was not). Or, if there has been a transformation, they may talk about that, perhaps saying that nothing was added or taken away (with the implication that they are still basing their judgment on whatever comparison they made before the transformation) or noting that something was added or subtracted (in which case it is often unclear whether the transformation alone is the basis for their judgment, or whether they are implicitly relating the transformation to the comparison they made before the transformation).

It is particularly telling to examine what children say when they are just beginning to move beyond earlier nonconserving responses. Instead of expressing uncertainty about which strategy is best for determining the answer to a known question, they seem to be struggling to reconcile different senses of "same" and/or "more." For example, after a class I observed in which a group of first graders had discussed a conservation-of-volume problem,[1] one boy came to the teacher still struggling to make sense of what happens when water is poured into a narrower container. "It's still the same," he said, "but when you pour it in here it's more." He seemed to be trying to express (and/or articulate for himself) the idea that the water was both the same and

---

[1]This class was part of a curriculum development project called Measure Up (Dougherty, 2003), which is developing a measurement-based curriculum for elementary school mathematics.

not the same—seemingly contradictory conclusions that he was not yet able to reconcile but that would be reconciled by realizing that the height changed but the volume did not. Inhelder et al. (1974) reported a very similar protocol from a length comparison task involving two rows of matches, one arranged in a zigzag and the other in a straight line, with an extra match in the zigzag line so that the endpoints of the two rows coincide. The child said, "The roads are exactly the same … except that you've put a bit more in the bottom one so that they're the same length" (p. 139). Like the child struggling with conservation of volume, this child is clearly struggling to reconcile two senses of "same"—here, same distance between endpoints versus same length of "road" (or same number of matches).

The notion that the child is struggling with an apparent contradiction (that the liquid in two containers, or the length of a zigzig road compared to a straight one, is both "the same" and "more") and develops a better understanding through his efforts to resolve that contradiction is, of course, very much in accord with Piaget's (1970) account of equilibration. The important point in this context, however, is that the resolution is achieved by distinguishing more clearly among aspects of quantity that the child had been subsuming in a rather diffuse notion of amount. It is because the quantitative relations are not the same for all quantitative dimensions that the contradiction arises, and correspondingly that contradiction is resolved when the child recognizes that there is more than one aspect of amount and quantities may differ on some but not others.

An important instructional implication of the hypothesis that development involves coming to differentiate more clearly among quantitative dimensions is the value of introducing children to mathematical vocabulary and corresponding measurement procedures that differentiate particular quantitative dimensions from others, and relatedly, to incorporate the consideration of a variety of quantitative dimensions (not just numerosity) in instruction. From a Vygotskiian perspective, language and symbol systems are cultural tools that support children's cognitive development. Consistent with that idea, the introduction of distinct terms for number, length, area, and so forth, and also of distinct procedures and tools for measuring those dimensions (including the conventional counting sequence, sticks that fit between two blocks, or tiles that can be overlaid on other shapes), may be very helpful to children who are just coming to recognize that one quantity can differ from another, and/or be like another, in a variety of ways and correspondingly, that a transformed quantity can differ from the pretransformation quantity in some ways while remaining unchanged in others.

Chapter 4

Understanding Units

A profound shift in thinking about counting comes with the recognition that counting is fundamentally a means of comparing quantities and, in that sense, a measurement tool. Like other forms of measurement, counting requires the choice of a unit. The units are usually taken to be objects—blocks or toy animals or crayons. They can also be parts of objects, like the legs on an insect or the sides of a triangle. In principle, provided we are consistent about what we take as a unit, we can count any sort of discriminable element in any kind of array. But we don't. There are two things in particular that we don't customarily do in counting. One is to count aggregates of separate individuals (unless they are grouped). Thus, although it seems natural to count the triads of squares in this row (there are three of them):

(a) ☐ ☐ ☐   ☐ ☐ ☐   ☐ ☐ ☐

it feels very odd to do the same here (again three, but they don't correspond to the spatial grouping of the squares):

(b) ☐ ☐   ☐ ☐ ☐   ☐ ☐   ☐ ☐

Of course, even in the latter case, if we are told to count triads or if we have a reason for wanting to know how many groups of three can be formed, we can count the array that way. But it seems far less natural to parse Array (b) into three entities than to parse Array (a) that way.

The other thing we don't customarily do is to count parts of things, when there are several such things. Thus, although it is fine to count the number of sides this triangle has,

(c)

or this rhombus:

(d)

it does not feel as natural to count the number of sides in an array consisting of both a rhombus and a square (seven sides altogether) as in this array:

(e)

Tellingly, this count feels more natural if we present the shapes not as solid figures but as outlines created by juxtaposing discrete line segments as in this array:

(f)

There is no principled reason why triads to be counted need to consist of closely spaced items, or why, in counting the edges of solid figures, we should not include multiple figures in a single count; and although they seem odd, we can carry out the counts in (b) and (e) as well as those in (a), (c), (d), and (f). But their oddness brings to light an aspect of counting that normally goes unnoticed: the parsing of an array into countable units. Counting triads of randomly spaced squares, like counting the edges in a triangle and a rhombus together, feels odd because it goes against the way we normally parse the arrays. When there are discrete items, our inclination is to treat each of those as a unit, unless there is a spatial basis for grouping them into aggregate units such as triads. Alternatively, when just a single object is presented, it is unproblematic to treat salient parts of it as units. What we don't find natural is to override salient discrete-object units in favor of counting either parts of those objects or aggregates that do not correspond to spatial groupings.

The reason this observation is important is that mathematical thinking requires a concept of *unit* that goes beyond our everyday notions of objects and groups of objects. Specifically, it requires flexibility in the choice of units, together with a concern for equivalences among units. The numerical value we get when we count an array, or when we measure a continuous quantity, depends on the unit we choose, and correspondingly it is critical to be consistent in our choice. For instance, we might count the same set of shoes as pairs, getting the numerical value 4, or as individual shoes, getting the value 8, but we cannot count some of them as pairs and others singly (getting some value between 4 and 8). Notably, in counting, it is the identity of the unit rather than its size that matters: Some of the shoes may be baby shoes and others large men's shoes, but we treat each of them as one shoe (or one half of a pair of shoes). Because the counts in (b) and (e) just shown do not violate the principle of using a consistent unit, there is nothing, in principle, wrong with them, but they seem odd because they involve disregarding the composition of the arrays in terms of discrete objects—squares, in (b), and shapes, in (e)—and adopting a different counting unit instead.

Gal'perin and Georgiev (1969) argued forcefully that the common practice, in teaching young children, of conflating mathematical units with the everyday notion of objects leads to several interrelated shortcomings in children's reasoning about units. Among these is a lack of concern for the size or fullness of units, which Gal'perin and Georgiev illustrated by describing 6-year-old children's performance on an exercise in which they were first asked to put five spoonfuls of rice in a pile, then to take four spoonfuls away from the pile, and then to state how many spoonfuls remained. Many children did not fill the spoon completely in taking spoonfuls from the pile, and so were left with what was obviously more than one spoonful after removing four spoonfuls from the original five, creating a conflict between children's observations and their knowledge that $5 - 4 = 1$. Only four children were able to identify their failure to take full spoonfuls as the reason for the discrepancy. The others either estimated the amount of rice, ignoring the inconsistency of their estimate with the subtraction fact $5 - 4 = 1$, or else insisted that just one spoonful remained even though they acknowledged that it looked like more.

While Gal'perin and Georgiev's (1969) focus was on units of continuous quantity, the issue of equivalent units applies also to the seemingly straightforward process of identifying units of counting. Thus, before examining in more detail how an understanding of units based on measuring instruments develops, research addressing how children think about units in counting is discussed.

COUNTING WITH UNITS OTHER THAN DISCRETE OBJECTS

Although the examples at the beginning of this chapter suggest that boundaries between objects have a substantial impact even for adults on the ways we think about enumerating an array, evidence from research with young children suggests that the impact of object boundaries is far more profound for them. In particular, a seminal paper on children's use of alternative counting units (Shipley & Shepperson, 1990) provided evidence of strong limitations on the kinds of units young children use in counting.

In their first experiment, Shipley and Shepperson (1990) asked children to count arrays composed of some intact and some "broken" objects. For example, an array might consist of four intact forks and one fork presented with the handle separated from the tines, so that it constitutes another two discrete pieces. The researchers varied the wording of the count request ("How many forks?" vs. "How many things?"), the homogeneity of the arrays (e.g., all forks or a variety of different objects), the familiarity of the items (forks vs. nonsense objects), and the spatial arrangement of the arrays (with separated parts aligned or appearing in different positions in the array). Across all these variants of the task, they found that children ranging from 3 to 6 years of age predominantly counted each discrete element separately, so that the separated handle and tines of a fork counted as two items. Counts that combined separated pieces and counted them as a single item increased with age, however, and accounted for about one third of the 5- and 6-year-olds' counts.

In a second experiment, 4-year-olds were asked to count the same kinds of arrays, but whenever a child counted the parts separately, the experimenter explicitly indicated that the two separated parts together formed one object and then asked the child to count the array again. This intervention led to some changes in children's counting, but most often that change consisted of omitting the separated parts from the count entirely so that only the intact objects were counted. Thus, even with explicit instruction, many children would not combine complementary but spatially separated parts of a fork or other object and treat them as a single unit in counting.

In a third experiment, Shipley and Shepperson (1990) asked children how many "kinds of toys" there were in displays consisting of several duplicates of each of several toys. Only two 3- and 4-year-olds, out of a sample of 44, made a single correct response on this task. Instead, the children typically counted each individual item in the set, resulting in a quantification of the discrete objects, not the classes. Again, performance improved markedly with age, and a majority of 5- and 6-year-olds were successful in counting the classes.

Sophian and Kailihiwa (1998) further investigated children's counting of units that do not correspond to discrete objects, focusing on children's ability to adapt their counting in response to questions that specified different units. In their first experiment, they showed children arrays composed of toy animals grouped into "families" and asked the children to count either the number of individuals in one family or the number of families. To ensure that children

understood the questions, each trial began with the child being asked to identify one exemplar of the unit in question (e.g., either one dog or the dog family) by placing it in a special location. When this was done, the experimenter
said, "Good, here is one dog/family. Now count all the dogs/families." Thus, a
valid exemplar was identified by the child and explicitly labeled as the unit to
be counted by the experimenter. Nevertheless, although children consistently
counted the appropriate individuals on the individual-count trials, the
4-year-olds appropriately counted the families on less than half of the family-count trials. Indeed, 55% of the 4-year-olds failed to produce a single count
of families. As in Shipley and Shepperson's (1990) work, however, performance improved rapidly with age, and fully 75% of 5-year-olds appropriately
counted the families on all eight of the family-count trials.

Two further experiments (Sophian & Kailihiwa, 1998, Experiments 2
and 3) used materials that were made to be taken apart into pieces and put
back together, like plastic Easter eggs, to construct arrays composed of
some intact and some separated objects (with the pieces of the latter always
in immediate proximity to each other, but not touching). As in Experiment
1, the focus was on whether children differentiated between questions about
these arrays that specified different units—in this case, pieces versus whole
objects. Thus, on each trial, the experimenter would either display a piece
of an object and ask, "How many pieces like this can we get from all these
things?" or she would display an intact object and ask, "How many whole
eggs can we get from all these things?" At both ages, children showed considerable hesitation on the first couple of trials of the testing session, apparently struggling to determine what to count. Once they decided on a unit,
however, they tended to stick with it thereafter in spite of the fact that the
experimenter's questions changed and she demonstrated the unit she
wanted the child to quantify on every single trial. As a result, none of the
4-year-olds showed clearly differentiated patterns of counting in response
to these two questions, and the 5-year-olds did only modestly better. Typically the 4-year-olds engaged in one of two types of counting and maintained it throughout the experiment: Either they treated whole objects as
the counting unit, in some cases omitting the separated objects (on 43% of
problems overall), or they treated each discrete item in the array as a unit,
regardless of whether it was a whole object or a piece (on 37% of the problems). Among the 5-year-olds, 40% of the sample did show differentiated
patterns of counting, but the majority of these children (25% of the sample)
did so by excluding the separated objects when they were counting wholes
and excluding the intact objects when they were counting pieces. Thus, they
avoided the conflict between the specification of units in the problem presentation and the notion of units as discrete objects by restricting their
counting to items that matched what they had been asked to count and that
in addition appeared in the array as discrete individuals.

In a follow-up experiment, in order to make the contrast between the two types of counting questions more salient, the "How many pieces …?" and the "How many whole …?" questions were each asked in turn about every array that was presented. This procedure elicited more counts of pieces from 4-year-olds (36% of their counts here, vs. just 21% in the previous experiment), but still only two 4-year-olds showed clearly differentiated counting even under these circumstances. A majority of 5-year-olds (61%) did so, however, treating whole objects as the unit when they were asked about wholes and pieces as the unit when they were asked about pieces.

Developmental Implications

Although the counting of arrays using units other than discrete objects is not in itself likely to be particularly central in mathematical development, the realization that the same materials can be partitioned into units in a variety of ways has profound mathematical ramifications that go far beyond counting. First, the dissociation of mathematical units from physical segmentation introduces the possibility of measuring continuous quantities, by thinking of them as composed of units that can be enumerated even though there are no physical demarcations between those units. Second, it provides the foundation both for forming higher order units, including the units based on powers of 10 that are the basis of our place value system, and for forming smaller units by partitioning the original unit into fractional parts.

The evidence of an extended developmental trajectory in children's differentiation of counting units from discrete objects also sheds new light on the question of the developmental significance of very early numerical abilities. The question of whether very young children, especially preverbal infants, represent numerical information in the same way or in very different ways from older children and adults has motivated extensive discussion of alternative representational systems that might enter into the processing of numerical information. The continuity thesis holds that the cognitive mechanism that underlies infants' numerical discriminations is isomorphic with the verbal counting process and so provides a conceptual foundation for learning to count (R. Gelman, 1998). A very different perspective on the question of the continuity of numerical reasoning from infancy through childhood and beyond, however, emerges from a consideration of the importance of units for numerical representations.

The heart of the continuity thesis is the postulation of a preverbal mechanism that uses analog magnitudes to represent numerical quantities and that embodies the same principles of one-to-one correspondence, stable order, and cardinality that underlie verbal counting (R. Gelman, 1998; cf. chap. 2). Although this preverbal mechanism was initially posited to account for findings of small-number discrimination in infancy, recently some researchers have proposed that infants form analog representations of large numerosities but are unable to use that representational system for numerosities less than four (Lipton & Spelke, 2004; Xu, 2003). Such a limitation presumably would undermine the usefulness of an analog representational system as a scaffold for learning to count verbally. Furthermore, two alternative accounts of preverbal numerical discriminations have been put forward, both of which differ from the continuity hypothesis in that they invoke mechanisms that do not map directly onto verbal counting, although they do persist in adult processing of objects and/or continuous quantities. One of these is the *object-file theory* (e.g., Simon, 1997; Xu, 2003), which holds that perceptual representations like those that underlie adults' individuation and tracking of objects allow infants to discriminate between small numerosities such as two versus three. Another account holds that what appear to be numerical discriminations in infants are in fact discriminations based on continuous quantitative properties of the stimulus arrays, such as total stimulus area or contour length (Mix et al., 2002).

Consideration of the developmental changes observed in children's reasoning about counting units indicates an even more profound caveat to the continuity thesis than those raised by alternative accounts of infant numerical discriminations. All of the infant numerical discriminations that have been demonstrated to date, whether or not they are attributable to a countinglike mechanism, differ from the kinds of counting abilities demonstrated by children in the early elementary school years in that they are based on numerical units defined by physical characteristics of the stimulus materials. Regardless of how infants represent numerical information, they do not appear to be capable of generating different numerical representations for the same quantity by adopting different units. What makes this advance possible is not just a switch from one representational mechanism to another but the emergence of an entirely new conception of units, and correspondingly of numbers. Once the child understands the possibility of adopting different units, number is no longer a physical property of a spatial array or temporal event sequence but a mathematical property of the relation between a total quantity and a unit.

USING UNITS IN MEASURING CONTINUOUS QUANTITIES

In counting, units are based on the identities of the items we are counting, whether those identities are defined at a very general level (e.g., things) or more specifically (e.g., legs). Because of this, the sizes of the units are generally irrelevant; in counting animals, for instance, a collection consisting of a horse and a dog is numerically equal to one consisting of a duck and a rabbit, even though the first pair is unquestionably larger on many dimensions of magnitude. The situation is very different when it comes to measurement of continuous quantities, however. Here, units are defined by their size, on some dimension of magnitude, and identifiable distinctions among parts that do not correspond to the boundaries between these size-based units are entirely disregarded. For example, when we measure the height of a ladder with a yardstick, we do not consider the segments defined by the placement of the rungs; we are only interested in the units formed by successive placements of the yardstick against the ladder.

As Gal'perin and Georgiev (1969) noted, young children are not initially clear about the importance of using constant units. Children readily divide a continuous quantity into pieces as a way of partitioning it into equal shares, but at early ages they are indifferent to the size of the pieces (K. F. Miller, 1984). Indeed, if, in allocating the pieces among recipients, the numbers of pieces do not come out even, preschoolers will "even out" the shares simply by cutting one of the pieces in the shortchanged share into two so as to increase the number of pieces in that share.

Barrett and Clements (2003) reported evidence that children have difficulty even in interpreting units that are marked for them on a linear quantity. In clinical interviews with four 4th-grade students, they asked the students about the lengths of various sections of a straw that was notched at regular intervals to divide it into 24 segments. Initially, the units were introduced by bending the straw to show two segments and labeling that *a length of two*, and then bending the straw to show just one segment and labeling that *a length of one*. But when a student was subsequently shown a 3-segment length, she asserted that its length was two, because there were only two notches within the segment. Likewise, she expressed confusion about why Barrett had labeled a four-section length *four* because there were only three notches. All four of the children Barret and Clements interviewed expressed similar confusion about whether the notches or the segments between them should be counted in determining the length of a section of straw. This type of confusion may contribute to the insensitivity to unit size noted by Gal'perin and Georgiev (1969) and by K. F. Miller (1984); to the extent that children focus on the boundaries between segments, rather than the segments between them, the issue of unit size cannot arise because the notches are being treated as points, not as entities with spatial extent.

Nunes et al. (1993, Experiment 1) obtained information about children's construction of units of linear measurement by presenting pairs of 6- and 8-year-old children with problems in which, without being able to see each other, they had to decide whether or not two lines, each visible to only one child in the pair, were the same length. In different conditions, the children were given different measuring instruments: either rulers or two pieces of string (one for each child) that were equal in length. As noted earlier (chap. 3), children had no trouble using the string to compare lengths provided it was equal in length to one or both of the lines to be compared. Of particular interest in relation to children's ideas about units of measurement, however, is their performance when this was not the case. Two such problems were presented: one in which the string was half the length of one of the lines (or both, when the lines were equally long), and one in which the string was twice as long as one or both lines.

When the string was half the length of one (or both) of the lines to be compared, children used it as a unit 43% of the time, iterating it and arriving at a correct conclusion about the relations between the lines by doing so. When the string was twice the length of one (or both) of the lines, however, the children used it appropriately as a measurement unit only 13% of the time, and they were not always correct in their conclusions about the relation between the two lines when they did so. When children were given a ruler (which was always longer than either line), they did far better, using it correctly 84% of the time. Indeed, even when one of the children received a "broken" ruler, which started at 4 cm instead of 0, they took that complication into account and made correct comparisons 63% of the time.

These results are interesting in at least two ways. First, they suggest that the ability to carry out standard measuring procedures with conventional instruments, and even adapt them appropriately to novel circumstances, does not necessarily imply that children appreciate the underlying concept of a *unit of measurement*—at least not well enough to apply it to nonconventional measures. And second, they indicate that developmentally, an understanding of the iteration of a given unit of measure against the quantities to be measured precedes an understanding of the creation of new units through subdivision.

Huttenlocher, Newcombe, and Sandberg's (1994) work on young children's coding of spatial location provides intriguing evidence of a form of mental partitioning that operates from a very early age. They presented children with problems involving locating a toy that had been hidden in a long and narrow sandbox (5 feet × 16 inches) that did not have any distinctive visual markings. After the object was hidden, the child was required to turn briefly away from the sandbox before being allowed to search, so that searches could not be based simply on maintaining a visual or physical orientation toward the point at which the object was hidden. The focus was on the position of children's searches along the length of the sandbox. Biases in children's search patterns suggested that as early as 1 to 2 years of age, children used the midpoint of the sandbox as a reference point. Specifically, children's searches were most accurate when the object's location was very close to one end of the sandbox or at the midpoint, and less accurate as the distance from these reference points increased. Interestingly, 4-year-old children showed a more complex pattern of bias, indicative of the subdivision of the sandbox into halves and the use of the midpoint of each half as well as the midpoint of the box as a whole as reference points.

Thus, their accuracy was greatest for locations at each end, at the midpoint, and halfway between the midpoint and the endpoints, and less accurate as the distance of the hiding place from the nearest of these points increased. Of course, the subdivisions were not being used as units of measure, in that they were not iterated against any other quantity. All the same, given the difficulties observed in tasks that, like Nunes et al.'s (1993), require the partitioning of a given quantity to create a unit of measure, it is striking that partitioning occurs spontaneously, and quite early in development, in the context of spatial coding.

RELATIONSHIPS BETWEEN UNIT SIZE, NUMBER OF UNITS, AND AGGREGATE QUANTITY

At the heart of understanding measurement units is an appreciation of how variations in unit size affect the outcome of a measurement operation. A charming illustration of children's initial lack of clarity about this occurred in interactions between a preservice teacher and a group of elementary school children about the lengths of snakes they had drawn on the playground (Kribs-Zaleta & Bradshaw, 2003). One student showed that her snake's length was 28 by partitioning it into 28 approximately equal units. Another child, however, drew a line all the way across the courtyard for his snake, and measured its length as 25 steps. The class puzzled over how that very long snake could be only 25 when the other snake was 28. Recess ended, terminating the discussion, before the class arrived at the understanding that the inconsistent results were obtained because the girl's units were very different from the boy's units. The steps the boy used as units were much larger than the subdivisions the first child had created.

Although the relation between unit size and number is an inverse one—the larger the unit, the fewer of them it takes to match a given quantity—young children may inappropriately conflate different aspects of "bigness" so that they expect the use of a "big" unit to result in a "big" number. Sophian (2002) obtained evidence of this kind of reasoning in a study in which children were asked to judge whether it would be possible to fit more small objects or more objects that were larger in size into a designated space. A sample problem can be seen in Figure 4.1. The child saw two plastic bears—one larger than the other—and a wooden bench. The question posed was whether more of the small bears or more of the larger ones could sit together on the bench. Initially, most 3-year-olds judged that more of the larger bears would fit. Despite these initial errors, however, a brief training process in which children had the opportunity to see the effects of placing successive small or large objects into corresponding containers or regions was quite effective in improving children's performance. After six such training trials, 3-year-olds averaged close to 60% correct and

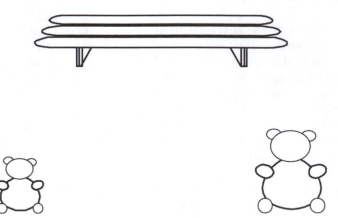

Figure 4.1.   A sample problem from Sophian (2002): Can more of the small bears or more of the larger ones sit together on the bench?

4-year-olds almost 70% correct, as compared to 36% correct at both age levels before the training.

These results, like the kinds of errors in quantitative reasoning discussed in chapter 3, appear to reflect a lack of differentiation between different aspects of quantities in children's initial reasoning. Specifically, before receiving the training trials, some children seem to have interpreted the question about whether more of one or more of the other would fit as something like, "Which is more?" and so they chose the larger bears. The training helped them to differentiate more clearly between two inversely related senses of more—taking up more space and fitting more within a given space—and thus allowed the children as a group to shift from choosing the larger objects to choosing the smaller ones on a majority of trials.

The inverse relation between unit size and number is particularly important for understanding the magnitude relations among fractions with different denominators. When children first learn about fractions, they often assume that unit fractions with larger denominators are larger in value than those with smaller denominators, for example, that $\frac{1}{4}$ is greater than $\frac{1}{3}$ because 4 is greater than 3 (e.g., Behr, Wachsmuth, Post, & Lesh, 1984). This error suggests a conflation of different aspects of magnitude in much the same way as the errors Sophian (2002) observed in children's initial expectations as to whether more smaller or larger units would fit in a given space.

In reasoning about the partitioning of physical quantities, it is not difficult for children to learn that the relation between the number of parts and the size of each part is an inverse one. Sophian, Garyantes, and Chang (1997) asked 5-, 6-, and 7-year-olds about the sizes of shares that would result from partitioning a fixed quantity of food (red lentils, which children were told represented bits of pizza) among different numbers of recipients. In an initial experiment, all three age groups tended to expect that a greater number of recipients would result in larger, rather than smaller, shares for each. In subsequent work (Experiments 3 and 4), however, a procedural change elicited much better performance from 7-year-olds; and while 5-year-olds were still incorrect initially, they improved rapidly when they were given the opportunity to actually partition the quantities among the recipients and compare the sizes of the resulting shares. Moreover, improved performance was not restricted to problems involving the particular numerical comparisons for which children had seen the outcomes. Thus, the children's thinking about the relation between the number of shares and the size of each share had changed and not just their expectations about the particular sharing scenarios they had observed.

Although these results indicate that the effect of more recipients on share size is understood fairly early in development (i.e., among 7-year-olds, even without training, and among 5-year-olds after a very brief training experience), the corresponding relation between denominator size and fraction magnitude remains a potent source of confusion much later in students' mathematics learning. The idea that fraction magnitudes increase rather than decrease as the size of the denominator increases is quite prevalent among fourth graders, and it can reappear much later when students are faced with cognitively demanding problems (e.g., Behr et al., 1984). Despite the emphasis on the partitioning of wholes into equal parts in early fraction instruction, many students do not attain a solid grasp of the implications of this idea for the relation between a fraction's denominator and the magnitude of that fraction. Their persisting difficulties are symptomatic of conceptual limitations of the part–whole conception of fractions, in particular, its lack of specificity with respect to constraints such as the need for the parts to be equal in size. Chapter 6 presents a fuller discussion of the limitations of the part–whole conception of fractions, and the corresponding advantages of conceptualizing fractions in a measurement framework that gives considerations of unit size a central place.

UNDERSTANDING HIERARCHIES OF UNITS

Although the magnitude of a given quantity can always be measured in more than one way, using different sizes of units and correspondingly getting different numerical results, there is a trade-off involved in selecting the unit we will use; measurement using large units is more efficient because we do not have to count a great many units, but small units give us more precision. Thus, in the United States, we use meters, feet, or yards to measure rope, but kilometers or miles to measure distances between cities. A distance stated in miles might easily be off by several yards, even if we specify the number of miles to two decimal places, but we accept that imprecision for the convenience of representing large distances simply. Of course, where great precision is required, it can be obtained simply by increasing the number of decimal places used in specifying the number of miles, or by specifying the number of whole miles and then characterizing the remaining distance in feet and inches.

As this example illustrates, the coordination of multiple levels of units makes it possible to attain both precision and efficiency. This principle is the foundation for place value representation, which aggregates groups of ones into tens and tens into hundreds, thereby making it possible to represent large numbers precisely yet also concisely. Likewise, it is the basis for fractions (including decimal fractions), which give us great flexibility in unit size because we can make the new fractional units as small as we like simply by increasing the number of parts into which we subdivide the original whole. Accordingly, Behr, Harel, Post, and Lesh (1994) argued that familiarizing children with the use of higher order units (units consisting of groups of more than one item) in whole-number arithmetic would help to prepare them for the transition to working with rational numbers. They maintained that traditional school arithmetic is based on the hidden assumption, "all quantities are represented in units of one" (p. 122), an assertion that is nicely illustrated by their discussion of a multistep problem, which asks how many bags with two marbles in each can be made from specified numbers of bags containing four marbles and six marbles, respectively. Behr et al. state that the traditional way of solving this problem is to determine the total number of marbles John has (representing the quantity in each bag in units of one to do so) and then dividing that total by two. An alternative approach, involving the use of a higher order unit, would be to determine the number of groups of two in each bag (which is straightforward, because all the bags contain an even number of marbles) and then sum the results.

To work effectively with higher order units, children need not only to understand the possibility of using units other than discrete objects but also to be able to coordinate distinct but hierarchically related units in representing quantities and in comparing them to one another. A very simple form of that coordination, but one that is nevertheless challenging for young children, can be seen in Frydman and Bryant's (1988) work on children's ability to construct equal amounts with different-sized units. Frydman and Bryant (1988) asked children to give equal numbers of bricks to two recipients, while stipulating that one recipient could only receive bricks two or three at a time (joined together as "doubles" or "triples") while the other received them singly. Thus, to solve the problems correctly, children had to adapt their usual one-to-one distribution strategies to take into account the different-sized units to be given to the two recipients. Four-year-olds successfully did this on just 18% of the problems. Their most common strategy, employed on 58% of the problems, was to ignore the difference in units and maintain a one-to-one correspondence between discrete items so that, for each single brick given to one recipient, the other recipient was given one "double" or "triple." Five-year-olds, however, succeeded on 68% of the problems, indicating a marked age-related improvement in the ability to take into account the difference in the sizes of the units allocated to the two recipients.

Problems that involve many-to-one counting, or determining the number of items needed to give several such items to each of a number of recipients, are closely related to the sharing problems studied by Frydman and Bryant (1988) but more demanding in a way that has an important bearing on the use of higher order units in arithmetic. Consider the problem of determining how many small blocks are needed to build a tower the same height as four large blocks, each of which is as tall as three of the small blocks. Although closely related to Frydman and Bryant's "triples" task, this problem requires children to think about the total number of small blocks needed to match several large ones rather than simply to match each large block in turn with the appropriate number of small blocks. The problem thus becomes one of converting between alternative units of measurement for the height of the tower. The problem states the height of the tower in one unit of measure—large blocks—and the child must convert that measure into one based on a different unit, that of small blocks. Similarly, Behr et al.'s (1994) alternative solution to the marbles problem involves converting between the units of four and six that are given in the problem and the units of two that are required for a solution.

Sophian and Madrid (2003, Experiment 1) found that 5- to 7-year-old children did quite poorly on block tower problems involving many-to-one relationships (presented as drawings, like the one in Fig. 4.2, so that the blocks could not actually be manipulated). The 7-year-olds averaged just 16% correct on an initial block of problems and the 5- and 6-year-olds less than 2% correct. Hypothesizing that the need to iterate the mapping of several small blocks to one large one was an important source of difficulty, Sophian and Madrid gave children a series of six training trials using actual blocks that could be manipulated. In one condition, these trials consisted simply of an opportunity to actually construct the towers and determine the number of small blocks required. In the other, the experimenter either verified correct responses or corrected erroneous ones by constructing a separate stack of small blocks for each of the big ones, and then counting all of the small blocks before combining the stacks into a single tower. Only the 7-year-olds improved with training, and they did so only in the second condition. This result is consistent with Sophian and Madrid's assertion that the iteration of the many-to-one mapping was initially problematic for the

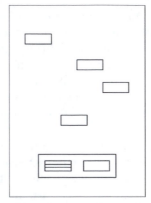

Figure 4.2. A sample problem from Sophian and Madrid (2003): The small blocks stacked on the left in the rectangle at the bottom of the page belong to Turtle, and the large blocks belong to Bear. If Bear stacks up all his blocks, his tower will be much larger than Turtle's. Then how many more of his small blocks will Turtle need so he can make a tower the same height as Bear's?

children, since the process of iterating the mapping between small and large blocks was highlighted in the separate-stacks training condition but not in the condition in which the heights of the towers were compared directly.

A second, closely related study, in which 7-year-olds explained their answers during training, corroborated this analysis of the separate-stacks training; 62% of the children who received this training, but only 5% of those who received the alternative whole-tower training, noted the need to add together multiple instances of the number of small blocks equivalent to a single large block; and another 17% of the children who received training based on separate stacks, but none of those who received whole-tower training, explicitly indicated the multiplicative character of the problems. Thus, children's explanations suggest that experience with the separate-stacks training, but not with the whole-tower training, elicited at least the beginnings of a form of reasoning in which several small blocks were aggregated into a composite unit to be iterated, and that this kind of reasoning is important to the coordination of different-sized units.

Composing and Decomposing Large Numbers

The coordination of different levels of units is a powerful way of grasping the quantitative significance of large numbers and numerical computations on them. Lampert's (1986) work on large-number multiplication with fourth-grade students nicely illustrates the use of several kinds of units to conceptualize the large quantities resulting from multiplying two-digit numbers. She began by inviting students to generate simple stories corresponding to multiplication problems, which they did easily, and then she helped them generate useful groupings for solving the problems. For instance, to solve the problem 28 × 65, a student proposed thinking of it as 28 glasses with 65 drops in each. Lampert then introduced another unit, jugs, which corresponded to 10 glasses or 650 drops, so that the quantity could be represented as two jugs and 8 glasses. As the class worked on figuring out how many drops that was, Lampert suggested a decomposition of the drops in the glasses into groups of 60 and 5 in order to make the computation easier, proposing that 5 drops from each glass be moved to a jar, leaving 60 × 8 drops in the glasses, plus the 40 that had been removed from the glasses. So the total is 1,300 for the two full jugs, plus 480 for the eight 60-drop glasses, plus the 40, or 1,820. A student in the class proposed another way of using the units the class had generated to solve the problem, based on the idea that 28 glasses was just two glasses short of three full jugs. So the problem could be solved by subtracting 2 glasses, or 130 drops, from the 650 drops that would make a full jug, leaving 520, and adding that to the 1,300 for the two full jugs. One of the strengths of Lampert's teaching method is that the numerical relation between the higher order units and the basic units always remains explicit.

The unschooled Brazilian children studied by Carraher, Carraher, and Schliemann (1985) used very similar strategies of grouping and decomposition in computing prices in the marketplace, although their groups were not typically based on units of 10. For instance, to determine the cost of 10 coconuts at 35 *cruzeiros* each, one child first determined that the cost of three coconuts was 105, then doubled that for six coconuts, and then added another 105 for three more coconuts and finally added to that the cost of a single coconut. In this solution, the original unit, an individual coconut, was aggregated into a collection of three coconuts. The new unit was iterated several times and ultimately the sum of those iterations was combined with one of the original units.

The coordination of hierarchically related units is especially important in reasoning about ratios and proportions. Lamon (1993) identified at least two kinds of higher order units that enter into students' solutions of proportion problems. One consists of forming a higher order unit that represents the combination of different elements that are being put into a ratio relation. Thus, asked about a class of 25 in which there are 3 girls in every group of 5, a student might determine the number of such groups in the class, treating the group as a unit to determine that the class consists of 5 groups, and then combine that information with the information about group composition to determine the number of girls and the number of boys in the class. Another approach is to treat the ratio itself as a unit (or as two linked units) and iterate its components. Thus, if one group consists of 5 children, 3 of whom are girls, then the other 2 are boys; and two groups would be 10 children, 6 girls and 4 boys; three groups would be 15 children, 9 girls and 6 boys; four groups would be 20 children, 12 girls and 8 boys; and five groups would be 25 children—the size of the class—of whom 15 would be girls and 10 would be boys.

Place Value

The place value system offers a systematic way of breaking down large numerical values into hierarchically related units. A crucial constraint imposed by place value representations, however, is that there can be no more than nine units at any level (because only one column is available for each type of unit and so numerical values greater than nine cannot be represented). This constraint is an important source of difficulty for children, who find the regrouping operations of "carrying" (when addition or multiplication operations result in the accumulation of more than nine units at any one level) and "borrowing" (temporarily creating more than nine units at a particular level in order to permit the subtraction of the number of those units specified in the subtrahend) far from transparent. A second major area of difficulty is in learning about decimal fractions, which extend the place value system to units smaller than one.

The errors children make in borrowing have intrigued researchers because they are often quite systematic, suggesting specific "bugs" in students' computational procedures (Brown & van Lehn, 1982). However, the bugs are characteristically nonsensical from a quantitative perspective, suggesting that students have assimilated elements of the correct procedures without regard for the quantitative meanings of those symbol manipulations (Resnick, 1982). In a sense, the meanings of the numerical symbols being manipulated are irrelevant in carrying out the operation of borrowing, because the procedure for borrowing from the next column is exactly the same regardless of which columns you are working with. Yet, it is the quantitative relation between the columns that entails certain constraints that students often fail to honor. For instance, if there is a zero in the column immediately to the left, students often incorrectly borrow one from the column to the left of that one and add 10 to the column they are working on just as if they had borrowed from the column to the immediate left. What makes this procedure unsound, of course, is that the column they are borrowing from here represents units 100 times larger, rather than 10 times larger, than the one to which they are adding 10.

Instructional efforts to promote understanding of the operations of carrying and borrowing often involve using physical materials, such as base-10 blocks, or materials that are packaged in groups of 10, to illustrate the idea of forming higher order units based on groups of 10 and then decomposing those units in order to "borrow" in subtraction (e.g., Bowers, Cobb, &

McClain, 1999; Fuson & Briars, 1990; Hiebert & Wearne, 1992). However, in her work on multidigit multiplication, Lampert (1986) adopted a different approach, emphasizing the decompositions implicit in place value representations and recording the successive subproducts of the component parts separately, so that the need for carrying did not arise. For example, 38×23 would be decomposed into $(30 + 8) \times (20 + 3)$, and a subproduct calculated for each pairing of a component of the multiplicand with the multiplier—that is, 8×3, or 24; 30×3, or 90; 8×20, or 160; and 30 times 20, or 600. These subproducts are then summed to get the overall product. Although the mathematical effect of summing the subproducts of 8×3 and 30×3 is the same as carrying a 2 in multiplying 38×3, the quantitative meaning of the subproducts is much more transparent than that of a carried "2" in the tens place.

Decimal fractions extend the place value system to create smaller units based on subdivision of the original unit into tenths, and successive subdivisions to create hundredths, thousandths, and so forth. The interpretation of decimals is quite difficult for students long after they have mastered place value representations for whole numbers. A large part of the difficulty appears to lie in understanding the role of the decimal point. A common error is to interpret the digits to the right of the decimal point like a whole-number representation (Hiebert, 1984a; Sackur-Grisvard & Leonard, 1985); thus students may judge .8 to be equal in value to .08 and .008; but .8 to be less than .80 and .80 less than .800. Relatedly, in adding decimal numbers, students often align the numbers from their right-most digit rather than from the decimal points, so that, for instance, 5.1 and .46 are summed to .97 (or to 9.7) rather than to 5.56 (Hiebert & Wearne, 1985). It is clear from these errors that children have not grasped the way that successive columns to the right of the decimal point specify fractional units based on partitioning the unit in the column immediately to their left into tenths.

Correspondingly, students have great difficulty translating between common-fraction representations and decimal representations. Thus, Hiebert and Wearne (1983, cited in Hiebert, 1984a) presented seventh graders with part–whole representations of fractions (shaded parts of a region) and asked them to express the quantities as decimals. The most common response was a decimal formed by expressing the quantity as a common fraction and then putting the numerator of that fraction to the left of a decimal point and the denominator to the right, so that for instance, a representation of $\frac{1}{4}$ would be expressed in decimal form as 1.4. This error is very different from the interpretation of decimal fractions (between 0 and 1) as whole numbers, suggesting that students may have multiple ways of thinking about decimal fractions that they draw upon in different circumstances and that are not well integrated with one another. The lack of coherence suggests that students have grasped two separate ideas about decimals—that they are an extension of the representational system we use for whole numbers, and that they correspond to common fractions—but they have difficulty coordinating the two and hence are not able to interpret correctly the place values of digits to the right of the decimal point.

Moss (2002; Moss & Case, 1999) was remarkably successful in helping fourth graders to attain an understanding of decimal fractions and their correspondences to common fractions by building on students' everyday knowledge of percents and on their ideas about halving. Thus, the students knew that one half was 50% and easily learned to represent that as .50, and that half of that was one fourth or 25%, which they learned to represent as .25. Interestingly, however, in order to extend the decimal notation to a third decimal place, they used a transitional notation in which they appended the notation ".5" to a two-digit decimal to signify half a percentage point more. Thus, having one fourth, they got one eighth, and its percent counterpart, $12\frac{1}{2}\%$, but initially they wrote the decimal equivalent as ".12.5," building on their knowledge that the decimal representation ".5" is equivalent to the common fraction "$\frac{1}{2}$." Although they quickly learned to omit the second decimal point and write ".125," the need for the transitional notation suggests that at least initially, despite their facility with two-digit decimals, students did not fully grasp the place-value meaning of the decimal numbers. Indeed, the interpretation of two-digit decimals as percents is entirely consistent with the interpretation of two digits to the right of the decimal as a kind of whole number. It is not clear from the published reports whether children were able to integrate digits to the left and right of the decimal point so as to represent, for example, the sum of .75 and .50 as 1.25 rather than .125, or whether they could translate mixed or improper fractions as well as proper fractions into decimal notation.

THE IMPORTANCE OF INCORPORATING THE CONCEPT OF UNIT IN EARLY MATHEMATICS INSTRUCTION

The concept of unit, although usually left implicit in elementary mathematics instruction, pervades topics ranging from counting and whole-number arithmetic to measurement and rational number. An important benefit of making it more explicit from the first years of mathematics instruction is that doing so allows us to identify profound conceptual connections among these topics. Furthermore, the identification of those links makes it possible to clarify some of the difficulties students encounter in their mathematics learning.

The concept of unit—the quantity to be treated as one in any act of quantification—is deceptively simple. At least three factors make it a challenging concept for the learner. The first is the need to distinguish the mathematical concept of unit from the everyday concept of object that is very often used to exemplify a unit. The second is that units are defined in somewhat different ways in different contexts, particularly in counting versus in measuring continuous quantities. And the third is the complexity that can arise in the use and coordination of multiple layers of units.

Although counting units need not be physically discrete objects, the fact that countable items can vary in size indicates that discreteness is a factor in defining units of counting in a way that it is not in defining measurement units. As a result, it is not surprising that even for adults discreteness has an effect, albeit not an insurmountable one, on how we parse arrays into countable units. The challenge children face is to appreciate that, although physical boundaries often influence our choices of units, that choice is not dictated by the physical properties of the material but can be changed to suit our purposes. The appreciation of this flexibility is critical for the construction of higher order units and fractional parts, both of which are powerful tools for extending the scope of quantitative reasoning. Through the use of higher order units, it becomes possible to think precisely about large quantities and about operations on those quantities. Through the use of fractional units, it becomes possible to obtain any desired level of precision in the representation of small quantities. But both of these extensions require coordinating multiple levels of units and mastering representational systems for keeping track of them. Too often, in the course of learning to use these representational systems, children lose track of their quantitative meaning, that is, of the levels of quantification that are being represented and how they are related to each other. The explicit representation of the different layers of units in these systems may be critical in helping students retain a quantitative understanding of the mathematics they are doing even as the representational systems they are working with become more complex.

Chapter 5

Relations Among Quantities in Arithmetic: Additive and Multiplicative Reasoning

Arithmetic is the study of numerical calculations, particularly the operations of addition, subtraction, multiplication, and division. In practice, these operations consist of a set of procedures that generate numerical outcomes. Conceptually, however, they are ways of representing relations among quantities, and an understanding of those relations is critical both to determining the appropriate operation(s) to perform in problem solving and to understanding why the procedures themselves work the way they do.

Two contrasting ways of thinking about relations among quantities are reflected in the operations of addition and subtraction, on one hand, and multiplication and division, on the other, and the contrast between the two hinges on differences in the way units are used. In addition and subtraction, relations between quantities are characterized in terms of a unit that is independent of either quantity. Thus, when we say, "John is six inches taller than his little sister Sarah," the unit we are using to compare them, inches, is related to the quantities we are comparing, heights, only in that it is a linear unit and the quantities being compared are linear. We could express the height relation equally well using some other linear unit—such as 15 cm, or half a foot. In contrast, in multiplication and division, we express relations among quantities by taking one quantity as a unit against which to describe the other. For instance, when we say John is three times as tall as Sarah, we are taking Sarah's height as a unit and using that unit to quantify John's height. Getting John's height, given a measure of Sarah's height in, say, inches, is essentially a matter of converting from a measure of John's height based on Sarah-units,

3, to a measure based on inches, which we obtain by multiplying 3 times the number of inches per Sarah-unit (i.e., Sarah's height in inches). A number of profound differences between additive relations (addition and subtraction) and multiplicative relations (multiplication and division) follow from this basic difference in the way relations between quantities are conceptualized.

Additive relations are basically binary, in that they involve operating on two quantities (the addends, or the subtrahend and minuend) to get a third (the sum, or the remainder). In contrast, multiplicative relations, because they are fundamentally proportional, involve relationships among at least four terms (as can be seen in the general expression of proportionality $\frac{a}{b} = \frac{c}{d}$). Multiplication and division problems can be expressed in binary form (e.g., a × b = c) only when one of the terms in the proportional relation is 1 (Vergnaud, 1983). Thus, for example, consider the multiplication problem: There are 6 sticks of gum in a package. If you bought 3 packages, how many sticks of gum would you get? On the surface, the solution is simply to multiply 6 × 3; but the underlying mathematical structure is the proportion,

> 6 sticks to 1 package = x sticks to 3 packages,

i.e.,

$$\frac{6}{1} = \frac{x}{3}.$$

Additive and multiplicative relations also differ in that additive relations always involve operating on two like quantities to obtain a result that refers to the same type of quantity (apples + apples = apples) whereas multiplicative relations may involve either comparing different types of quantities (e.g., sticks vs. packages of gum) or combining like quantities to obtain a different type of quantity (e.g., area; Vergnaud, 1983).

A central thesis of this chapter is that the conceptual differences between additive and multiplicative relations derive from the fundamental difference between comparing two quantities by means of a common unit that is independent of either of them and comparing them by using one as a unit against which to measure the other. The two sections that follow consider the major findings concerning the development of additive reasoning and of multiplicative reasoning, respectively, in light of this idea. The discussion of additive reasoning focuses on children's understanding of the part–whole relations that are the conceptual core of both addition and subtraction. The main goal of the discussion of multiplicative reasoning is to clarify the profound conceptual differences between it and additive reasoning and at the same time to illuminate the conceptual connections between the two. The chapter closes with a brief discussion of the developmental and instructional ramifications of understanding the relation between additive and multiplicative reasoning in terms of different ways of thinking about relations between quantities.

ADDITIVE REASONING

Three interrelated lines of research address children's understanding of additive relations: (a) research on children's interpretations of addition and subtraction story problems; (b) research on children's understanding of the relations between a set and its subsets, termed part–whole or class inclusion relations; and (c) research on children's knowledge about the commutativity and associativity of addition and the inverse relation between addition and subtraction. All three of these topics are linked by the idea that addition and subtraction characterize the quantity of a set based on its part–whole relations to other sets (Vergnaud, 1982). All addition and subtraction problems can be understood as a matter of either finding the whole, given the parts, or finding a part, given the other part and the whole (or as a series of such determinations, in the case of multistep problems). Although some kinds of arithmetic problems can be solved in other ways, a generally accepted conclusion is that the ability to solve a full range of arithmetic problems requires an understanding of this part–whole structure (e.g., Briars & Larkin, 1984; Riley, Greeno, & Heller, 1983), and that this structure is also the conceptual foundation for understanding additive commutativity, associativity, and inversion (Resnick, 1989).

Problem Solving

Asked to give an example of a typical subtraction problem, most of us would probably say something along these lines: "John had three apples, then he ate one. How many apples did he have left after that?" This is called a "change" problem, because it describes an initial quantity that is changed by an arithmetic operation, resulting in a different final quantity. It is, by far, the most common type of subtraction problem in first-grade mathematics textbooks in the United States (Stigler, Fuson, Ham, & Kim, 1986). Indeed, so closely is subtraction associated with change that school children often read the subtraction sign "–" as "take away" instead of "minus."

Several classification systems have been developed to characterize the structural properties of addition and subtraction story problems (e.g., Carpenter, Hiebert, & Moser, 1981; Nesher, Greeno, & Riley, 1982; Vergnaud, 1982). These classification systems are of interest because they help to illuminate the different possible ways of thinking about addition and subtraction, and, together with data on children's solution patterns, shed some light on the development of those ways of thinking.

One distinction that has been made is between problems that involve a dynamic event and problems that describe static situations. A static counterpart to the change problem in the previous paragraph is the following: John has three apples. One apple is green, the other apples are red. How many red apples does John have? It turns out that, within subtraction problems, those that involve determining the result of a change are substantially easier than those that involve static relations—Carpenter et al. (1981) reported success rates of 72% versus 47%—whereas within addition problems, those that involve determining the result of a change are slightly more difficult than those that involve a static relation—79% versus 86% correct, in Carpenter et al.'s study. (See Ibarra & Lindvall, 1982, for similar results from a study of kindergartners.) These results suggest that, for young children, addition and subtraction may not be simple opposites but reflections of somewhat different ways of thinking about quantities. For subtraction, the notion of acting on an initial quantity and changing it appears to be primary, whereas for addition, the notion of a totality seems to be what is important.

Change problems increase greatly in difficulty when it is the initial quantity rather than the final one that must be determined (Hiebert, 1982). Final-unknown change problems, like their static counterparts, are typically solved by creating representations of the sets in a way that directly corresponds to the problem description (Carpenter et al., 1981). Initial-unknown problems, of course, are not amenable to that strategy because the child does not know how large to make the first set.

Another important distinction is between problems that involve the characterization of a single overall quantity and problems that involve a comparison between two nonoverlapping quantities. Here is an example of the latter: John has three apples. Joey has one apple. How many more apples does John have than Joey? This class of problems is particularly interesting, as it suggests a conceptual basis for subtraction in the comparison of quantities. The most common strategy used to solve compare subtraction problems directly models the mapping of one set onto another. Two sets of counters with the numerosities indicated in the problem are created and put into one-to-one correspondence with each other, and then the leftover items from the larger set are counted to find the answer to the problem (Carpenter et al., 1981). Clearly, this strategy is a direct extension of the nonnumerical comparison of quantities, in which the child goes beyond identifying one quantity as greater than the other to determine how much greater it is. The role of comparison processes is much less apparent in children's solutions to addition compare problems, however. These, like other addition problems, are most often solved by creating two sets corresponding to the values in the problems and then counting all the items together (Carpenter et al., 1981).

Subtraction compare problems appear to be a bit more difficult than subtraction change problems for first-grade children to solve. Carpenter et al. (1981) reported that 72% of a sample of first graders correctly solved subtraction problems involving determining the final value after a change transformation, whereas 67% correctly solved compare problems involving determining the numerical difference between two collections. Similarly, in a study with kindergartners who had received extensive problem-solving practice, Carpenter, Ansell, Franke, Fennema, and Weisbeck (1993) obtained success rates of 73% and 67% on the two types of subtraction problems.

Hudson (1983), however, argued that the difficulty of compare problems stems largely from children's difficulties interpreting the "How many more?" question. He reported that the large majority of errors consisted of stating the numerical values of one or both of the sets, an error pattern that strongly suggests that children confused the "How many more" questions in these problems with the simpler and more familiar question, "How many?" Furthermore, Hudson (1983) showed that when the task was modified to make clear the comparison question that was being posed, even preschool children were able to solve the problems successfully. In the modified task, children were shown pictures of stimuli such as birds and worms (arranged in different configurations on opposite sides of the page) and asked: "Suppose the birds all race over and each one tries to get a worm. … How many birds won't get a worm?" (p. 85). This wording, of course, makes explicit the idea of mapping the sets onto each other. In one experiment (Hudson, 1983, Experiment 2) 83% of a sample of preschoolers and 96% of a sample of kindergartners responded correctly to at least six of the eight "Won't get" problems. In contrast, only 17% of the preschoolers and 25% of the kindergartners got as many as six out of eight problems correct on corresponding problems posed with the standard "How many more" wording. De Corte, Verschaffel, and De Win (1985) reported similar findings from a study with first- and second-grade children.

In principle, the comparison-of-quantities perspective encompasses addition as well as subtraction compare problems. The process of comparing two quantities leads to the identification of a third quantity, the difference quantity, which together with the two given quantities forms a part–part–whole structure that embraces both addition and subtraction. The *difference quantity* is the quantity that, if added to the smaller quantity, makes it equal to the larger, or, if subtracted from the larger, makes it equal to the smaller. However, it is unclear from children's counting-based solution strategies whether children think about addition compare problems in this way, or simply interpret them as a complex way of asking about the result of combining two sets. In either case, it is clear that reasoning about comparing two sets applies more directly to subtraction compare problems than to addition compare ones. In subtraction compare problems, the two quantities given in the problem can be directly compared to one another and the difference between them thereby identified. In addition compare problems, the comparison is between the combination of the two given quantities and a third, equivalent, quantity. The comparison process plays no role in the solution beyond indicating that the two given quantities are to be combined. An implication of this observation is that, insofar as comparison processes are especially intuitive for young children, subtraction compare problems may be expected to be solved more readily than addition compare problems. The available data are strikingly consistent with this idea: Carpenter et al. (1981) reported that first graders correctly solved 29% of subtraction compare problems but only 10% of addition compare problems.

Taken together, the data on young children's performance across different types of addition and subtraction problems suggest that three distinct intuitions inform their early reasoning about addition and subtraction. The most basic intuitive idea underlying addition is that of a totality, which encompasses two (or more) component quantities. A second intuition, one that applies to both addition and subtraction but appears to be particularly salient in relation to subtraction, is that of an initial quantity that is changed by either putting more items into it or taking some items away. Finally, a third powerful idea is that of comparing quantities by mapping them onto one another, giving rise to a comparison form of subtraction. School textbooks give much more attention to the first two of these ways of thinking about addition and subtraction than to the third, as combine problems are the most common type of addition problems and change problems (with the final quantity unknown) are the most common type of subtraction problem in U.S. first-grade texts (Stigler et al., 1986). Children's facility with subtraction compare problems even before they begin formal schooling, however, suggests that ideas about the comparison of quantities that enable children to determine the magnitude relations even among unenumerated quantities remain an important element of their thinking about arithmetic relations among numerical quantities.

Models developed to account for developmental patterns in students' addition and subtraction problem solving have converged on the idea that, although some problems can be solved on the basis of simpler kinds of reasoning, facility with a full range of arithmetic problems requires an understanding of their part–whole structure (e.g., Briars & Larkin, 1984; Riley et al., 1983). On this view, the difficulties beginning elementary school students have with problems such as change subtraction problems with the initial set unknown arise because they have not yet developed a cognitive part–whole schema. This position, however, needs to be reconciled with evidence that even preschool and kindergarten children display part–whole knowledge in some contexts (e.g., Sophian & McCorgray, 1994; Sophian & Vong, 1995).

Additive Part–Whole Relations

A useful starting point for considering what young children know about part–whole relations and how that knowledge changes as their mathematics learning progresses is Resnick's (1989, 1992) accounts of the emergence of quantitative knowledge from early-developing schemas that represent basic relations between quantities. Specifically, Resnick posits that before children begin formal schooling, they have several schemas that provide a crucial foundation for the development of quantitative knowledge. These include a part–whole schema that reflects the additivity of material quantities; an increase and/or decrease schema; and a comparison schema. The part–whole schema represents the fact that material can be cut into pieces without changing the original quantity, and the pieces can be put back together in different ways also without affecting the quantity. The increase and/or decrease schema allows children to identify changes that increase quantity, changes that decrease quantity, and changes that leave quantity unchanged. And the comparison schema allows children to determine perceptually that one quantity is larger than another. These schemas are termed *protoquantitative* because, according to Resnick, they are initially independent of children's knowledge about counting, which also develops during the preschool years. Truly quantitative knowledge arises from the integration of children's protoquantitative additive schemas with their knowledge of counting, resulting in a quantified part–whole schema.

Any characterization of early knowledge about relations among material quantities as unquantified is, of course, open to question in light of the research into infants' numerical knowledge (see chap. 2), which suggests that there may not be a point in development at which material quantities are entirely unquantified. Because the results from research on infants' knowledge about number are still controversial, no firm conclusions about the issue can be drawn; and in any case it is unclear to what extent Resnick's (1989, 1992) ideas about the role of counting knowledge hinge on the explicit use of counting terms or could be satisfied by the operation of a nonverbal counting mechanism such as Gallistel and Gelman (1992) posited. What is of great interest in Resnick's account is the idea that the origins of children's knowledge about part–whole relations and relative magnitudes are independent of enumeration processes, stemming instead from children's ideas about physical materials. This aspect of her account accords with the comparison-of-quantities perspective.

Research on young children's knowledge about additive part–whole relations has been inspired in large part by Piaget's (1952) account of the development of *class inclusion knowledge*, that is, knowledge that a superordinate set is necessarily greater in magnitude than the individual subsets that comprise it. According to Piaget, class inclusion is one of several quantitative concepts that are attained only with the development of concrete operational reasoning (typically around 5 to 7 years of age). In support of this thesis, Piaget reported that preschool-aged children, asked to identify which is larger between a superordinate set and the larger of two subsets within it (e.g., "Are there more daisies or more flowers?" given four daisies plus two flowers of another kind), typically indicate the subset (daisies) rather than the superordinate (flowers). Like other claims about preoperational reasoning, however, the claim that preoperational children do not understand class inclusion has been the subject of considerable debate and empirical research (e.g., Markman, 1979; McGarrigle, Grieve, & Hughes, 1978; Sophian & McCorgray, 1994; Wilkinson, 1976).

McGarrigle et al. (1978) were able to elicit correct class inclusion judgments by introducing a salient feature that applied to all the elements of the superordinate class and then including an adjective designating that feature in the class inclusion question to help children identify the items to which the superordinate term referred. For instance, showing children a collection of toy cows, some of which were brown and all of which were lying down, or "sleeping," they asked, "Are there more brown cows or more sleeping cows?" More often than not, preschool children answered this question correctly ("More sleeping cows"). McGarrigle et al.'s interpretation was that the salience of the sleeping feature, which characterized the entire set, helped children overcome the tendency to interpret the question as one about the relation between the two subsets (more brown cows or more cows that aren't brown?). However, because there is no logical relationship between the numbers of sleeping cows and the numbers of brown cows, it is unclear how this clarification could facilitate logical, as opposed to empirical, solutions of the problem. That is, the adjective "sleeping" helped children to identify the designated classes, so that they could compare them empirically, but it is not clear that those empirical solutions constitute evidence of logical knowledge of class inclusion relations.

Sophian and McCorgray (1994) contrasted class inclusion problems with noninclusion problems, which involved the same superordinate and subordinate classes. Thus, on all trials children saw collections composed of three types of items, two of which were subsets of a common superordinate category while the third was not (e.g., pears, bananas, and cows). On class inclusion trials, the children were asked to compare the superordinate category with one of its subsets, for example, fruits versus bananas, whereas on noninclusion problems they were asked to compare the superordinate with the unrelated set, for example, fruits versus cows. Five- and 6-year-old children reliably chose the correct set on both class inclusion and noninclusion problems. However, 4-year-olds were successful only on the noninclusion problems, indicating that inclusion relations were a source of difficulty above and beyond other demands of the problems, which were comparable across the inclusion and noninclusion problems. Still, even the positive results from 5-year-olds are difficult to reconcile with theoretical analyses of elementary school children's arithmetic problem solving, which invoke deficiencies in part–whole understanding as a major source of difficulty in solving certain classes of arithmetic word problems (Briars & Larkin, 1984; Riley et al., 1983).

These results indicate the need for a more developmental analysis of children's early knowledge about relations between sets than Resnick (1989, 1992) offered. They support the presence of part–whole knowledge in preschool children, but only in the latter part of the preschool period. Furthermore, contrary to Resnick's (1992) distinction between early un-quantified knowledge about part–whole relations and later quantitative knowledge, there is evidence that preschool children can reason appropri-ately, if not precisely, about the numerical ramifications of the part–whole relations among sets.

Sophian and Vong (1995) presented 4- and 5-year-old children with story problems in which a character had gathered a number of objects at a park and, on his way home with them, met either a "friend," who gave him an additional item, or a "monster," who took away one of the items he had. Children were either shown the number of items the character started with and asked how many he had when he got home (final-unknown problems) or vice versa (initial-unknown problems). Initial-unknown problems have been found to be much more difficult for school children than final-un-known problems (Carpenter et al., 1981; Hiebert, 1982), and their diffi-culty has been attributed to the need for a conceptual understanding of the part–whole relations in the problems in order to be able to reason backward from the final to the initial quantity (Riley et al., 1983). Sophian and Vong, however, found that 5-year-olds (but not 4-year-olds) responded to both initial-unknown and final-unknown problems in a way that indicated an ap-preciation of whether the initial quantity would be larger or smaller than the final quantity. Although children's responses were often numerically in-accurate, the direction of the response (i.e., whether it was greater or smaller than the number given in the problem) indicated some understand-ing of the part–whole relations in the problems. The pattern of results is dis-played graphically in Figure 5.1. Within the final-unknown problems, both age groups appropriately gave answers that were greater than the initial value more often when the character had received an extra object from a friend than when he had lost one to a monster (these answers are repre-sented by the light-colored bars in the figure; a converse pattern held for answers that were less than the initial value, which are represented by the dark-colored bars). Within the initial-unknown problems, 5-year-olds (but not 4-year-olds) appropriately gave answers that were greater than the final value (again, represented by the light-colored bars) more often when that value represented the situation after the character had lost an object to a monster than when it represented the situation after the character had gained an object from a friend.

Although studies of young children's reasoning about part–whole relation-ships have focused on change situations (initial-unknown and final-unknown problems) and on combine or totality situations (class inclusion problems), the

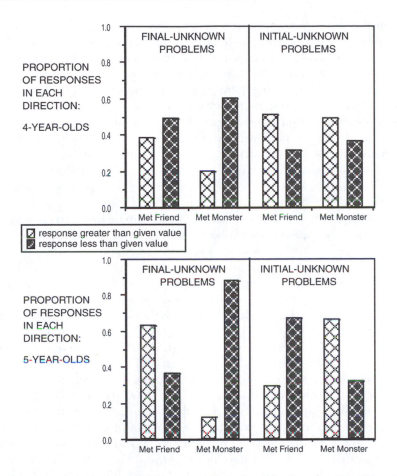

Figure 5.1.   Response patterns across problems involving increase (Met Friend) versus decrease (Met Monster) events. In the final-unknown problems, the task is to determine the quantity after the increase or decrease event, given information about the original quantity; in the initial-unknown ones, it is to determine the quantity before the increase or decrease event, given information about the final quantity. (Data from Sophian & Vong, 1995.)

part–whole structure also applies, in a somewhat different form, to compare situations. In these situations, the comparison of two quantities results in the identification of a third, difference, quantity. Taken together, the two compared quantities and the difference quantity form a part–whole structure in which the two smaller quantities can be understood as parts of a whole (their union), which is equal in magnitude to the third quantity. This part–whole interpretation makes the inverse relation between addition and subtraction particularly clear: Equating the smaller of the original quantities to the larger one less the difference quantity is equivalent to equating the larger of the original quantities to the smaller one joined with the difference quantity. Furthermore, because comparison processes do not depend on enumeration (we can identify the physical magnitude of a difference between continuous quantities such as line segments just by aligning them), this way of understanding part–whole relations need not be tied to numerical computation.

The developmental convergence between Sophian and McCorgray's (1994) results for class inclusion problems and those of Sophian and Vong (1995) for initial-unknown change problems suggests that the development of part–whole knowledge may in fact be closely tied to the development of related numerical knowledge. It may be through mapping numbers into sets, and thereby observing how numerical relations correspond to relations among physical quantities, that children gain insight into the idea that a set may be compared with a subset within it.

The conclusion that part–whole knowledge develops over the preschool period, and through the integration of numerical knowledge with knowledge about relations among physical quantities, fits well with Resnick's (1989, 1992) account of the development of quantitative knowledge, if we consider part–whole knowledge of the kinds demonstrated by Sophian and McCorgray (1994) and Sophian and Vong (1995) as early forms of quantitative, rather than merely protoquantitative, knowledge. That conclusion, however, raises the question of why children in the early elementary grades have so much difficulty with addition and subtraction problems whose solution requires the abstraction of a part–whole structure from the specific relations among quantities that are described in the problem. It seems likely that the solution to this apparent discrepancy lies in the recognition that conceptual knowledge is not all-or-none but becomes increasingly robust, flexible, and accessible with development (Sophian, 1997). At least three factors can be identified that could contribute to differences in children's success rates across different types of arithmetic problems without requiring the emergence of a new form of conceptual knowledge to account for the mastery of the more difficult problems.

One factor is cognitive complexity. Early successes on problems thought to require part–whole knowledge are observed only under conditions that minimize the demands of the task, for instance, by providing pictorial stimuli that both represent the critical numerical information and also support children in grasping the relations among the quantities (e.g., pictures of birds and worms, in Hudson's, 1983, work; pictures of the initial, change, and final scenarios in Sophian and Vong's, 1995, work).

A second factor is linguistic. Systematic errors in children's comprehension of standard arithmetic word problems are evidenced in distortions in the retelling or recall of the problems (Cummins, 1988, 1991; De Corte & Verschaffel, 1987).

Finally, limited familiarity may contribute to children's relatively poor performance on certain types of arithmetic problems. The problems on which children have been found to do best are the very ones that occur most often in arithmetic textbooks, particularly in the first grade (Stigler et al., 1986). Correspondingly, the problems on which difficulties attributed to the lack of part–whole knowledge have been observed are ones that children encounter relatively infrequently. Of course, the relationship between problem frequency and student performance is likely due at least in part to the selection of relatively simple problems for inclusion in the texts, but it may also be the case that differential exposure contributes to the differences in children's performance across problem types.

Principles of Commutativity, Associativity, and Inversion

The part–whole structure nicely integrates three important principles of addition and subtraction: the principles of commutativity of addition ($a + b = b + a$), associativity of addition ($a + [b + c] = [a + b] + c$), and the inverse relation between addition and subtraction ($a + b - b = a$). Commutativity and inversion are both quite transparent in the way in which addition and subtraction apply to part–whole structures. Essentially, *commutativity* is a manifestation of the principle of conservation; the whole is not affected by how we position the parts. *Inversion* is the mathematical reflection of the physical reversibility of actions of joining and separating: If I join something else with an initial quantity, all I need to do is take it away again to get back to what I had initially (and vice versa). *Associativity* is a bit more complex in that it entails applying the idea of decomposition, not only to the whole, but also to at least one of the original parts. Thus the structure, part + part = whole, becomes, (subpart + subpart) + part = whole. Those subparts and parts can then be rearranged without affecting the total, again in accordance with the principle of conservation. Thus, (subpart + subpart) + part = subpart + (subpart + part).

Consistent with the idea that an understanding of the commutativity and associativity of addition, and of the inverse relation between addition and subtraction, follows from an understanding of its part–whole structure, which is present at least in rudimentary form by about 5 years of age, the available developmental evidence indicates that young children have a grasp of at least the principles of commutativity and inversion as early as 5 years of age. Associativity has received little direct investigation, but computational strategies that correspond to the principle of associativity have been found to be fairly common by 6 years of age.

Interest in young children's knowledge about the commutativity of addition was stimulated by the observation that in adding pairs of numbers, even kindergarten children quickly move from counting-on procedures for adding that reflect the order of addends to more efficient ones that treat commuted pairs of addends equivalently (Groen & Resnick, 1977). In the earlier form of counting-on, the child takes the first addend as a starting point and makes a number of counting increments corresponding to the second addend (e.g., for 3 + 5, the child would make five counting increments beyond 3: "4, 5, 6, 7, 8"). In the more efficient strategy, termed *min* because it minimizes the number of counting increments required, the child starts with the larger of the two addends and makes a number of counting increments corresponding to the smaller addend, regardless of the order in which the two addends are presented. There is some question of whether the use of min really reflects an understanding of commutativity or merely a work-saving technique that is not informed by conceptual considerations (Baroody & Gannon, 1984). However, at least two other lines of evidence support the view that children do understand commutativity as early as 5 years of age. First, using a task in which children had to judge whether or not two sums were equal, Sophian and McCorgray (1994, Experiment 2) showed that even when the numerosity of one quantity was unspecified (but known to be the same in the two sums being compared), 5- and 6-year-olds correctly judged that sums consisting of the same two quantities taken in different orders were equal. Second, several studies have examined children's ability to judge whether a second problem could be solved without computation by looking back at a previous result, and to explain their judgments (Baroody & Gannon, 1984; Canobi, Reeve, & Pattison, 2003.) The results from these studies indicated that a majority of 5-year-olds made correct judgments, although they were considerably less likely to be able to justify them.

Knowledge of inversion has been studied by examining children's performance on three-term problems that include both an addition and a subtraction. Bryant, Christie, and Rendu (1999) compared children's solution for problems such as 14 + 7 – 7, in which the inverse relation between adding and subtracting the same number makes computation unnecessary, with their solution times for problems such as 9 + 9 – 4, which had comparable results but could not be solved without computing partial results. Their finding that children as young as 5 years of age were more successful on the inversion problems than on the control problems supports the conclusion that children recognize the inverse relation between addition and subtraction quite early. Similar evidence has since been obtained with preschool (4-year-old) children as well (Rasmussen, Ho, & Bisanz, 2003).

Associativity is implicit in a decomposition strategy that consists of breaking down one addend into a sum of two smaller numbers and then grouping one of those numbers with the other addend so as to generate an easier number combination. For instance, 12 + 2 may be transformed into (10 + 2) + 2 and then into 10 + (2 + 2) or 10 + 4. Siegler (1987) reported that this type of computational strategy was fairly common among first and second graders, although rare among kindergartners.

MULTIPLICATIVE REASONING

School children are often introduced to multiplication as a process of repeated addition; and studies of children who have received little formal schooling indicate that they too tend to approach multiplication as a process of repeated addition (e.g., Carraher, Carraher, & Schliemann, 1985). Several investigators, however, have argued that multiplication is better characterized in terms of one-to-many mappings (Confrey, 1994; Park & Nunes, 2001). That perspective aligns well with the emphasis here on understanding multiplication in terms of the use of one quantity as a unit for the other, because the quantity that is iterated in a many-to-one mapping is functioning as a higher order unit (cf. chap. 4). An implication is that the conceptually important links between multiplicative and additive reasoning are better understood in terms of the way units enter into all numerical characterizations of quantities than in terms of the computational correspondence between multiplication and repeated addition. Because the relation between unit size and numerical value is always inversely multiplicative, the need for multiplicative reasoning arises as soon as we consider the numerical ramifications of using different units of quantification.

Ratios and Units

The earliest evidence of proportional reasoning in young children has come from studies of children's ability to identify equivalent spatial proportions. Even infants are sensitive to certain kinds of spatial proportions; if an object is partially overhanging the edge of another object on which it is resting, the proportion of the object that protrudes beyond the edge determines how they react when the object either remains in place or falls off (Baillargeon, Needham, & DeVos, 1992, cited in Baillargeon et al., 1995). Similarly, Sophian (2000b) obtained evidence that preschool children are able to identify which of two stimuli is the same in its spatial proportions (i.e., height-to-width ratio) as a larger sample stimulus (cf. chap. 3). However, this kind of matching is less complex than many other kinds of multiplicative reasoning in that it does not involve considering relations across different types of quantities. All of the quantities in spatial ratios are of the same type: lengths, areas, or volumes. The relations among these quantities could, of course, be represented with operations of multiplication and division. But what is powerful about the multiplicative operations is that they are not restricted to expressing relations among like quantities; one could equally well represent the equivalence between the ratio of height to width of a rectangle and the weights of a sack of flour and a sack of sugar.

What makes the latter proportion obscure to very young children, but straightforward to represent with the operations of multiplication and division, is that it requires the explicit quantification of the multiplicative relation between quantities. When young children compare spatial ratios, the comparison is a holistic, perceptual, one; they don't calculate how many times the width of a rectangle can be iterated along its height, they just see that it is very tall for its width. As a result, they have only a global idea of the relation between height and width to compare to another rectangle's height and width. There is no way to map such a representation onto the relation between two weights, even assuming that the relation between the weights could be perceived as readily as the height–width relation. Multiplicative reasoning gains its full power only when one quantity is explicitly quantified using the other as a unit because this operation results in a numerical value for the relation between the quantities, which can then be compared with other values representing the multiplicative relations between other pairs of quantities, regardless of what kinds of quantities they were. The numerical ratio provides an abstract representation of the relation between two quantities (the measured quantity and the unit used to measure it) that can be compared across all sorts of quantities.

Reasoning About Many-to-One Relations

Many-to-one correspondences arise whenever several items of one kind must be mapped onto each single item of another kind, for example, in putting three flowers in each of a number of vases (Piaget, 1952). Although 5-year-old children can construct many-to-one mappings easily enough— for instance, they can give several small items to one recipient each time they give a single larger item to another recipient (Frydman & Bryant, 1988)—anticipating the numerical consequences of a series of many-to-one mappings is substantially more difficult. These problems amount to problems of conversion between units: How many large units are equivalent to a given number of small ones (or vice versa)?

To study children's ability to reason, not only about individual many-to-one mappings (e.g., two of these items for one of these), but about the numerical consequences of a series of such mappings, Sophian and Madrid (2003) asked children to determine how many small blocks would be needed to build a tower the same height as one made of several large blocks. This problem is equivalent to stating the height of the tower in small units instead of the original larger units. Sophian and Madrid found that children below 7 years of age were unable to solve this type of problem, and 7-year-olds succeeded only after receiving a series of training problems that encouraged them to think of the several items that together corresponded to a single larger item as together comprising a new type of unit to be iterated (cf. chap. 4).

These results are consistent with findings from Carpenter et al.'s (1993) work with kindergarten children who had had extensive experience with arithmetic problem solving. The children in their study solved both multiplication and division problems involving many-to-one relations by using tally marks or counters to represent a series of many-to-one groupings matching the information in the problem (6 pieces of gum to a package, 3 packages; 15 guppies, 3 in each jar) and then counting the appropriate unit to determine the unknown value (18 pieces of gum; 5 jars).

Multiplicative Situations and Conceptualizations of Multiplicative Relations

Several investigators have attempted to classify different types of multiplication and division problems or situations (e.g., Greer, 1992; Kouba, 1989; Nunes & Bryant, 1996; Vergnaud, 1983). A major difficulty in developing a clear classification system lies in distinguishing between different types of multiplicative situations, on one hand, and different ways of thinking about a multiplicative situation, on the other. A given multiplicative situation may be amenable to more than one type of multiplicative thinking, and different types of multiplicative situations may be amenable to the same form of multiplicative thinking.

Perhaps the clearest distinction among multiplicative situations is the one Vergnaud (1983) draws between "isomorphism-of-measures" problems and "product-of-measures" problems. Isomorphism-of-measures problems involve relations among different types of quantities, such as items purchased and currency paid, or durations and distances. They can generally be conceptualized as a matter of either mapping the relation between the two types of quantities from one pair of values (e.g., a purchase of a single item for 10 cents) to another (e.g., a purchase of three items for 30 cents) or of applying the same scalar relation to the two quantities (e.g., a purchase of three times as many items will cost three times as much). Product-of-measures problems consist of area problems (height × width) and Cartesian products, in which the number of distinct pairings of elements from two sets is the product of the number of elements in each set (e.g., the number of outfits that can be formed with three different skirts and four different blouses is 12). Whereas in isomorphism-of-measures problems, two different types of quantities are being related to determine an unknown value on one of those dimensions, in product-of-measures problems, two quantities are being related to generate a product that is a different type of quantity from either of them (measured in a different type of unit). For instance, the Cartesian product resulting from pairing skirts and blouses is neither a number of skirts nor a number of blouses but a number of outfits.

Despite this profound difference, both classes of problems can be conceptualized in terms of many-to-one mappings. For instance, just as costs can be related to items purchased by thinking about a many-to-one mapping between some number of cents (or other currency unit) and each individual item purchased, the outfit problem can be solved by thinking about the many-to-one mapping of the alternative blouses onto each skirt in turn (or vice versa). That is, there are four outfits corresponding to Skirt A (formed by pairing it with each of the possible blouses), four more corresponding to Skirt B (paired with each of the possible blouses), and four more for Skirt C. Bryant, Morgado, and Nunes (1992, cited in Nunes & Bryant, 1996) provide evidence that in fact children often approach Cartesian product problems in just this way.

Area measurement, too, can be conceptualized as the iteration of enough equal rows, each consisting of a number of units of area sufficient to span the width of a target area, to cover the length of the target area. Indeed, evidence from a study of children's strategies for measuring area (Nunes, Light, & Mason, 1993, Study 2) suggests that this conceptualization may be more intuitive for children than a product-of-measures conceptualization. Nunes et al. asked 8- to 10-year-old children to decide whether two rectangular areas that could not be directly compared were equal in area or, if not, which one was larger. They provided the children with rulers and bricks by means of which to measure the rectangles. Although the children tended to start out by using the rulers, they were much more successful when they used the bricks. With the rulers, they had a strong tendency to add their length and width measurements and compare the sums. There was nothing in their conceptualization of how two linear measures combine to determine area to guide them in identifying the appropriate arithmetic operation to apply to their measurements. Using the bricks, however, they typically constructed an equal-groups interpretation of the area problem (how many bricks per row times the number of rows), which led them to correct multiplicative solutions. The equal-groups solution with bricks, although it still involves the measurement of length and width, avoids the need to shift from linear units to area units that is entailed by the use of rulers, and, in doing so, lends itself well to an equal-groups interpretation, which makes it clear that the relation between length, width, and area is multiplicative rather than additive.

Clearly, some types of problems are more explicit than others about the presence of equal groups or many-to-one mappings among the quantities. Yet even problems that do not explicitly mention equal groups can often be conceptualized in that way; thus it may be more appropriate to think about equal groups as a way of conceptualizing a broad range of multiplicative situations than as a distinct class of problems or situations. For example, Greer (1992) distinguishes "equal-groups" problems from "multiplicative comparison" problems, which involve statements like "n times as many" (Greer, 1992, p. 277). However, as Sophian and Madrid's (2003) block-tower problems illustrate, a good way of understanding such multiplicative comparisons is to interpret them in terms of a series of equal groups. For instance, to understand the statement "There are 3 times as many girls as boys in the class" a student might picture the class arranged so that each boy is paired with a trio of girls.

Two distinct interpretations of division problems derive from the equal-groups conceptualization of multiplication (and hence, equivalently, from the conversion-between-units conceptualization). They differ in whether the quantity to be determined is the number of items per group (partitive or sharing division) or the number of groups of a specified size (quotitive or measurement division). Children as young as kindergartners can solve both kinds of division problems (Carpenter et al., 1993); if manipulatives are provided, they generally do so by creating physical models of the grouping situation described in the problem.

A limitation of equal-groups conceptualizations, however, is that they are difficult to apply to multiplicative relations among fractional quantities. Although it is conceivable to have half a group (particularly given the understanding that groups are fixed in size), that idea is far from intuitive for young children. Indeed, a common problem in understanding division by a fraction is to confuse division by $\frac{1}{2}$ with division into halves or taking half of a quantity, both of which amount to multiplying by $\frac{1}{2}$ or dividing by 2 rather than dividing by $\frac{1}{2}$. However, any equal-groups problem can be understood as a matter of applying a different unit of quantification to a quantity that is given in the problem, and this conceptualization readily encompasses operations with fractions as well as with whole numbers. From this perspective, individual items and groups of items are alternative units in terms of which a given quantity can be described, and multiplication and division convert values based on one type of unit into values for the same quantity based on the other type of unit.

Principles of Commutativity, Associativity, and Inversion

Despite the structural differences between addition and multiplication, multiplication, like addition, is characterized by principles of commutativity ($a \times b = b \times a$), associativity ($a \times [b \times c] = [a \times b] \times c$), and inversion ($a \times b \div b = a$). Children's knowledge of these principles as they apply to multiplication has received very little empirical study, however, and that work appears to have examined only the commutativity of multiplication (Baroody, 1999; Nunes & Bryant, 1995).

The connection between commutativity, associativity, and inversion and the proportionality structure of multiplication is much less clear than the connection between the corresponding principles for addition and the additive part–whole structure. Indeed, even the algebraic expression of these principles uses a binary structure rather than the quaternary proportional structure that is at the heart of multiplicative relations. (An expression of commutativity in proportional terms would be the statement: if $\dfrac{a}{b} = \dfrac{c}{d}$, then $\dfrac{a}{c} = \dfrac{b}{d}$.)

Children's reasoning about multiplicative commutativity, likewise, appears to be based on a binary interpretation of multiplication. Baroody (1999) studied the role of commutative relations in children's learning of basic multiplication facts. He examined patterns of posttest performance of third-grade children (mean age: 8 years, 5 months) who initially had virtually no knowledge of a target set of multiplication facts and then received practice on a subset of those facts. On the posttest, the children did significantly better on multiplication facts that were commuted versions of practiced facts than on different nonpracticed facts, but not as well on the commuted facts as on the specific facts that had been practiced. Baroody's (1999) interpretation of these results is based on the idea that children learn multiplication combinations by forming associative links between pairs of numbers and their products (Siegler, 1988), a form of multiplication knowledge that is clearly binary rather than proportional in structure. Within this framework, children's success on computed versions of learned multiplication combinations suggests that associative links are generalized from particular multiplication combinations to commuted variants of those combinations.

Nunes and Bryant (1995) obtained further insight into children's reasoning about the commutativity of multiplication by contrasting their understanding of commutativity in two physical contexts. In one, the multiplication described a spatial array (rows × columns), which could simply be rotated to transform the original problem into a commuted counterpart. In the other, the multiplication described a quantity composed of a number of equal groups. In this case it would be necessary to rearrange the items into different-sized groups in order to transform the original problem into a commuted counterpart. Nunes and Bryant's finding that children were substantially less likely to recognize the equivalence of commuted problems in the latter case suggests that children rely heavily on their understanding of physical situations and the relations between them in reasoning about multiplicative commutativity.

One study has examined adults' (university undergraduates') understanding of the inverse relation between multiplication and division, comparing performance on three-term problems involving first multiplication and then division with performance on corresponding problems involving first addition and then subtraction (Robinson & Ninowski, 2003). The inversion problems were interspersed with control, noninversion problems, so that participants' sensitivity to the inversion principles could be inferred from quicker and more accurate responses to the inversion than to the control problems. Not surprisingly, strong differences between inversion and control problems were obtained in both problem sets; the inversion problems elicited much quicker responses and far fewer errors than their noninversion counterparts. However, participants began using the inversion strategy to respond to inversion problems without step-by-step computation earlier within the set of addition and subtraction problems than they did in the multiplication and division problem set, suggesting that their understanding of the inversion relation between multiplication and division was not as strong as their understanding of the inversion relation between addition and subtraction.

THE CONCEPTUAL RELATION BETWEEN ADDITIVE AND MULTIPLICATIVE REASONING

Because additive relations are so much less complex than multiplicative ones, it is natural to think of them as the starting point for arithmetic reasoning. Indeed, it is widely assumed that children must build on their understanding of addition and subtraction in learning multiplication and division. But the perspective developed here suggests that the connection between additive and multiplicative reasoning is not a direct building-block connection. Rather, they are closely linked because an understanding of multiplicative relations depends on an understanding of the concept of a unit that is generally developed first in the context of additive reasoning.

In order to represent numerically a relation between quantities, whether that relation is an additive or a multiplicative one, we need to choose a unit; and as soon as we do so both additive and multiplicative ways of thinking about quantities come into play. Any numerical quantification involves additive relations because the act of measuring entails thinking of the total quantity as composed of a series of pieces and of the pieces as combining to make the whole. At the same time, any numerical quantification involves a choice of units, and an understanding of how the numerical value and the size of the unit combine to specify the magnitude of the quantity entails multiplicativity.

Approached via the idea of many-to-one correspondence, the contrast between additive and multiplicative reasoning is a fairly subtle one: the difference between thinking of a packet of candy, for example, as the sum of five individual candies versus as a composite unit that is in a one-to-many relation to the basic unit of an individual candy. However, this shift entails being explicit about the unit of quantification in a way that is often neglected in additive reasoning.

Mack (1995) nicely illustrated students' carelessness about units in her work on fraction addition and subtraction. Her students learned to think of fraction addition and subtraction (with common denominators) as the addition and subtraction of whole numbers, but with reference to fractional parts instead of wholes. However, their failure to recognize the importance of specifying the unit led them to make errors such as giving 4 as the sum of $\frac{1}{5} + \frac{3}{5}$.

Such carelessness about units is likely to be less problematic in whole-number addition and subtraction because the unit is generally constant, but it can be seen there as well. In some unpublished research, I once gave first-grade children the following story problem: "Some children are jumping into a sandbox. One jumps in with both feet; three jump in on one foot. How many footprints do they make?" The children were required to specify the unit as well as the numerical value in their answers. A very common answer was "4 children." The children who responded this way failed to notice that the numerical value they were asked to determine was not based on the same unit as the numbers given in the problem. Thus, they simply added the numbers given in the problem (a shortcut that is no doubt reinforced by the fact that in the early elementary school years, addition is very often adequate to solve the problems they are given).

All numerical representations are representations of the ratio between the quantity they describe and the unit of quantification used to measure it. In this sense, the seeds of multiplicative reasoning are already contained in the first act of enumeration. But the importance of this idea does not become clear until we consider alternative units of quantification, and as soon as we do that, it becomes necessary to deal with multiplicative relations. In instruction, it is natural to want to sidestep this complexity initially and familiarize children with addition and subtraction before introducing multiplication and division. But the danger when we do so is that we obscure the very ideas that children will later need to grasp when we do teach multiplication and division.

Although addition and multiplication are similar in several important ways, seeing multiplication as a simple extension of addition (and division correspondingly as an extension of subtraction) has serious conceptual drawbacks. Both addition and multiplication are operations that can be carried out on two numbers to get a third number; both are commutative and associative; each has an inverse operation (subtraction, division) and an identity element (0 for addition, 1 for multiplication); and, when the second addend (for addition) or the multiplier (for multiplication) is greater than the identity element, both operations represent an increase in magnitude. Yet, encouraging children to build directly on what they know about adding and subtracting in learning to multiply and divide obscures the profound difference between the proportional structure of multiplication and division and the part–whole structure of addition and subtraction. Furthermore, it misrepresents the real conceptual relation between additive and multiplicative reasoning and thus the ways in which children's early additive reasoning can affect their later ability to make sense of multiplicative relations.

Chapter 6

Understanding Fractions

Like other numbers, *fractions* are fundamentally representations of magnitude. Nevertheless, children find it much more difficult to interpret fractions than whole numbers as representations of magnitude. There are two major obstacles to understanding fraction magnitudes. The first is appreciating that the two numbers that comprise a fraction (numerator and denominator) together specify a single magnitude (Behr et al., 1984). The second obstacle is understanding how that magnitude is related to the magnitudes of the numerator and, especially, the denominator (Behr et al., 1984; Ohlsson, 1991). The potential for confusion about this relationship is apparent from the observation that the relative magnitude of two fractions in some cases does correspond to the relative magnitudes of the numbers within them (e.g., $\frac{2}{5} < \frac{3}{5}$ and $\frac{2}{3} < \frac{4}{5}$), but very often does not (e.g., $\frac{2}{3} > \frac{2}{5}$, $\frac{3}{4} > \frac{5}{8}$, and $\frac{3}{4} = \frac{6}{8}$ even though $3 < 5$, $4 < 8$, and $3 < 6$).

Not surprisingly, children have little difficulty understanding magnitude relations among fractions that share a common denominator. Correct judgments in such cases may be simple generalizations of children's knowledge of whole-number magnitudes. The inverse relation between the denominator of a fraction and the magnitude of the fraction as a whole is less transparent, however. Given two fractions with equal numerators, elementary school students often expect the fraction with the larger denominator to be greater rather than smaller in value (Behr et al., 1984). Although this misconception generally declines by the end of elementary school, it persists among some students even in high school (Stafylidou & Vosniadou, 2004).

Conceptually, the inverse relation between denominator size and the magnitude of a fraction is intimately related to the idea of a unit of measure.

Fractional units are obtained by partitioning the original unit into a number of equal parts, and the denominator indicates the size of the new units by specifying the number of parts into which the whole was partitioned. The more parts, the smaller each one is; hence the inverse relation between the size of the denominator and the magnitude of the fraction as a whole.

A fundamental conceptual foundation for understanding fractions, then, is the idea that fractions describe a quantity by specifying a fractional unit of measure (via the denominator of the fraction) and indicating how many such units correspond to the quantity in question (via the numerator of the fraction). Commonly, this idea is presented to students by representing fractions as segments of a circle, or some other shape, that has been divided into equal parts. This way of conceptualizing fractions, however, is vulnerable to two serious sources of confusion. First, it uses the concepts of "part" and "whole" in a very different way from that in which they have been used previously, in the context of addition and subtraction, and the contrast may not be clear to students, resulting in confusion about what actually constitutes a part and a whole, and about how fractions fit with the knowledge students have about whole numbers. Second, it fails to make clear important constraints on the composition of wholes and parts that are critical to understanding both the magnitude relations among fractions and the meaning of arithmetic operations on fractions. For example, although students are told that fractional parts must be equal, there is nothing in the idea of cutting a whole into parts that indicates why their size cannot vary. It is only when these parts are understood as measurement units, the size of which will determine the numerical value obtained for a given quantity, that it becomes clear why it is essential that the sizes be uniform.

The central thesis of this chapter is that an inadequate understanding of fractional parts as units of measure is the primary conceptual reason why students find fraction learning difficult and confusing. In the first three sections of the chapter, several other hypotheses that have been advanced to explain students' difficulties with fractions are discussed. First, the idea derived from counting-based accounts of numerical development, that fractions are problematic because they do not conform to the ideas about numbers that are the basis for earlier forms of numerical thinking, particularly counting, is examined. Second, the idea that fractions are conceptually complex in that they involve a cluster of distinct, albeit interrelated, subconstructs is briefly discussed. And third, the idea that the information-processing demands of fractions overwhelm students, particularly in the elementary grades, is considered. These perspectives are not incompatible either with each other or with my own emphasis on the importance of understanding fractional units. However, although there are elements of truth in each of them, in my view, they do not provide a satisfying account, either individually or in combination, for the difficulties that students have with fractions. In noting the limitations of each, I hope to clarify the need for the alternative view to be developed in the two subsequent sections of the chapter. These first examine the conceptual difficulties that arise within the part–whole model of fractions as it is customarily used to explain fractions to elementary school students, and then elaborate on the conceptual advantages of conceptualizing fractions from a measurement perspective.

The final two sections of the chapter address instructional issues. The thesis derived from the counting-based view of mathematics development, that the difficulties children have with fraction learning are a function of the lack of congruence between fractions and the way counting works, suggests that fractions are likely to pose substantial conceptual difficulty no matter how they are taught. The kinds of considerations developed in this chapter, however, suggest that it may be possible to avoid much of the confusion students experience in learning about fractions by identifying the conceptual ideas on which an understanding of fractions depends and ensuring that they are adequately developed in early mathematics instruction.

Although instructional studies have not been designed to directly test these alternative positions, the instructional research that has been done certainly has a bearing on any account of children's fraction learning insofar as it provides information about what instructional approaches, if any, are effective in fostering a sound understanding of fractions. Accordingly, two recently developed experimental curricula are described, both of which have met with considerable success in teaching rational number concepts to fourth- and fifth-grade students. Although the curricula differ markedly from each other in a number of ways, they share an emphasis on developing students' understanding of the magnitudes that fractions represent.

The final section of the chapter addresses the conceptual links between fraction learning and earlier mathematical learning, highlighting the potential ramifications of the way in which whole-number arithmetic is taught for later fraction learning.

FROM COUNTING NUMBERS TO FRACTIONS

A counterpart to the claim that the process of learning to count builds on principles derived from an innate nonverbal counting mechanism (cf. chap. 2) is the attribution of the difficulties children have with fractions to the lack of fit of those same principles with the properties of fractions (R. Gelman, 1991). In particular, it has been suggested that the contrast between counting, which children generally find unproblematic, and fractions, which seem to be much more challenging for children, stems from the fact that whereas learning to count is facilitated by innate structures, fraction learning is adversely impacted by those same structures because fractions do not work the same way that counting numbers do. For example, because fractions, unlike counting numbers, do not form a sequence in which each number has a fixed successor, the one-to-one and stable-order principles that are important to counting may become a potential source of confusion when children encounter fractions.

R. Gelman (1991) reported research on kindergarten and first-grade children's interpretations of pictorial and numeral representations of fractions designed to test the thesis that children try to assimilate fractions to their ideas about counting. Among the findings were (a) that children read fraction symbols such as $\frac{\text{``}1\text{''}}{2}$ as concatenations of whole numbers (e.g., "one and two" rather than "one half"); (b) that they incorrectly judged unit fractions with larger denominators to be greater rather than smaller than those with smaller denominators (e.g., they said that $\frac{\text{``}1\text{''}}{4}$ was more than $\frac{\text{``}1\text{''}}{2}$), and (c) that they were unable to correctly place pictorial representations of proper and mixed fractions (e.g., $\frac{1}{3}$ of a circle, $1\frac{1}{2}$ circles) on a number line on which the values 0, 1, 2, and 3 were marked (also with circles).

Consistent with R. Gelman's (1991) analysis, Vamvakoussi and Vosniadou (2004) found that just over half (9 of 16) of a sample of ninth graders expressed the view that fractions form a series (or perhaps multiple such series) within which successive fractions do not have any other fractions between them. These students, for example, asserted that there is only one fraction between $\frac{3}{8}$ and $\frac{5}{8}$, the fraction $\frac{4}{8}$. Similarly, they asserted that there are no other fractions between the two decimals .005 and .006, but that there are eight between .01 and .001, because .01 is the same as .010, and so, starting with .001 one could generate intermediate decimal fractions by incrementing the last decimal place to .002, .003, and so on through .009. Vamvakoussi and Vosniadou (2004) argued that a conceptual reorganization is needed for students to progress from this way of thinking, which reflects children's knowledge about counting, to an appreciation of the density of fractions. Several students in their sample (4 of 16) did recognize that there are infinitely many fractions between some pairs of given fractions but denied it in other cases. Only one student consistently asserted, across five different pairs of decimal and/or common fractions, that there were infinitely many fractions in between the given ones. These results are particularly striking because the ninth graders who participated in the study had already received considerable instruction in fractions. The incorrect notion that fractions form a series with a specific successor to each member of the series and no fractions in between the successive fractions persisted in spite of instruction in common fractions, decimal fractions, and real numbers, including explicit instruction in how to find fractions that are intermediate between two given fractions!

However, a study that examined students' understanding of the density of fractions from a somewhat different perspective (Smith, Solomon, & Carey, 2005) provided evidence that even elementary school children do have some understanding of the density of rational numbers. Smith et al. focused on children's grasp of the idea that numbers are infinitely divisible. Thirty percent of the third- through sixth-grade children in their sample (15 of 50) responded to an initial question as to how many numbers there are between zero and one by saying that the number was infinite, or that the numbers went on forever; and another 22% ($n = 11$), although they did not refer to infinity, did say that there are a great many numbers between zero and one (e.g., "lots," "hundreds," or "millions"). Most of the latter students ($n = 8$) went on, in response to a subsequent question, to endorse the idea that the fractions are in fact infinite by stating that one could divide in half forever (beginning with one) without ever getting to zero.

Two alternative explanations for the divergence between these results and the evidence of a much more limited understanding of fraction density among the ninth-grade students in Vamvakoussi and Vosniadou's (2004) study seem plausible. One is that students fail to generalize the insights into the infinity of fractions between zero and one that they expressed in Smith et al.'s (2005) study to other intervals between numbers. Alternatively, it may be that characteristics of the questions posed in the two studies led students to respond in different ways. Smith et al. probed students who initially responded that there are no numbers between zero and one by asking them about the number one half, whereas it appears that Vamvakoussi and Vosniadou accepted students' initial responses without any probing. Thus, it may be that the presentation of pairs of numbers that could easily be construed as members of a systematic series led students to presuppose that the investigator wanted them to consider only other numbers in that series rather than all possible numbers. In contrast, in Smith et al.'s study, when students initially assumed that the investigator wanted them to consider only whole numbers, the investigator's follow-up query as to whether or not $\frac{1}{2}$ was a number between zero and one helped to clarify that fractions as well as whole numbers were to be considered. Although these alternative interpretations of the divergence between the two studies suggest substantially different conclusions about the scope of children's understanding of fraction density, neither account is consistent with the view that children's knowledge of the discreteness of counting numbers dominates their thinking about fractions to such an extent that they have no conception of the density of fractions.

In contrast to the view that fundamental differences between counting numbers and fractions interfere with fraction learning, Steffe (2002) viewed children's ideas about counting as a potentially constructive factor in the development of fraction schemes. Specifically, he maintained that fraction schemes can emerge from the reorganization of earlier counting schemes in response to problems that the earlier schemes either did not solve or solved less well than the newly reorganized schemes. From this perspective, it is worth noting that, although the students in Vamvakoussi and Vosniadou's (2004) study were incorrect in asserting that certain fractions have no other fractions between them, and others have only a finite number of fractions between them, their use of counting-based sequences to generate pseudosuccessive fractions did enable them to identify at least some intermediate fractions for many pairs of fractions.

Vamvakoussi and Vosniadou (2004) also reported other data that fit well with the idea that counting knowledge can contribute in constructive ways to the understanding of fractions. In addition to questions pertaining to the density of fractions, they asked children about algebraic properties of numbers, in particular about the existence of an *opposite* (a number that, added to a given number, results in a sum of 0) and an *inverse* (a number that, multiplied with the given number, results in a product of 1) for a decimal fraction (.02506) and an irrational number ($\sqrt{3}$). A large majority of their sample (14 of 16) correctly affirmed the existence of an opposite and an inverse for both of these numbers, even though the students were typically unable to indicate what those opposites and inverses were.

Early Forms of Fraction Knowledge

An important consideration for any account of the relation between counting knowledge and knowledge about fractions is that the development of fraction knowledge begins long before fraction symbols are introduced in the elementary grades. At least two kinds of fraction knowledge have been demonstrated in preschool children. Children know that the term *half* refers to one of two parts (Hunting & Davis, 1991a); and they can partition a quantity into roughly equal parts through a process of distributive counting (Frydman & Bryant, 1988; Hunting & Davis, 1991a; K. F. Miller, 1984). Moreover, the same sorts of evidence that have been adduced in support of nonverbal knowledge about positive whole numbers in infancy can also be adduced in support of nonverbal knowledge about fractional values.

Of course infants have not yet learned what the words "one half" or the symbol $\frac{\text{"1"}}{2}$ means, but neither have they learned the word "two" or the symbol "2." Insofar as any numerical knowledge has been demonstrated in infancy, the evidence has consisted of demonstrating that infants react differentially to physical quantities in ways that correspond to numerical differences between them. And the same kind of evidence can be adduced for fraction knowledge. Baillargeon and her colleagues (Baillargeon,

Needham, & DeVos, 1992, cited in Baillargeon et al.,1995) have shown that infants $6\frac{1}{2}$ months of age are sensitive to the relations between different portions of a supported object in interpreting relations of physical support. Specifically, they found that infants looked more at an "impossible" test event, in which a box remained supported when only 15% of its bottom surface was in contact with a supporting platform, than at a "possible" event, in which 70% of the bottom surface of the supported object was in contact with the supporting platform. These results indicate that infants react differentially as a function of quantitative properties of what they see that we (as adults) represent with fractions. Of course, this differential looking does not constitute evidence that infants have formed any explicitly numerical representation of the unsupported portion of the object—but neither does differentiation between arrays of two versus three objects constitute evidence of the formation of an explicitly numerical representation of the arrays. The differentiation that Baillargeon et al. (1992) demonstrated is not very precise, because 15% and 70% are very different in magnitude, but it depends on the multiplicative relation between two quantities in the same way that fractions do.

When Less Is More

An important, and potentially confusing, aspect of fractions is the inverse relation between the denominator of the fraction and its value. In a series of studies investigating the beginnings of this kind of knowledge in early childhood, Sophian et al. (1997) asked 5- and 7-year-old children to compare pairs of sharing scenarios and to determine which alternative in each pair would result in a larger portion for an individual recipient. Not surprisingly, even 5-year-old children had no trouble recognizing that if different total quantities were shared among equal numbers of recipients, the recipients who shared the larger quantity would get larger portions than those who shared the smaller quantity. Consistent with R. Gelman's (1991) report of overgeneralizations from whole-number knowledge, however, the children incorrectly expected that sharing equal total quantities among different numbers of recipients would result in larger portions when the quantity was shared among a greater number of recipients than when it was shared among fewer recipients.

Nevertheless, in a subsequent study (Sophian et al., 1997, Experiment 4), 5-year-old children proved able to learn the inverse relation between number of recipients and share size from a brief series of demonstration trials. The demonstration trials consisted simply of asking the child to decide which of two sharing scenarios, differing only in the number of recipients, would result in a larger share for a toy character. After the child made a choice, the experimenter invited him or her to observe the outcome of both sharing scenarios. The experimenter then shared out two equivalent quantities among different numbers of recipients and asked the child which way of sharing resulted in a bigger share for the toy character. After just eight such trials, the children had reversed their initial expectations. Just 26% of their responses to a set of pretest sharing problems were correct, whereas their performance on similar posttest problems, administered after the demonstration trials, averaged 71% correct. Thus, by observing the results of alternative sharing scenarios, the children quickly learned that sharing a given quantity among more recipients would reduce rather than increase the amount each recipient got.

This finding may account for a discrepancy between the results of Sophian et al.'s (1997) initial experiment and a nearly parallel experiment by Correa, Nunes, and Bryant (1998). In their task, 5- to 7-year-old children were again asked to compare alternative sharing scenarios involving different numbers of recipients. They gave the children the option of judging that both sharing scenarios would result in the same size shares, but this was the least common response at all ages, accounting for 19% of responses at 5 years and dropping to just 2% by age 7. More importantly, correct choices of the alternative with fewer recipients were more frequent than any other response at all ages, accounting for 56% of the responses of 5-year-olds and fully 87% of those of 7-year-olds. (Correa et al. noted that at 7 years, choices of the incorrect alternative accounted for a high percentage of children's errors, but because the overall error rate was very low for that age group, occurrences of that error were even less frequent for them than for younger children.) In this respect, the data are at odds with those of Sophian et al., who found a preponderance of incorrect choices of the scenario involving more recipients at both 5 and 7 years of age. The strong effect of demonstration trials that Sophian et al. (1997) found, however, suggests that the divergent results may stem from the fact that in Correa et al.'s study the experimental tasks were presented only after a prior control task, in which children observed the specific numerical outcomes of sharing eight blocks in one case among two rabbits and in another case among four rabbits. This task may have functioned much like the demonstration trials in Sophian et al.'s training study, allowing children to observe that increasing the number of recipients results in each getting a smaller share.

In a further study by Kornilaki and Nunes (2005), 5-year-old children were about equally likely to assert that sharing a quantity among a larger number of recipients would result in larger shares (incorrect) as that it would result in smaller shares (correct) than sharing the same quantity among a smaller number of recipients. By 7 years of age, however, correct reasoning predominated (without any training) and there were very few occasions in which children claimed that a greater number of recipients would result in larger shares.

There is no question but that inappropriate generalizations from whole-number knowledge occur in children's thinking about fractions, as they do in young children's thinking about the results of sharing among different numbers of recipients. It is a big leap, however, from such generalizations to the conclusion that children have innate structures that support learning to count but are inconsistent with what they must later learn about fractions. Clearly, children have learned quite a lot about counting and whole numbers at a time when they as yet know very little about fractions, and it is hardly surprising that they make use of what they do know in trying to interpret what is unfamiliar nor that, in doing so, they make some errors as well as some correct extrapolations. Accordingly, it is clearly desirable instructionally to illuminate the connections between counting numbers and fractions, and to help children understand why they are alike in certain ways and different in others. Because the mathematics of fractions is by no means discontinuous from the mathematics of counting numbers, children's knowledge about counting has to be a foundation for fraction learning rather than an obstacle to it.

FRACTION SUBCONSTRUCTS

Several conceptual analyses of fractions have emphasized the number of distinct, albeit interrelated, subconstructs or interpretations connected with them. Kieren (1988), for example, identified four subconstructs comprising the concept of *rational number*:

- *Measure*, the interpretation of fractions as representations of magnitudes that can be intermediate between whole numbers of units (e.g., magnitudes between 0 and 1).
- *Quotient*, the interpretation of a fraction as the numerical value obtained by dividing one whole number by another.
- *Ratio number*, the interpretation of a fraction as representing the relative magnitude of two nonoverlapping quantities (as in a recipe that calls for three eggs for every two cups of flour).
- *Multiplicative operator*, the interpretation of a fraction as representing an extending and/or contracting or stretching and/or shrinking function applied to some object, set, or number (so that, e.g., taking $\frac{2}{3}$ of a quantity stretches that quantity by a factor of 2 but then shrinks the "stretched" quantity by a factor of 3 so that the end result is smaller than the original quantity).

Behr et al. (1992) discuss, in addition to the quotient and operator subconstructs, a part–whole subconstruct, which involves interpreting fractions as representing one or more parts of a whole, where the parts are formed by partitioning the whole into a number of equal units.

While the initial purpose of analyzing fraction subconstructs was to clarify the objectives of fraction instruction, it has also been suggested that the multiplicity of interpretations or subconstructs that students must consider is an important factor in the difficulties students have with fractions (English & Halford, 1995; Ohlsson, 1991; Ni, 2001). The interpretation of fractions as representations of magnitude, however, remains fundamentally the same across the various subconstructs that have been discussed. Although different subconstructs involve interpreting the numerator and denominator of a fraction in somewhat different ways, the principles by which these two values combine to determine the magnitude of the fraction as a whole remain the same for all of them.

Thus, for example, within the part–whole subconstruct, the denominator represents the number of parts into which the original unit is partitioned, and the numerator represents the number of those parts corresponding to the quantity being represented. The magnitude of the fraction decreases as the denominator gets larger, because the size of each part is decreasing, and the size increases as the numerator gets larger because more parts of that size are being included. Within the quotient interpretation, similarly, the numerator represents the dividend and the denominator the divisor of a division operation. The quotient decreases as the divisor increases and increases as the numerator decreases. The operator interpretation directly represents these inverse effects of numerator and denominator in terms of extending or stretching, on one hand, and contracting or shrinking, on the other.

Thompson and Saldanha's (2003) characterization of fractions in terms of the conception of two quantities as being in a "reciprocal relation of relative size" likewise underscores the conceptual coherence of fraction subconstructs. Their perspective, like the one advanced here, begins with the notion that fractions are fundamentally representations of magnitude. In addition, in recognizing that in order for one amount to be $\frac{1}{n}$ the size of another, the latter amount must be n times the size of the former, they emphasize the close link between fraction knowledge and multiplicative reasoning about many-to-one relations.

THE INFORMATION-PROCESSING DEMANDS OF FRACTIONS

A number of accounts of fraction learning have called attention to the complexity of the information processing entailed in reasoning about fractions. Ohlsson (1991), for instance, argued that the concept of *equivalent fractions* is central to fraction arithmetic, and that it in turn entails a "schema of constancy under multiplicative compensation" (p. 39), that is, an appreciation of the fact that the inequality between the numerators of two equivalent fractions is offset by a proportionally equivalent inequality in the denominators. Kamii and Clark (1995) also emphasize the importance of multiplicative thinking in understanding fractions, but for them multiplicative thinking is closely related to the idea of one-to-many correspondence. It entails a hierarchical cognitive structure such that each individual item at one level corresponds to a group of items at the next lower level. Thus, for example, understanding the equivalence between $\frac{1}{4}$ and $\frac{3}{12}$ depends on appreciating that each of the four parts of a whole (fourths) may itself consist of three subparts (twelfths of the whole). Although these are very different perspectives on fraction equivalence, both entail the coordination of two relations (the relation between numerators and the relation between denominators, from Ohlsson's perspective; the relation of parts to whole and subparts to parts, from Kamii & Clark's perspective) and so might be expected to require considerable information-processing capacity.

English and Halford (1995) analyzed the information-processing demands of different mathematical tasks in terms of the number of distinct elements that need to be kept in mind simultaneously in order to successfully perform the task. They argue that different fraction subconstructs entail different information-processing demands. Conceptualizing an array as a ratio, for instance identifying a 3:4 ratio between red and blue counters in an array, involves just binary relations, because only the two subsets need to be related to one another. In contrast, conceptualizing the same array as corresponding to the fraction $\frac{3}{7}$ entails ternary relations, because the child must relate three sets: the total set (all the counters) and each of its subsets (the red counters and the blue ones). Understanding equivalence relations between two fractions, as in the expression $\frac{1}{2} = \frac{3}{6}$, entails quaternary relations, because the relations among all four of the quantities must be considered. Similarly, English and Halford suggest that quotient interpretations of fractions are more demanding cognitively than part–whole ones because they involve a more complex series of mappings. In order to understand the sharing of three pizzas among four people as entailing that each person gets $\frac{3}{4}$ of a pizza, for example, children must map the number of people onto the fraction name, fourths, then map the fraction name onto the partitioning of the pizzas into four pieces each, and then map the pieces onto the people to determine that each will get three pieces, and because each piece is $\frac{1}{4}$ of a pizza, each person's share will be equivalent to $\frac{3}{4}$ of a pizza.

Although the notion that fractions are cognitively demanding is intuitively appealing (and designing instruction so as to avoid overtaxing students' information-processing capacities, as English & Halford, 1995, recommend, may well be helpful), the empirical evaluation of effects of information-processing demands is complicated by the fact that those information-processing demands are affected by a number of factors other than the objective task structure. Processes of *chunking* (recoding a multidimensional concept into fewer dimensions) and/or *segmentation* (breaking a task into a series of steps, each of which is not too demanding in its information-processing requirements) can dramatically alter the information-processing demands of many tasks. Furthermore, in their analysis of fraction tasks, English and Halford note that differences in the salience of critical elements of formally similar tasks can markedly affect their information-processing demands. Thus, for example, area models of fractions (such as a partitioned rectangle) are held to be lower in their information-processing demands than set models (such as an array of red and blue counters) because the whole is more salient in the area model and the nonselected parts (e.g., the nonshaded segments) are less salient. The greater salience of the whole in the area model enables students to focus just on the critical relation between the selected parts and the whole; whereas, because the whole is less salient than the parts in set models, a portion of students' limited processing resources is spent processing the nonselected parts. It might be possible to reduce the cognitive demands of set models by choosing materials that, like the sleeping cows in McGarrigle et al.'s (1978) work on class inclusion (cf. chap. 5), make the whole more salient. But that possibility only underscores the point that the information-processing demands of any particular task cannot be specified in the absence of independent measures of factors such as the salience of its key elements. Correspondingly, although the idea that information-processing constraints contribute to students' difficulties with fractions is certainly a plausible one, it is quite difficult to evaluate empirically.

A second important limitation of information-processing analyses of students' difficulties with fractions is that they focus on how individuals perform a particular task or set of tasks rather than on what they understand about a given subject matter. Even though it seems clear that some kinds of conceptual knowledge are more complex than others, it is unclear how, if at all, one might analyze the information-processing demands of a particular body of conceptual knowledge (as distinct from the information-processing demands of particular tasks used to assess that knowledge). As a result, the notion that information-processing demands make fractions difficult for students offers little insight into the conceptual aspects of fraction learning that educators are increasingly recognizing as critical (e.g., Byrnes & Wasik, 1991; Kilpatrick, Swafford, & Findell, 2001).

An empirical study of the effects of individual differences in working memory (which might be expected to be an index of information-processing capacity) and in conceptual knowledge about fractions on student performance on fraction tasks (Hecht, Close, & Santisi, 2003) provides little support for the view that information-processing limitations are central to students' difficulties with fractions. The study focused on individual differences in the performance of fifth-grade students on three fraction tasks: (a) the computation of fraction sums and products; (b) the estimation of fraction sums; and (c) the solution of one-step word problems involving fraction addition, multiplication, or division. Individual differences in working memory were assessed with a counting-span task, and individual differences in conceptual knowledge were assessed with tasks requiring students (a) to provide fraction bar representations (e.g., $\frac{2}{3}$) for pictorially presented fractions (shaded regions of a polygon or set of polygons) and vice versa; (b) to provide a pictorial result for a fraction addition problem presented pictorially; and (c) to indicate the larger of two numbers presented in fraction-bar form or as whole numbers (e.g., $\frac{1}{2}$ vs. 1).

Two aspects of the results speak to the question of the role of information-processing limitations in students' difficulties with fractions.

First, although working memory was a significant predictor of student performance on the outcome measures, its effects were independent of, and smaller than, the effects of conceptual knowledge. Each of the three outcome measures correlated much more highly with the measure of conceptual knowledge (*r*s ranging from .64 for fraction computation and .66 for word problems to .75 for fraction estimation) than with the working memory measure (*r*s ranging from .16 for fraction estimation to .40 for fraction computation and .46 for word problems).

Second, structural equation modeling indicated that the effects of working memory that were found were mediated by effects of individual differences in students' knowledge of simple arithmetic facts and not by effects of individual differences in conceptual knowledge about fractions. This pattern of results not only indicates that individual differences among students in working memory have little to do with their conceptual understanding of fractions but also suggests that, insofar as working memory affects performance on fraction tasks, it does so primarily by influencing students' facility with the basic whole-number arithmetic facts that enter into fraction computations.

PARTS AND WHOLES IN UNDERSTANDING FRACTIONS

Instruction in fractions typically begins with the idea of dividing a whole into parts. The number of parts in the whole becomes the denominator of the fraction, and the number of those parts that make up the quantity being described becomes the numerator. Although this is a sound interpretation of a fraction, it is a source of confusion in understanding that a fraction has a single value because it identifies separate quantitative referents for the numerator and denominator. Furthermore, as Thompson and Saldanha (2003) note, it suggests that the parts represented by the numerator are a subset of the parts comprising the whole that are represented by the denominator—an implication that makes improper fractions like $\frac{6}{5}$ difficult to understand.

An even more fundamental problem is that notions such as two out of five parts fail to capture constraints on the nature of the parts and their relation to the whole that are critical to understanding how the numerator and denominator of a fraction determine its magnitude. If we picture receiving two cookies from a plate containing three, or five cookies from a plate containing eight, it is hard to escape the idea that the latter quantity is greater. The plate has more on it, we get more to eat, and there is also more left over for someone else! In order to compare fraction magnitudes, we need to recognize that the focus is on the relation between the parts and the whole, not on the size of either one. Whatever the whole is, it counts as 1, and the size of each part is $\frac{1}{n}$, where n is the number of parts, no matter how big the original whole was. Therefore, increasing the number of parts in the whole along with the number of those parts that are included in the quantity being described—as in a comparison of two cookies out of three versus five cookies out of eight—does not necessarily make the fraction itself larger.

This is a critical difference between part–whole reasoning as it applies to additive structures versus to fractions. In additive structures, the numerical size of each part is free to vary independently of the other part, and the whole, which is the aggregate of the parts, changes as the sizes of the parts change. In the case of fractions, the whole is the unit against which a quantity of interest is being measured, and fractional subunits are created by partitioning that whole into equal segments. Because fractions describe a quantity relative to a whole, the size of the whole cannot be changed without also changing the relation between the quantity of interest and that whole, and thus the fractional value of the quantity of interest.

Another crucial, but often unstated, aspect of the part–whole interpretation of fractions is apparent from errors students often make in adding and subtracting fractions. The fractional parts being added or subtracted must be parts defined in relation to the same whole. It is for this reason that the wholes (represented by the denominators) are not added, only the parts. But, as Silver (1986) noted, students not only make the error of adding denominators as well as numerators—so that the sum of $\frac{1}{2} + \frac{2}{3}$, for example, is

reported to be $\dfrac{(1+2)}{(2+3)}$ or $\dfrac{3}{5}$—they conceptualize fractions in a way that sup-
ports this error. Asked to sketch fraction addition problems, students often shaded one half of one circle and one third of another; then they counted all the shaded parts for the numerator and all of the parts, shaded and un-shaded, for the denominator (in effect adding the denominators as well as the numerators). This illustration violates both the principle that all fractional parts must be equal in size (because here some are thirds of the original unit and some are halves) and the constraint that fractions to be added or subtracted must express parts defined in relation to a common whole and hence, that the whole does not increase when they are added. Similarly, students readily generated stories that fit their incorrect procedure for fraction addition. For instance, if a player gets one hit out of two times at bat in one inning, and two hits out of three times at bat in the next, his total hit rate is three out of eight. The procedure of adding denominators as well as numerators works in cases like this because what is being done is not in fact to add two fractional parts of the same whole but to create a weighted average of fractional parts of two different wholes.

FRACTIONAL MEASUREMENT UNITS

From a measurement perspective, fractions derive from the construction of new units that are smaller than our original unit so as to be able to give a more precise numerical description of the quantity we are measuring (Davydov & Tsvetkovich, 1991). If we are being paid by the hour for a job that takes between 4 and 5 hours to complete, we do not want to receive just 4 hours' pay. We also want part of an hour's pay for the time beyond 4 hours that we put in. To determine how much pay we deserve for that time, we need to use a unit smaller than an hour, and we can create such a unit by thinking of an hour as not just a single unit of time but as a collection of smaller units such as tenths of an hour or quarter hours. Because the fractional parts are to serve as units of measurement, they must be equal in size. However, depending on the number of parts into which the whole is partitioned, that size can be smaller or larger and, correspondingly, measurements based on it will be more or less precise.

The denominator of a fraction indicates the size of the parts represented by the fraction indirectly, by specifying the number of parts into which the whole has been partitioned to create those parts. Hence the size of the denominator is inversely related to the size of the fractional unit. Because children as young as 5 years of age can learn within a few trials that partitioning a fixed quantity into a larger number of shares makes each quantity smaller than it would be if fewer shares were created (Sophian et al., 1997; cf. chap. 5), this perspective on fraction magnitudes provides an intuitive foundation for understanding that fractions with larger denominators are, other things being equal, smaller in value than those with smaller denominators.

The notion of smaller units created through partitioning also provides an intuitive basis for grasping a more subtle aspect of fraction magnitude, the fact that the effect of denominator size on the magnitude of the fraction is a multiplicative one. An error that many students make is to expect additively equal changes to the numerator and denominator of a fraction to result in an equivalent fraction. Thus, for instance, they are likely to incorrectly judge that $\frac{2}{7} = \frac{4}{9}$ because the numerators of the two fractions differ by the same amount as the denominators, that is, the numerator of the first fraction has been increased by 2 to get the numerator of the second fraction, and the denominator has likewise been increased by 2 (Behr et al., 1984). This judgment suggests an awareness that the numerator and denominator of a fraction must change together to maintain its value, but a lack of appreciation that the changes must be multiplicatively, rather than additively, equivalent.

Sophian and Madrid (2004) further investigated students' reasoning about fraction magnitudes by presenting them with two pairs of nonequivalent fractions at a time and asking them to decide in which pair the fractions were more nearly alike in magnitude and to explain the reasoning on which their decisions were based. Thus, for example, are $\frac{3}{4}$ and $\frac{4}{5}$ more nearly alike, or less nearly alike, in magnitude than $\frac{7}{8}$ and $\frac{8}{9}$? Seventh graders often responded to this type of problem by maintaining that all of the fractions were the same because, in each case, just one piece was left out of the whole. These students lost sight of the importance of considering the size of each piece in this context. Other students noted that the same number of parts would be left but they also realized that the parts would be smaller in the fractions with the larger denominators, and so concluded correctly that those fractions would be more nearly the same in magnitude. By considering the size of the fractional units, these students were able to appreciate that two pairs of fractions that differ by the same amount in their numerators and in their denominators are not equally different in their magnitudes.

This insight by itself, however, does not indicate that the changes in numerator and denominator must be proportionally equal for two fractions to be equal in value, or why. The measurement model in which new units are generated by partitioning an initial unit into smaller (equal) parts, offers more insight. Given a whole that has already been divided into equal parts, a simple way to increase the number of parts is to split each of the existing parts into still smaller parts. This process is multiplicative in that there is a many-to-one relation between the smaller parts being created and each of the original parts. And exactly the same many-to-one relation that holds for the total number of parts in the whole also holds for the number of parts in the portion that is being represented with a fraction: Each of the original parts in that portion has been split into several of the new smaller parts. As a result, in generating a new fractional representation of a quantity by splitting the original fractional units into smaller ones, the number of parts corresponding to the represented quantity—the numerator of the new fraction—increases multiplicatively by the same factor as the number of parts in the whole—the denominator of the new fraction—does.

This understanding of fractions, however, depends critically on the constraint, noted in the preceding section, that the whole must remain constant irrespective of the number of fractional pieces into which it is partitioned. Without this constraint, there is no need for splitting to create a larger number of pieces in a whole, and, correspondingly, there is no principled relation between the number of fractional pieces (the denominator of the fraction) and the size of those pieces; one could simply join additional pieces to the whole, changing the number of pieces but not their size. If we describe a portion of cookies, for example, two cookies, as a fraction of a larger plate of cookies, that fraction changes from being $\frac{1}{2}$ of the cookies on the plate (given four cookies on the plate) to being $\frac{2}{5}$ just by someone putting another cookie on the plate. Although the portion described is still the same, two cookies, clearly we cannot conclude that $\frac{1}{2} = \frac{2}{5}$. Although both fractions represent the same two cookies, they represent those quantities in relation to different wholes and so their magnitudes are not the same.

Because of the emphasis in instruction on finding common denominators in order to add or subtract fractions, students tend to treat fractions with different denominators as incommensurable rather than learning to interpret the denominator as a source of information about the fraction's magnitude. Indeed, when adding or subtracting common-denominator fractions, they often treat the fractional part like a whole-number unit, acting as if the denominator were just a tag (much like an object label, such as *blocks*) indicating what sorts of things were being added or subtracted (Mack, 1995). Worse, they act as if this tag were optional or implicit, leading to confusions between whole numbers and fractions such as adding $2 + \frac{3}{8}$ and getting $\frac{5}{8}$ (because the 2 is assumed to mean $\frac{2}{8}$), or adding $\frac{1}{5} + \frac{2}{5}$ and getting 3 (because the 5 is dropped in reporting the result).

Conversely, in working with different-denominator fractions, because of the need to convert to common denominators in order to add or subtract, children sometimes conclude that it is not possible to make any meaningful comparison between different-denominator fractions. For example, in a study in which fifth- and seventh-grade students were asked to evaluate alternative ways of comparing common-denominator fractions and different-denominator fractions (Sophian & Madrid, unpublished data), several students judged it not very smart to compare $\frac{1}{3}$ and $\frac{1}{4}$ by reasoning that the fraction with the larger denominator would be smaller in value. They asserted that fractions could be compared only by converting the fractions to a common denominator, such as twelfths.

The measurement model of fractions clarifies the flaw in both of these approaches: We cannot disregard the units we are combining when some are fractional units and some are wholes, any more than we could if working with larger composites like dozens versus individuals. Just as two dozens plus three individuals do not make five (dozens or individuals), $2 + \frac{3}{8}$ does not equal either 5 or $\frac{5}{8}$. At the same time, knowing the sizes of the units can be informative about relative magnitudes even when we are comparing different units. Because dividing a unit three ways makes for larger parts than dividing it four ways, we know that $\frac{1}{3}$ is greater than $\frac{1}{4}$.

Of course, if the numerators as well as the denominators of two fractions differ (particularly if both differ in the same direction), the comparison is much more difficult because the change in unit size must be weighed against the change in number of units. Even in such cases, however, it is in many cases possible to draw conclusions about relative magnitude with a minimum of calculation (and without converting to a common denominator). For instance, capitalizing on the multiplicative relations between the numerator and the denominator within each fraction, one might try to identify a familiar fraction that is greater than one fraction and less than the other. Thus, $\frac{5}{14}$ must be greater than $\frac{11}{34}$ because the first is greater than $\frac{1}{3}$ and the second is less. Alternatively, one might estimate the multiplicative relation between numerators (or between denominators, whichever has more convenient values) and then check whether the multiplicative relation between the other part of the fractions is greater or less. Thus, reasoning that way, one might note that 11 is just over twice 5, and because 34 is considerably more than twice 14, the denominator has increased by a greater proportional amount than the numerator, making $\frac{11}{34}$ smaller in magnitude than $\dfrac{5}{14}$. Students' ability to generate and carry out such strategies might serve as a good indication of "fraction sense," an appreciation of the space of magnitude relations within which any fraction can be situated.

This kind of facility in reasoning about fraction magnitudes is the exception rather than the rule, however. In Sophian and Madrid's (2004) study of students' reasoning about the degree of similarity in the magnitudes of paired (nonequivalent) fractions, across 20 problems in which paired fractions differed both in their numerators and their denominators, just one seventh grader in a sample of 24 (4%) and seven university students out of 35 (20% of a sample recruited without regard to students' major field of study) reliably identified the more similar pair of fractions, selecting the pair with the smaller difference in values on 15 or more of the 20 problems (binomial probability = .04). The most common response pattern among the other students was to try to identify a pair in which there was a smaller additive difference in either the numerators or denominators (e.g., choosing $\dfrac{3}{7}$ vs. $\dfrac{4}{7}$ over $\dfrac{2}{9}$ vs. $\dfrac{4}{9}$ because $4 - 3$ is less than $4 - 2$; and $\dfrac{1}{4}$ vs. $\dfrac{1}{5}$ over $\dfrac{1}{7}$ vs. $\dfrac{1}{9}$ because $5 - 4$ is less than $9 - 7$). Fifteen seventh graders (63%) and 10 university students (29%) responded this way on at least 13 of the 16 problems in which there was a greater additive difference in one pair than the other (binomial $p = .02$).

SUCCESSFUL FRACTION INSTRUCTION

Although several theorists have posited cognitive-developmental factors that contribute to the difficulties students have with fractions (e.g., English & Halford, 1995; Ohlsson, 1988), because the development of fraction knowledge is closely intertwined with school instruction, it is difficult to separate general developmental constraints from effects of instructional practices. A valuable source of information in endeavoring to make such a distinction comes from instructional research in which new methods of teaching are evaluated. Evidence of effective instructional innovations not only sheds light on how teaching and learning might be improved but also speaks to the more fundamental question of whether widely observed difficulties are an unavoidable consequence of cognitive limitations (together with the cognitive complexity of the material to be learned) or only a function of the ways in which that material has been taught in the past.

Two innovative approaches to fraction instruction are therefore described in some detail here. These are the curriculum developed by the Rational Number Project (RNP; Cramer & Post, 1995; Cramer, Post, & del Mas, 2002), which emphasizes the development of conceptual understanding through the use of concrete models for fractions, and the work of Moss and Case (1999), which uses children's familiarity with percents as a starting point for developing understanding of fraction magnitudes. Although these curricula differ in many ways, they share a focus on helping children to interpret fractions as representations of magnitude.

The Rational Number Project

The work of the RNP represents what has probably been the most sustained effort to understand and improve fraction learning and teaching in the United States. The experimental fraction curriculum developed through this project (Cramer & Post, 1995; Cramer et al., 2002) incorporates multiple physical models for fractions, encouraging the development of conceptual knowledge by making translations between and within different modes of representation. Mathematical symbols and computational procedures are taught only after a conceptual foundation is established through this work with physical models.

In an initial study (Cramer & Post, 1995), 49 fourth-grade students who received this curriculum and 34 students who received curricula based on commercial texts discussed a fraction estimation problem ("Tell me about where $\frac{11}{12} - \frac{4}{6}$ would be on this number line [on which values from $\frac{1}{2}$ to 2 were marked at intervals of $\frac{1}{2}$]"). The results supported the expectation that the experimental students would develop a richer conceptual understanding of rational numbers than the other students. Not only were the RNP students more likely to arrive at correct answers to the problems (75% of the RNP students vs. 47% of the controls), they were much more likely to give a sound explanation for their response (45% vs. 6% of the controls).

Subsequent work (Cramer et al., 2002) corroborated these results with a sample of over 1,600 fourth- and fifth-grade students drawn from 66 classrooms that were randomly assigned to either the RNP curriculum or a curriculum based on one of the two commercial texts used by the district. The RNP curriculum covered the same topics as the commercial texts, but devoted more time to helping students understand the meaning of fractions by relating them to concrete models and less time to developing their symbolic computational skills. Posttest comparisons indicated that the two groups did not differ in their performance on fraction addition and subtraction computations, despite the very limited time devoted to this topic in the RNP curriculum, but the RNP group outperformed the control group on subscales measuring conceptual knowledge, knowledge about fraction ordering, estimation, and the ability to transfer learned skills to novel tasks. Interview data indicated that the RNP students used mental images of fractions to solve order and estimation problems involving fractions, whereas the control students tended to rely on standard procedures.

A Curriculum Building on Percentages

Moss and Case (1999) developed an experimental curriculum for rational numbers based primarily on a developmental analysis that led them to posit that rational number understanding, like whole number understanding, results from the integration of numerical schemas with global (nonnumerical) schemas that initially develop separately (see also Resnick & Singer, 1993). Their approach was to build on children's existing numerical and nonnumerical knowledge in order to help children integrate the two and then elaborate their numerical schemas. They used the fullness of beakers of liquid as a physical model of fractions, and, because the children already had some familiarity with percentages, began their instruction with percentage representations of different levels of fullness. Initial instruction built upon children's natural tendency to use a halving strategy to help them determine the locations for different percentages of fullness. Later, computational problems were presented in which children had to determine the numerical value for the quantity of liquid needed to fill a bottle with a numerically specified capacity to a certain percentages of fullness, (e.g., to fill a 900-ml bottle 75% full). At first, children solved these problems on the basis of their halving strategy. Thus, to calculate 75% of a 900-ml bottle, they would note that half of 900 ml, or 50%, is 450 ml and half of that, or 25% of 900 ml, is 225 ml, and then they would sum those figures to determine that 75% of 900 ml is 450 + 225, or 675 ml. Later, in an analogy to money, they incorporated a strategy of dividing by 10 to get 10% into their computations. Only after students had developed considerable facility working with percentages were other rational-number representations introduced—first, two-place decimals; then multiplace decimals; and finally fractions represented with the fraction bar.

To evaluate the effectiveness of their instructional program, Moss and Case (1999) compared the performance of two groups of children on a Rational Number Test administered immediately before and after the instructional sequence. The experimental group received the experimental curriculum for twenty 40-minute instructional sessions presented weekly over 5 months. The control group received twenty-five 40-minute lessons in rational numbers following the instructional sequence in a widely used textbook. The sequence began with fractions, introduced as referring to parts of a whole and illustrated with pie-chart diagrams. Decimals were introduced, beginning with tenths, only after students had learned to compare fraction magnitudes and to identify equivalent fractions. Both curricula were taught in the same general style, drawing heavily on manipulatives and encouraging group work and discussion.

The results provided strong evidence for the greater effectiveness of the experimental than the control curriculum. In particular, the experimental students showed markedly (and reliably) greater gains from pretest to posttest than the control students did on five subcategories of items:

- "Nonstandard" computation items, for example, "How much is 10% of $.90?"; "What is $\frac{1}{2}$ of $\frac{1}{8}$?" (However, a subcategory of "standard" computation items did not show group differences; these included, "What is $\frac{1}{3}$ of $\frac{1}{5}$?" and "How much is $3.64 - 0.8$?" Although the distinction between these and the nonstandard items is not clear to me, it suffices to note that some computation items yielded group differences but others did not.)
- Compare and order items, for example, "Draw a picture to show which is greater, $\frac{2}{3}$ or $\frac{3}{4}$"; "Which is bigger, tenths, hundredths, or thousandths?"
- Misleading appearance items, for example, "Find $\frac{3}{4}$ of a pizza (predivided into eighths)"; "What number should go at point A [corresponding to one of the markers dividing the interval between 0.1 and 0.2 into tenths, on a number line extending from 0 to 0.3]?"
- Word problems, for example, "Joan is 100% taller than her daughter Jessica. Jessica's height is what percentage of Joan's?"; "These CDs are marked down from $8.00 to $7.20. What is the discount as a percentage of the original price?" and,
- Items involving translating between different rational number representations, for example, "How many is .5 of all the blocks?"; "What is $\frac{1}{8}$ as a decimal?"

What the Programs Share

Although the programs differ in many ways, they share an emphasis on helping children to develop a strong grasp of the magnitudes of fractions. Both rely heavily on working with concrete representations of fractions (principally pie diagrams in the RNP curriculum, partially filled beakers in the Moss and Case, 1999, curriculum) and connecting them with fraction symbols (ordinary fractions in the RNP curriculum, percentages in the Moss and Case one) before introducing purely symbolic work. Neither program appears to be explicit about the idea that fractions entail constructing new measurement units, but they do treat fractions as measures in that the instruction they present is grounded in the use of fractions to represent physical quantities. Moreover, both programs emphasize understanding the correspondence between different representational systems, in particular, common fractions and decimals, and the process of translation may serve to illuminate the way in which different units, obtained by partitioning wholes into different numbers of parts, are used in forming fractions.

The successes reported through the use of these innovative instructional approaches strongly suggest that fractions are not inherently beyond the cognitive reach of fifth-grade students. Clearly, students at this grade level can master much of the material that has traditionally caused confusion, including magnitude relations between different-denominator (and different-numerator) fractions and translations between decimal and common fractions, provided the material is presented in a way that emphasizes the understanding of fractions as representations of magnitude. It is particularly noteworthy that neither program appeared to result in learning that was restricted to just one or two of the different subconstructs identified by Kieren (1988) and others. More systematic evaluations of students' ability to generalize ideas learned in relation to certain subconstructs to problems involving other subconstructs would be useful in further addressing the question of whether the conceptual differences between the different subconstructs are an important obstacle to generalizable learning.

Although the results that have been reported to date are very positive, a caveat is that both programs have been evaluated only in terms of immediate student achievement. We do not know how well students retain what they have learned or how effectively they progress to more advanced topics. Furthermore, the assessment instruments inevitably reflect the researchers' own judgments about what is important and may not adequately assess aspects of fraction knowledge that are important from other perspectives. In particular, neither assessment provided information specifically on children's understanding of fractions as involving the construction of new units of measurement. Of course, it might be argued that that is not important so long as the students can apply fractions appropriately to physical quantities, understand the magnitude relations between them, and operate effectively with them. Ultimately, this issue can only be resolved in the context of a longer term vision of what we want students to learn, not only about fractions but about mathematics as a whole.

MATHEMATICAL DEVELOPMENT THROUGH THE ELEMENTARY YEARS

Fractions are the culmination of the "mathematics of numbers"—the knowledge that children have been developing since they began to count about the use of numbers to represent relationships among quantities. An influential thesis has been that fractions are difficult to learn because they must be superimposed on the basically incompatible way that children think about whole numbers, a way of thinking that is grounded in the counting procedure with its implications that each number has a successor and that these successive numbers map in a one-to-one fashion into the elements of a set (R. Gelman, 1991). A difficulty with this thesis, however, is that it suggests that the difficulties students experience are intrinsic to the nature of fractions, and thus that understanding fractions is likely to be a challenge for students no matter how they are taught. That implication is inconsistent with the successes of new approaches to fraction instruction such as those of Moss and Case (1999) and of the RNP (Cramer & Post, 1995; Cramer et al., 2002). Although it is almost certainly true that fraction learning is more dependent on explicit instruction than learning to count is, it is now clear that the judicious use of concrete representations to help students understand fractions as representations of magnitude can markedly facilitate the fraction-learning process. The shared emphasis on understanding fraction magnitudes in the instructional methods developed by the RNP and by Moss and Case (1999) strongly supports the view that fractions, like whole-number concepts, build critically on understanding the principles of representing magnitudes numerically.

Indeed, the fact that fractions represent relations between two quantities does not separate them from whole numbers, which also represent the relation between a target quantity and a chosen unit. Just as the transition from additive to multiplicative operations on whole numbers consists principally of a shift in the way units are used, the shift from whole numbers to fractions consists essentially of the introduction of a new way of constructing units—by partitioning the original unit into equal segments. Even this is only the mirror image of the construction of aggregate units such as the "tens" and "hundreds" needed to understand place value notation.

An important implication of these observations is that the kind of instruction about whole numbers students receive in the early elementary school period may have a substantial impact on how much difficulty they subsequently have making sense of fractions. Findings that U.S. students perform reasonably well in comparison to other countries in fourth grade, but less well in eighth to twelfth grades (Calsyn, Gonzales, & Frase, 1999), should not lead us to be complacent even about the first years of mathematics instruction. An important possibility is that the way whole-number mathematics is taught in the early grades does not adequately develop their understanding of the concepts needed to understand fractions and other mathematics topics in later years, thus setting the stage for relatively low levels of achievement in middle school and high school even though students appear to be doing well in the first years of mathematics instruction. In particular, a failure to fully develop the concept of *unit* and its relation to all numerical quantification may set in place a way of thinking about numbers that does not have immediate adverse effects on children's performance but that seriously hampers their ability to make sense of more advanced material.

This possibility is very difficult to evaluate empirically, because to do so would require following students who had received different elementary school curricula into middle and high school in order to determine whether their mathematics learning at those levels differed as a function of the elementary curriculum they had received. In the absence of such data, an analysis of the relations between the conceptual analyses of fraction learning presented earlier in this chapter, on one hand, and ideas about whole numbers, on the other, provides a basis for evaluating the plausibility of the idea that characteristics of early mathematics instruction may affect later fraction learning. The thrust of the present analysis is simply that fraction learning depends on thinking about numbers in ways that may or may not be effectively developed in work with whole numbers. In order to improve long-term mathematics learning, it is important that early curricula be evaluated, not only with respect to their immediate success, but also with respect to their conceptual contribution to later mathematics learning (Sophian, 2004).

Behr et al. (1994) argued that the concept of units of quantity spans the additive and multiplicative conceptual fields and thus provides a cognitive bridge from whole-number arithmetic to the learning and understanding of rational numbers. This idea led them to criticize the practice of focusing on "singleton" units (units corresponding to individual objects) in whole-number arithmetic, which they argued fails to familiarize students with the use of different unit types, a way of thinking about numbers that will be of great importance when the students encounter fractions. Developmental studies of early numerical reasoning support this idea in two ways. First, they provide evidence that children's initial ideas about units are mathematically inadequate, in that they conflate the concept of a unit with the idea of a discrete object (Gal'perin & Georgiev, 1969; Shipley & Shepperson, 1990; cf. chap. 2, this volume). And second, the research indicates that young children's ideas about units are quite responsive to instruction. Although they often have difficulty reasoning about composite units in contexts such as problems involving many-to-one correspondences, they make rapid progress when instruction in the use of such units is provided (Sophian & Madrid, 2003).

With the child's earliest acts of assigning a numerical value to a quantity, he or she makes use of the powerful process of using a unit of measurement to arrive at a numerical representation of a quantity of interest. This process remains central as children learn to carry out first additive and then multiplicative operations on whole numbers, and again as they learn to work with fractions in the middle and late elementary school years. The heart of elementary school arithmetic, whether with whole numbers or fractions, is the concept of a unit and an understanding of how it enters into the process of assigning numerical values to quantities.

Chapter 7

Implications for Developmental Psychology

From infancy, children are sensitive to quantitative relations in the world around them. Already in the first months of life, they discriminate between different auditory or visual stimuli on the basis of their quantitative properties, and by early in the second year, they distinguish between sequential presentations of two quantities in which both quantities are equal to each other, the second is less than the first, or the second is greater than the first (cf. chap. 2). With the assignment of numerical values to quantities, however, a form of quantitative thinking emerges that differs profoundly from these preverbal quantitative discriminations. In order to arrive at a numerical representation of a quantity—regardless of whether it is a verbal or a nonverbal one—it is necessary to apply some kind of unit to that quantity, and that introduces the possibility of using a smaller or a larger unit and with it the need to recognize that the numerical value that is obtained is a function of the chosen unit as well as of the quantity being represented. The many kinds of numerical knowledge that develop across early and middle childhood—from counting to adding and subtracting, then multiplying and dividing and knowledge about rational numbers and fractions—are profoundly interconnected because of their common dependence on the concept of unit.

The claim that the introduction of numerical symbols transforms mathematical thinking is shared by a number of accounts of mathematical development (e.g., Geary, 1995; Resnick, 1989, 1992; Saxe, 1979; Steffe, Cobb, & von Glasersfeld, 1988; Wynn, 1995). The present perspective shares with several of these accounts the recognition that with the acquisition of number words, the child enters into the system of mathematical practices and meanings that his or her culture has developed. It places particular signifi-cance, however, on a set of mathematical practices and meanings that must be present in any cultural system for representing quantities numeri-cally—those pertaining to the concept of unit. Although it is possible to count discrete objects without recognizing that alternative units might have been used, understanding the quantitative meaning of counting funda-mentally involves recognizing that the numerical value that one obtains by counting indicates the relation between the total quantity and the unit that is used to enumerate it. Moreover, that relation is fundamentally multipli-cative; to say that a quantity consists of n units is equivalent to saying that the magnitude of the total quantity is n times that of the unit. Thus, even as the dependence of numerical representations on units sets them apart from nonnumerical reasoning about quantities, it links them not only to additive but also to multiplicative reasoning, and hence to an understanding of frac-tions as well as of the natural numbers.

Several developmental ramifications of this perspective are considered in the succeeding sections of this chapter. First, its implications for the in-fluential idea that the development of mathematical knowledge is sup-ported by innate domain-specific mechanisms are examined. Second, two recurrent ideas about domain-general sources of developmental change in mathematical thinking are addressed: first, the idea that language acquisi-tion plays an important role in the development of mathematical knowl-edge, and second, the notion that age-related increases in processing capacity allow for more advanced forms of mathematical thinking. The chapter closes with a reprise of the main points of contrast between the counting-first and comparison-of-quantities perspectives and an evalua-tion of the evidence bearing on their divergent accounts of children's devel-oping mathematical knowledge.

ORIGINS OF THE CONCEPT OF UNIT AND ITS RAMIFICATIONS FOR DOMAIN SPECIFICITY

When children first learn to count, they most often count discrete physical objects—in effect, treating each physically separate item as a unit. It is only a small step from that to counting distinct parts of an object like the eyes in a face, the legs of a table, or the hands on a clock; and doing so still need not entail any explicit knowledge of the concept of unit or of the role of units in numerical representation. It is a considerably more challenging advance to count entire groups of objects, such as classes or families, as individual items (Shipley & Shepperson, 1990; Sophian & Kailihiwa, 1998). This ad-vance sets the stage for the recognition that units are applied to a quantity rather than intrinsically determined by that quantity, and thus for the emer-gence of a mathematical concept of unit. In itself, however, the mere act of enumerating groups rather than individual objects does not imply an understanding of units. Although the very young child may count various kinds of entities, in effect treating them as units, doing so is not equivalent to having a concept of unit, which entails recognizing that the numerical value obtained for any quantity depends on the unit that is used to measure (or count) it as well as on the magnitude of the quantity itself.

The learning of collective terms, which represent entities composed of multiple discrete objects (i.e., terms such as *pair* or *bunch*), may be a significant precursor to the development of a concept of unit in this sense.[2] Because pairs are defined in part by physical characteristics—for instance, two matching sneakers or two matching high-heeled dress shoes might well be considered a pair but one sneaker and one high-heeled shoe probably would not be—the concept of pair is not as abstract as the mathematical concept of unit. Other collection terms likewise imply some featural or spatial relationship, which is not necessary for a mathematical unit: *Bunch* implies physical proximity, *family* implies genetic or at least social relatedness, and so forth. Nevertheless, the acquisition of concepts such as pair introduces the child for the first time to the idea that a single "entity" is not necessarily a single discrete object, which in turn introduces the possibility of quantifying a given array of objects in more than one way. A particularly important advance in numerical reasoning occurs with the coordination of two or more hierarchically related units in a numerical representation. Understanding the multiplicative relations among measures (e.g., the relation between a measure based on pints vs. liters) depends fundamentally on such coordination. So, too, does the understanding of place value representations of whole numbers, in which individual units are coordinated with aggregate units, and of fractions, which entail coordinating whole units with fractional units obtained by partitioning a whole into equal parts. Most children do not have experience with the results of applying different units to a given quantity until the introduction of measurement in the early elementary school years, and they do not have experience with the coordination of more than one type of unit in a single numerical representation until they are taught about place value and fraction representations. It is on these two elaborations of the basic idea of using a unit of quantification to obtain a numerical value for a quantity that an understanding of the whole of multiplicative relations, including fractions, depends.

In the child's earliest counting, she or he takes for granted that any physically separate item is "one" and thus that each such item gets its own number tag in the counting process. At this point, the child is executing a procedure that is constrained entirely by physical aspects of the material to-

---

[2]I am indebted to Dan Berch for calling my attention to the potential importance of collection terms for the conceptual differentiation of mathematical units from physical objects.

gether with the child's knowledge of the count string and the process of mapping that string onto objects. Even when the child learns to measure a continuous quantity, using perhaps a standard measuring instrument like a ruler or perhaps the iteration of smaller objects (as in lining up paper clips along a strip of paper to determine its length in paper clips), from the child's perspective, the activity is constrained by the rules he or she has been told to follow (e.g., line up the paper clips so they touch but don't overlap; then count how many) and not by a concept of unit. It is only when the child herself or himself must understand how different numerical values result from applying different units to the same quantity that the concept of unit becomes essential.

If this kind of problem is never posed to the child, he or she may progress all the way to fractions without ever having considered the role of units in forming numerical representations of quantities. The evidence that children learn quickly from experience with different units, and yet without instruction show little progress over the preschool period (Sophian, 2002), is consistent with the idea that children often do not encounter the kinds of experiences that are needed to develop their understanding of mathematical units. Furthermore, the import of much of the discussion of arithmetic learning in chapters 5 and 6 is that a learning trajectory in which the significance of one's choice of unit is never explicitly considered makes for serious deficits in children's understanding of school arithmetic. In particular, it is likely to result in the lack of a clear understanding of the difference between additive and multiplicative operations, and the lack of a sound foundation for understanding fractions.

An important developmental implication of this analysis is that the development of mathematical concepts is to a very large extent a function of the instruction the children receive—and this is true not only for relatively advanced material, like fractions, but even for seemingly simple knowledge, such as knowledge of how to count. Counting may mean different things to different children, and correspondingly contribute in very different ways to further mathematical development, depending on the opportunities they receive to gain insight into the role of units in the counting process and in the interpretation of its outcomes.

In this respect, mathematical development is not heavily canalized. *Canalization* refers to an evolutionary process that establishes an expected developmental pathway that all children are likely to follow unless their phenotype or their environment deviates markedly from the norm in critical ways. Language acquisition, for example, is well canalized in that it takes very large deviations, such as deafness or the absence of an opportunity to interact with other people, to interfere with its normal course of development. Early phases of mathematics development look canalized, in that it is rare for children not to learn to count or to acquire basic additive concepts provided they interact with others who have these kinds of knowledge. But the conceptual knowledge underlying children's mathematical abilities, particularly their knowledge about units, can vary greatly depending on the kinds of experiences that they have had, and correspondingly the development of mathematical thinking can take very different paths.

Co-optation and the Distinction Between Biologically Primary and Biologically Secondary Cognitive Abilities

Geary (1995) introduced a distinction, derived from an evolutionary perspective on cognition, between biologically primary and biologically secondary cognitive abilities. Geary (1995) proposed that some cognitive abilities have evolved because they confer a biological advantage, increasing the adaptive fitness of the organism, whereas other cognitive abilities have become valuable only because of cultural developments that are too recent, from an evolutionary perspective, for those abilities to be directly supported biologically. The former abilities tend to be either innate or acquired with a minimum of effort. The latter, however, depend on the co-optation of cognitive capacities that originated in the service of more basic cognitive abilities, and because that co-optation is effortful, they typically are acquired only with explicit instruction and practice.

Geary (1995) suggested that although the skeletal principles that underlie counting are likely to be biologically primary, learning the relationship between number names and the associated quantities is probably biologically secondary. This distinction appears to be based on the observations that, on one hand, "counting is a pan-cultural activity" (p. 29) but, on the other hand, the terms used for different numerosities "vary from culture to culture, and must be memorized" (p. 37). However, because all vocabulary, and much of grammar, is likewise culturally specific, this interpretation implies that language itself is biologically secondary—a position that is inconsistent with Geary's (1995) own account of spoken language as a biologically primary ability, and with many other well-established arguments for the existence of a strong biological foundation for language acquisition (e.g., Pinker, 1995). In general, because all cultures must employ some set of number terms to carry out the counting process, just as all cultures must employ some set of vocabulary terms to engage in the use of language, it seems unpromising to rely on cultural variation in the particular terms as a basis for distinguishing between biologically primary versus secondary abilities in either realm.

However, Geary (1995) was clearly struggling with an important issue in attempting to draw this distinction. Although virtually all people engage fairly effortlessly, at least under certain circumstances, in determining the numerosity of small collections of discrete objects, it seems clear that the act of assigning a numerical value to a quantity is not always so simple or universally understood. The research on the counting of items other than discrete objects, reviewed in chapter 4, is one example. In attempting to distinguish between biologically primary and biologically secondary aspects of counting, Geary (1995) raised the important question of what accounts for the range of difficulty across different kinds of counting tasks. An interesting alternative to Geary's (1995) perspective on this issue is the possibility that it is the use of units, particularly the use of units in an explicit and flexible way, which distinguishes secondary mathematical abilities from primary ones.

Saxe and Moylan's (1982) study of measurement among the Oksapmin people, who live in an isolated region in Papua New Guinea, is relevant to this issue because it provides information about how people come to understand the importance of unit size. The Oksapmin people use points on the arm as referents to describe length, for instance, to indicate the lengths of the string bags they make. Because different people's arms are of different sizes, this measurement system results in measurement units that vary in size for different people. Saxe and Moylan (1982) examined children's and adults' awareness of this issue. They found that although unschooled adults recognized that a string bag would reach a higher point on child's arm than on an adult's, for the most part, unschooled children (mean age 8.4 years) expected the bag to come to the same place on both. Samples of school children, in Grade 2 and Grade 6, performed intermediately. By Grade 6, 30% still consistently predicted that the bag would come to the same place on an adult's arm as on a child's, although nearly half, 45%, made the correct prediction on at least three of the four test items.

These results suggest that an understanding of how the use of different-sized units affects measured outcomes is not necessarily a product of formal instruction in mathematics but it does depend on extensive experience with measurement. Insofar as the experiences that allowed the unschooled adults to arrive at an understanding of measurement units are presumably based on the practices of their culture, one can certainly say that the knowledge they achieve is a product of culture, a conclusion that is consistent with Geary's (1995) characterization of secondary mathematical abilities as culturally variable. However, it is unclear from what nonmathematical context the concept of a unit might have been "co-opted."

Perhaps the distinction that is needed is not one between biologically primary versus secondary abilities but rather between concepts whose acquisition depends on less versus more specialized kinds of experiences. Although the formation of numerical representations of quantities is pervasive, and always entails the use of some type of unit (without necessarily possessing a concept of unit), the opportunity to discover the consequences of using different units, and thus to begin to construct a concept of unit, may arise much less frequently. Accordingly, the acquisition of knowledge about how unit size affects the outcome of a measurement operation is slow and perhaps nonuniversal.

Domain-Specificity

Conceptual domains are defined by the uniqueness of the concepts and explanatory constructs used to reason about them (Gopnik & Wellman, 1994). For example, within the domain of naïve psychology (i.e., the psychology that people without academic training in the science of psychology use to understand themselves and others), constructs such as desires, beliefs, and intentions are invoked to explain why people behave the way they do. These constructs are not invoked to explain the behavior of inanimate objects, however; instead, physical constructs such as force are used. The distinctness of the explanatory constructs used in the two cases indicates that naïve psychology and naïve physics are distinct conceptual domains.

A major premise of R. Gelman's (1991) counting-based account of mathematical development has been that number is a core cognitive domain, supported by innate structures that call children's attention to number-relevant features of the events they experience. Specifically, she asserted that children have a preverbal counting mechanism that essentially provides a conceptual framework for learning to count verbally and acquiring other kinds of numerical knowledge, such as number conservation. This thesis is closely related to, but not identical with, a number of other accounts of innate cognitive structures for processing numerical quantities, notably Dehaene's (1992, 1997) postulation of an innate analog system that generates approximate representations of numerical quantities.

It is sometimes suggested that to question the existence of rich domain-specific mathematical knowledge in infancy is to endorse a strong empiricist view, according to which mathematical development is entirely a function of experience. But this conclusion is flawed in that it equates the absence of innate cognitive functions that are specific to mathematics with the absence of any innate cognitive functions that contribute to mathematical development. Two cognitive functions that are not specifically numerical but that nevertheless are likely play an important role in getting mathematical thinking started are (a) the ability to detect perceptual similarities and differences, and (b) the ability to segment the visual field into distinct objects. The apprehension of perceptual similarities and differences is not specific to the domain of mathematics, in that perceptual differences among stimuli can be as informative about other domains of development (e.g., the distinction between animate and inanimate) as about the quantitative relations on which mathematical thinking is based.

Likewise, the ability to segment the field into distinct objects is most directly associated with visual perception and perhaps with the domain of physical knowledge, but it also plays a crucial role in the development of numerical knowledge inasmuch as discrete objects are the first type of unit children use in counting. Although the assumption that units are defined by the physical characteristics that segment the world into discrete objects is inadequate in the long run, object segmentation processes nevertheless make a critical contribution to mathematical development in providing an initial basis for numerical quantification.

The notion that there are innate domain-specific mechanisms that support the acquisition of numerical knowledge is an extension of Chomsky's (1959) profound insight, which he articulated in relation to language development, that the acquisition of different systems of knowledge may involve distinct acquisition mechanisms that are highly specialized for acquiring particular kinds of knowledge. Chomsky's introduction of the idea of domain specificity was in response to the prevailing concern at the time with the specification of general laws of learning that apply equally to any content. Given the complexities of language, and the limitations of the language children hear (most notably, the imperfections pervading everyday speech, and the lack of correction of many kinds of errors), Chomsky argued that an all-purpose learning mechanism would not be capable of acquiring human language. The alternative he envisioned was a specialized mechanism, informed by a priori knowledge of the way languages work, that would draw children's attention to relevant aspects of the speech they heard and guide them in formulating productive hypotheses about the rules of language. Nearly half a century after Chomsky (1959) made this proposal, however, and notwithstanding enormous progress in genetic research in that time, the question of how such a priori knowledge might be incorporated in the genome remains problematic (Johnston & Edwards, 2002). And yet, over the same period of time, the idea of domain-specific acquisition mechanisms has been applied to a variety of other cognitive domains as well as language. Counting is one of them. Yet, although a strong case has been made that counting is more than a rote performance, nothing like the learnability argument proffered for language has been developed for it. There is no indication that the rules of counting have anything like the complexity of the rules of grammar.

None of the current accounts of innate systems for representing numerical quantities addresses the issue of how spatial or temporal stimuli are segmented into units, although it has been noted that stimuli need not be sharply separated for evidence of numerosity discrimination to be obtained (Wynn, 1996). Indeed, it is not clear whether the analog system that Dehaene (1997; cf. Dehaene, 2002) posits, which he interchangeably refers to as a "number sense" (or "number system") and a "quantity system," is specifically numerical, and hence dependent on some form of segmentation into units, or equally applicable to continuous (unenumerated) and discrete quantities. Indeed, the relation between the preverbal processing of discrete (numerical) and continuous quantities is an important issue to which little empirical research has been directed. In a classic paper based on research with rats, Meck and Church (1983) posited a common mechanism underlying timing and numerical processing, an idea that has had a strong influence on accounts of infant numerical processing (Gallistel & Gelman, 1992). However, it is not clear whether this mechanism could also underlie the processing of spatial rather than temporal kinds of continuous quantities, such as length and area.

Recognition of the critical role of units in numerical representation introduces a new perspective on the question of the domain specificity of the mechanisms underlying infants' sensitivity to numerical information. Because numerosity is always relative to a unit, any form of numerosity detection presupposes some mechanism for identifying the units within a temporal sequence or spatial array. For infants, that mechanism appears to consist of the perceptual processes by which the visual world and the temporal flow of experience is parsed into individuated objects and events. Thus, young children show a strong tendency to focus on discrete objects in their counting (Shipley & Shepperson, 1990). However, so long as the perceptual individuation of objects and events is the sole basis for identifying units, numerical knowledge is clearly intertwined with basic perceptual knowledge about objects and hence does not constitute a distinct domain. Numerical reasoning cannot be clearly differentiated from reasoning about objects until the concept of *mathematical unit* has been distinguished from that of a *discrete physical object* (Gal'perin & Georgiev, 1969) so that the child can use units that are not dictated by the physical properties of objects.

The notion that special kinds of experiences are needed for the differentiation of the concept of unit from that of discrete object (as argued in the preceding section) contrasts with accounts invoking the operation of a biologically specified, domain-specific acquisition mechanism in its implications for interindividual variation. The domain-specificity hypothesis suggests that virtually all individuals should acquire the same knowledge given experiences that are within the normal range for the species. In contrast, the notion that acquisition depends on specialized kinds of experiences suggests that individuals will vary widely in the knowledge they acquire as a function of the particulars of their experience. One way to distinguish between these two positions empirically, then, is to examine the degree of consistency across individuals in the knowledge they acquire given exposure to the same representational system.

In the case of language learning, for example, it would clearly be a serious challenge to the notion of a biologically specified language acquisition device if research were to reveal that some children acquired a full-fledged transformational grammar for their primary language while others (who did not have any biological impairment) acquired only a simple phrase-structure grammar for the same language. With respect to mathematics learning, similarly, it is a challenge to the domain-specificity position to find that children who have grown up using the same system for representing numbers (e.g., the English language and the Arabic numerals) acquire very different sorts of numerical knowledge. It is not just that some individuals are more successful at mathematics learning than others but that they have arrived at very different understandings of the same mathematical material. Insofar as these differences extend to concepts that are central to the domain of mathematics, as the concept of unit surely is, it seems clear that the acquisition of mathematical knowledge (beyond the very elementary knowledge that does not entail an understanding of units) cannot be accounted for by domain-specific elements of a biological heritage that is shared by virtually all children.

This analysis leaves open the question of whether there is any neural structure in the infant's brain that constitutes specifically a "number acquisition device" (analogous to Chomsky's, 1959, classic notion of a "language acquisition device"). The postulation of neural structures dedicated specifically to the processing of numerical information is not necessarily incompatible with the recognition that the concept of unit plays a critical role in the development of mathematical knowledge, provided one allows for a close interconnection between the numerical system and the perceptual system that segments experience into distinct (hence enumerable) objects and events. A further question, however, is whether the processing of specifically numerical information is developmentally prior to the nonnumerical processing of quantitative relations. This, of course, is the issue on which the counting-first and comparison-of-quantities perspectives differ.

The comparison-of-quantities perspective questions whether the acquisition of numerical knowledge entails the operation of an innate mechanism that is dedicated exclusively to numerical processing. At the same time, it does assign a critical role to other kinds of special-purpose mechanisms, most notably the perceptual mechanisms that subserve the segmentation of the world into separate objects and the tracking of several of those objects over time. (Interestingly, this mechanism appears to be important to language learning as well, in that early word learning appears to be guided by a "whole-object constraint"; Markman, 1990.) Thus, the comparison-of-quantities perspective suggests a developmental account that is intermediate between the classic notion that the brain is a general learning machine and the Chomskyan (1959) notion that it contains a number of domain-specific acquisition mechanisms. It discards the notion of sharply delineated domains of development (and with it the notion that answers to the question of whether cognition gets its structure from nature or nurture may vary across domains) not because of any claim that the acquisition process is the same for all kinds of knowledge but because the mechanisms that support learning of different kinds of knowledge overlap in ways that blur the boundary lines between domains. If such diverse pieces of knowledge acquisition as learning to predict the location of an object that is moved from one hiding place to another, learning to count four kittens, and learning that each of those four entities is called a "kitten," all build on mechanisms of object segmentation, how can we conclude that mechanisms for acquiring knowledge about the physical world, about language, and about number are domain-specific? Conversely, given the significance of the concept of unit for many kinds of numerical knowledge, what justification is there for considering counting and other numerical abilities part of the same domain as mathematical reasoning that does not involve the use of units, for example, comparing the depth of two holes by inserting a long stick into each one in turn? In short, although knowledge acquisition is informed by cognitive mechanisms that have quite specific functions, the scope of application of those mechanisms does not necessarily correspond to the boundaries of the domains into which mature conceptual knowledge is organized. The basic insight that the processes of knowledge acquisition may differ for different kinds of knowledge is not undermined by this observation, but the idea that we have innate domain-specific knowledge is. The idea that knowledge acquisition builds on a variety of mechanisms designed to process specific kinds of information rather than on a single general learning mechanism need not imply the existence of mechanisms dedicated to particular conceptual domains and imbued with innate knowledge about the content of those domains.

DOMAIN-GENERAL PROCESSES IN THE DEVELOPMENT OF MATHEMATICAL KNOWLEDGE

The claim that the acquisition of mathematical knowledge builds on mechanisms that have quite specialized functions, if not functions that correspond fully to adult conceptual domains, is not incompatible with the postulation of important links between the development of mathematical knowledge and more general developmental processes. Two ideas, in particular, that have emerged repeatedly in discussions of mathematical development and that are not incompatible with the conclusions about specialized mechanisms drawn in the preceding section, are (a) that language acquisition plays an important role in the development of mathematical knowledge, and (b) that mathematical development is constrained by developmental changes in fundamental information-processing capabilities.

Language as a Sociocultural Tool in Mathematical Development

Children acquire knowledge of the first counting terms—in English, the words *one*, *two*, and *three*, and perhaps several others—individually as terms in their language rather than as elements in the counting string. The most telling evidence for this conclusion is longitudinal data on early numerical language (Durkin, Shire, Riem, Crowther, & Rutter, 1986; Wagner & Walters, 1982), which indicates that children use the word "two" before the word "one." (Apparently divergent results are reported by Wynn, 1992b, who found that all of the children in her sample of 2- and 3-year-old children knew the cardinal meaning of the word "one," as assessed by their accuracy in giving the experimenter the specific number of items she requested, but only 30% demonstrated an understanding of "two" in this fashion. However, it should be noted that success on Wynn's [1992b] give-a-number task may not be indicative of initial learning of number word meanings. Counting out a specified number of items requires enumerating the objects being given and comparing that value to the number requested by the experimenter, whereas simply using a number word to designate a numerosity or comprehending such a statement involves only mapping a stated number word onto a collection of items.)

In Vygotskiian theory, language is an important sociocultural tool that both embodies culturally important knowledge and facilitates the transmission of that knowledge to the young people within the society. The sociocultural tools that language provides that bear on the development of mathematical thinking are by no means limited to the terms for the first several natural numbers.

Language also interfaces with numerical development in shaping the way children parse arrays into countable entities. In learning new words, children start with the assumption that they are labels for discrete objects, just as in counting they start with the assumption that the count terms are assigned to discrete objects. Children's word learning quickly progresses, however, to include words for parts of objects, such as "leg," and for groups of objects, such as "pair" or "family." An interesting, albeit untested, hypothesis is that this linguistic progress contributes to the developmental differentiation of the mathematical concept of unit from the everyday concept of object. By fostering the parsing of arrays into entities other than discrete objects, the expansion of children's vocabularies to include terms for parts of objects and for collections of objects may provide opportunities for children to recognize that the unit of counting is not dictated solely by the physical characteristics of an array.

Language may also contribute to the development of mathematical thinking through its provision of terms that distinguish among different dimensions of quantity—for instance, the terms *length*, *width*, *area*, *density*, *weight*, or *mass*, and *volume*. Young children often focus on length when asked about area (Hobbs & Bacharach, 1990; Ravn & Gelman, 1984); this confusion and others like it appear to play a major role in the well-known errors young children make on quantity conservation tasks (cf. chap. 3). In the process of learning the distinct meanings of terms for different quantitative dimensions, children gain insight into the distinctions among those dimensions, which in turn provides the basis for coming to understand the interrelations between them.

The clearest evidence for the importance of linguistic tools for mathematical development comes from studies comparing children's developing mathematical knowledge across cultures that differ in the structure of their numerical representational systems. In particular, Asian languages such as Chinese and Korean are completely regular in the way they represent numbers greater than 9, whereas the names for the numbers 10–15 are highly irregular in English and other European languages. Corresponding to this linguistic difference, researchers have found greater mastery of the count sequence beyond 10 among Chinese than among English preschoolers (Miller, Smith, Zhu, & Zhang, 1995) and also greater understanding of the tens-plus-ones composition of large numbers among Asian as compared to European and U. S. first graders (Miura et al., 1994).

Asian languages are also more explicit than European languages about the part–whole relations represented by fractions; for instance, a literal translation of the Korean term for "one third" is, "of three parts, one" (Miura, Okamoto, Vlahovic-Svetic, Kim, & Han, 1999, p. 358). Correspondingly, Miura and her colleagues found that Korean students make much more rapid progress than U.S. students in learning to map written fractions to geometric part–whole representations. In the middle of first grade, both Korean and U.S. students performed poorly (means were 22% and 21% correct respectively), but the performance of the Korean children increased rapidly over the next year whereas that of U.S. children did not. By the beginning of second grade, 25 of 33 Korean children, but only 1 of 20 U.S. children, correctly answered all eight of the fraction problems Miura et al. (1999) presented.

Language continues to have an impact on children's mathematical thinking—albeit not always a positive one—as schooling progresses. When children first encounter arithmetic word problems, for instance, they are often confused as to the meaning of statements such as, "John and Bill have eight marbles altogether" (Cummins, 1988, 1991). Often, this confusion is resolved through the adoption of a "keyword" strategy that looks for certain linguistic terms that signal which arithmetic operation to perform (Schoenfeld, 1985). For instance, the term *altogether* typically signals either addition or multiplication; the term *left* or *remaining* signals subtraction. Although not infallible, this strategy works on the types of problems that occur most often in school texts. Conceptually, however, it is impoverished in that it bypasses the process of identifying the part–whole relations in the problems, which is crucial to developing the "problem schemas" that support the formation of mental representations of the problem situations (Dean & Malik, 1986; Kintsch & Greeno, 1985).

Capacity Limitations and Developmental Malleability

A recurrent developmental question is whether there are age-related cognitive constraints that limit the kinds of thinking children are capable of at various ages. From a Piagetian perspective (Piaget, 1969, 1970), because conceptual development is a constructive process in which the child must discover new ways of thinking for himself or herself, learning—at least, conceptually rich learning—is constrained by the child's current cognitive abilities. Indeed, Piaget warned educators against teaching concepts to children before they were able to construct those concepts for themselves, suggesting that doing so would deprive the children of the opportunity to discover the concept himself or herself. "Each time one prematurely teaches a child something he could have discovered for himself," he wrote, "that child is kept from inventing it and consequently from understanding it completely" (Piaget, 1970, p. 715). Accordingly, analyses of the complexity of different mathematical concepts, considered in relation to the stages of logico-mathematical thinking identified by Piaget, have been the basis for conclusions about the ages at which those concepts should be taught. Kamii (1985), for instance, argued that addition is an appropriate instructional objective for first graders but subtraction is better left for second grade, and place value for even later.

From a somewhat different perspective, information-processing considerations have also been the basis for conclusions as to what types of mathematical thinking children are cognitively capable of at different ages (e.g., English & Halford, 1995). English and Halford's analysis began with the idea, based on the performance of children of different ages on various information-processing tasks, that children's information-processing capacity increases with age. In particular, they posited that at early ages, children may only be capable of a making a single cognitive mapping, as in mapping the sequence of counting words onto a collection of objects, and as they get older, they acquire the information-processing capacity to handle more complex mappings and thus to perform mathematical tasks whose information-processing demands were too great for them at early ages.

The sociocultural perspective of Vygotsky (e.g., 1978) contrasts with both of these perspectives in that it emphasizes the contributions that social interactions, including schooling, make to children's cognitive development and correspondingly it views young children's capabilities as considerably more malleable than either the Piagetian or the information-processing views do. Because Vygotsky considered individual development to result from the internalization of knowledge that is initially embodied in the interactions between the child and others, especially more knowledgeable members of the community, his theory called attention to the possibility that the kinds of instruction children receive may limit their development as well as the reverse. Davydov (1975), in particular, developed this perspective on early mathematical thinking, suggesting that the cognitive limitations Piaget identified as characteristic of young children might be a function of the cultural and instructional background of the children. In particular, he suggested that errors such as nonconservation, which result from overreliance on salient perceptual features, might stem from young children's lack of familiarity with mathematically sound ways to compare quantities. This led him to propose methods of early mathematics instruction designed to foster a better understanding of measurement, and he found that these methods of instruction indeed had a marked impact on children's performance on Piagetian tasks.

Although Davydov's (1975a) focus was on the cognitive capabilities of young children, a parallel line of reasoning might be developed about the cognitive limitations of older children and the implications of those limitations for instruction in multiplicative relations and fractions. Capacity-based analyses of students' difficulties with fractions invoke the formal-operational structure of proportionality (Inhelder & Piaget, 1958) and/or the idea that working with fractions often entails coordinating multiple mappings (English & Halford, 1995). A crucial question for understanding the developmental significance of these analyses, however, concerns the malleability of the limitations that are often observed in children's reasoning about fractions. Although capacity limitations are presumed to be a function of biological characteristics of the organism, fixed biological constraints need not imply fixed capabilities. In fact, it is not unusual for accounts of cognitive development that consider information-processing limitations an important factor in age differences to recognize that those information-processing limitations may be as much a function of how information is encoded as of biological characteristics of the brain (e.g., Case, Kurland, & Goldberg, 1982).

Spinillo and Bryant's (1991) research on children's reasoning about part–part and part–whole relations presents an interesting challenge to a capacity-based account of the development of proportional reasoning. Spinillo and Bryant hypothesized that second-order reasoning, or reasoning about the relation between two relations, is dependent on children's familiarity with the first-order relations. In proportional reasoning, the first-order relations are the ratios between part and whole in individual stimuli. However, Spinillo and Bryant argued that children's difficulties in comparing these ratios are not due to any intrinsic limitation on second-order reasoning but rather to lack of familiarity with the first-order part–whole relations. In support of this hypothesis, they demonstrated that 6- and 7-year-old children were able to solve proportional matching problems that could be solved on the basis of part–part relations (i.e., by noting which of two parts was greater in each stimulus). Thus, for example, the children correctly judged that pairs of arrays, both of which were $\frac{5}{8}$ blue (but different in size and configuration), were the same (both were "more blue than white"), while pairs in which one array was $\frac{3}{8}$ blue and the other was $\frac{5}{8}$ blue were different (because the former was "more white than blue" and the latter "more blue than white"). The same children, however, could not discriminate pairs of arrays that were both $\frac{5}{8}$ blue from pairs in which one was $\frac{5}{8}$ blue and the other $\frac{7}{8}$ blue, because in both cases there was "more blue than white." The positive findings for problems involving the ratios $\frac{3}{8}$ and $\frac{5}{8}$ show that the comparison of two first-order relations is not intrinsically beyond young children's information-processing capacities and hence indicate that we need to look elsewhere to understand why children have difficulty with the problems that juxtapose $\frac{1}{8}$ and $\frac{3}{8}$ or $\frac{5}{8}$ and $\frac{7}{8}$. Certainly, the greater familiarity of part–part relations could make the information-processing demands of the two types of problems different, and hence Spinillo and Bryant's familiarity-based account is not antithetical to a processing capacity account. But the point is that we cannot attribute children's difficulties with proportionality judgments to the intrinsic information-processing demands of comparing two first-order relations given that they are able to compare first-order part–part relations. Spinillo and Bryant's results suggest that it is only because young children lack familiarity with part–whole relations that they have difficulty comparing two part–whole relations.

Extending Spinillo and Bryant's (1991) ideas about familiarity to the issue of why students have trouble understanding fractions generally, one might conjecture that the problem is not that fractions intrinsically require greater information-processing capability than the students have, but rather that students lack adequate familiarity with the types of units that must be coordinated to understand fractions. Ensuring that children are familiar with the role of units in numerical representation generally, and with the construction of fractional units through the partitioning of larger units, then, could have a marked impact on children's ability to reason effectively about fractions. To fully evaluate that possibility, however, would entail changing existing instructional practices to make units in general and fractional units in particular more familiar to children and then examining the consequences of that instructional change for children's performance with fractions. In this respect, developmental research is inseparable from instructional research.

THE DEVELOPMENTAL ORIGINS OF MATHEMATICAL KNOWLEDGE: A REPRISE

The two perspectives juxtaposed at the beginning of this book—the counting-first perspective and the comparison-of-quantities perspective—posit different starting points for the development of mathematical knowledge and correspondingly different conceptual transitions over the course of mathematical development. All of the lines of research considered in this book, from studies of the nonverbal quantitative discriminations of infants to investigations of middle-school and even university students' understanding of fractions, have a bearing on these alternative accounts.

Starting Points for Mathematical Development

From the counting-first perspective, mathematical development begins with knowledge about how to count, and that knowledge remains the conceptual core of mathematical thinking for many years. In contrast, the comparison-of-quantities perspective suggests that the origins of mathematical cognition lie in the perception of magnitude relations—equal, less than, and greater than—between quantities. The most direct evidence bearing on these issues is the extensive research on young infants' perception of numerosity and related quantitative properties of stimuli, such as contour length and surface area (cf. chap. 2). Although the conclusion that infants discriminate between small numerosities was considered well-established for many years, it has received new scrutiny in light of recent evidence that what appear to be numerical discriminations may in fact be based on continuous properties such as contour length. At the same time, studies controlling for continuous variables have yielded the surprising finding that infants may be able to discriminate widely spaced large numerosities but not small numerosities that differ by the same ratio. Neither the nonnumerical comparison-of-quantities account nor the accumulator model of preverbal counting offers a ready explanation for these results. Hence, at present, the only firm conclusion that can be drawn from the infancy research is that infants are able to make some kinds of quantitative discriminations from an early age. Efforts to specify the cognitive mechanisms by which they do so will surely remain a major focus as research on infants' quantitative abilities continues.

In lieu of the emphasis the counting-first perspective places on numerical knowledge, the comparison-of-quantities perspective calls attention to children's reasoning about continuous quantities as an important aspect of their early mathematical development. It is clear that, like numerical reasoning, reasoning about continuous quantities begins in the first year of life and undergoes profound developmental change in early and middle childhood (cf. chap. 3). Children develop an understanding of the distinctness of different quantitative dimensions (such as length vs. area) and, thereafter, of interrelations among dimensions. As their understanding of measurement grows, knowledge about continuous quantities and knowledge about number become integrated.

Conceptual Transitions in Mathematical Development

Another important divergence between the counting-based and comparison-of-quantities perspectives lies in their characterization of the conceptual transitions that occur in the development of mathematical thinking across early and middle childhood. Because the counting-based perspective holds that preverbal counting provides the conceptual framework for learning to count verbally, it suggests that the acquisition of verbal counting does not entail substantial conceptual change. (An exception to this generalization is Wynn's, 1992b, discussion of the developmental significance of how preverbal representations of number, which are magnitude-based, differ from verbal ones, which are only arbitrarily linked to the numerosities they represent.) However, as a consequence of its claim that children's understanding of number derives from counting, the counting-first perspective suggests that the acquisition of knowledge about fractions does pose a major conceptual hurdle. Conversely, the comparison-of-quantities perspective suggests that the introduction of number involves a profound conceptual transition (because of the dependence of number on the concept of unit), but that, once that transition has been made, the transition from whole numbers to fractions does not involve substantial conceptual change. That is because multiplicative reasoning has its roots in the iteration of a unit in order to generate a numerical representation of a quantity, a process that applies both to whole-number representations and to fractions.

These alternatives are not easy to distinguish empirically, in part because on either account the kinds of new knowledge that pose a conceptual challenge to children's prior ways of thinking are acquired only slowly, over an extended period of time. From the counting-first perspective, the crucial new knowledge that must be incorporated in children's mathematical thinking is knowledge about fractions, but, although even preschool children demonstrate some knowledge about fractions (Hunting & Davis, 1991b), an appreciation of the key conceptual idea that fractions are infinitely dense is not fully developed even at 15 years of age (Vamvakoussi & Vosniadou, 2004). Likewise, from the comparison-of-quantities perspective, the crucial new knowledge that children must incorporate in their thinking is that numerical representations of quantities are relative to the unit that is used, but, although children have already begun to use number words in the first half of their second year of life (Durkin et al., 1986), their understanding of the role of units in the numerical representation of quantities is still very shaky several years later (e.g., Sophian & Kailihiwa, 1998). On both accounts, then, the child's acquisition of new knowledge entails a conceptual reorganization, but because the knowledge acquisition process is an extended one, strong predictions cannot be made about when corresponding conceptual changes will take place.

Advocates of the counting-first perspective find support for their position in the widespread evidence that children have a great deal of difficulty with fraction instruction (e.g., R. Gelman, 1991). However, that phenomenon in itself does not constitute a strong basis for distinguishing between alternative theoretical accounts. Because counting is clearly an activity with which children have had extensive experience before they learn about fractions, difficulties stemming from the differences between fractions and counting numbers are to be expected on almost any account of mathematical development. The counting-first and comparison-of-quantities perspective do make distinct predictions about fraction learning insofar as they emphasize different points of contrast between fractions and counting numbers. The counting-first perspective puts particular emphasis on the difference between the density of fractions and the successor relations among counting numbers, whereas the comparison-of-quantities perspective emphasizes differences in the way in which units are used in the two kinds of numbers. Correspondingly, the counting-first perspective predicts confusion about whether there are other numbers between two seemingly adjacent numbers (such as 0 and 1, or $\frac{1}{5}$ and $\frac{2}{5}$), whereas the comparison-of-quantities perspective predicts confusions about the magnitude relations among different-denominator fractions (such as $\frac{1}{8}$ versus $\frac{1}{9}$), which derive from the way in which the denominator specifies a fractional unit. These contrasting predictions are not very helpful in deciding between the accounts, however, as the available evidence indicates that both kinds of confusions are commonplace (cf. chap. 6).

A major tenet of the comparison-of-quantities perspective is that the concept of unit on which all numerical representations depend is by no means transparent to young children. This tenet is not inconsistent with the existence of some sort of preverbal counting mechanism, but it is much more central to the account of mathematical development that emerges from the comparison-of-quantities perspective than to the account offered by advocates of the counting-first perspective. There is abundant evidence that the significance of units is, in fact, far from transparent to young children (cf. chap. 4). Four- and five-year-old children have difficulty identifying the appropriate unit to use in response to a numerical question and in the absence of specific training, they have difficulty appreciating how changes in unit size affect a numerical outcome. Moreover, the concept of unit has a strong bearing on later difficulties in mathematics learning, including the conflation of additive and multiplicative relations (cf. chap. 5) and confusion about the magnitude relations among fractions with different denominators (cf. chap. 6).

An important question is to what extent the difficulties children have with the concept of unit are a function of prevailing instructional practices, and to what extent they may reflect the intrinsic difficulty of this abstract and complex concept. My own view is that it should be possible to construct instructional programs in a way that enable children to achieve, from an early age, a concept of unit that is adequate to support all the arithmetic learning expected of them in the elementary and secondary years. This view is based in part on the success of experimental training in facilitating young children's performance on unit-related tasks (Sophian, 2002), and even more strongly on my observations in a first-grade class that was using the Measure Up curriculum (Dougherty, 2003; Dougherty, Okazaki, Zenigama, & Venenciano, 2005). The children in that class readily referred to the issue of what the unit is in discussing the numerical values of quantities. But a full evaluation of the issue cannot be made until the sequelae of different methods of instruction can be examined. What we know at this point is that, in the absence of instruction that explicitly familiarizes students with the concept of unit, a full understanding of units develops very slowly and correspondingly that continuing limitations on that understanding continue to affect children's mathematical thinking for many years.

What Have We Learned?

Although a wide range of research on children's developing mathematical knowledge bears on the contrasting claims of the counting-first and comparison-of-quantities positions, none of that research—individually or collectively—is decisive in choosing between the positions. In part, this state of affairs reflects the difficulty of making strong empirical predictions on the basis of accounts of developmental processes that occur over many years. Additionally, very little of the research to date was even designed to differentiate between theoretical alternatives; instead, it was very often designed simply to provide evidence of kinds of knowledge or kinds of confusions that were postulated from a single theoretical perspective. It is to be hoped that the recognition that more than one viable perspective on children's developing mathematical knowledge exists will result in efforts to obtain empirical evidence that can distinguish more clearly between the alternatives. Already, the juxtaposition of the comparison-of-quantities perspective to the counting-first perspective has been useful in calling attention to aspects of children's developing mathematical thinking whose importance was not widely recognized and thus in giving us a greater appreciation of the conceptual richness of the child's journey into mathematics.

Chapter 8

Implications for Mathematics Education

An implication of the theory that children's acquisition of knowledge about whole-number arithmetic is guided by innate counting structures is that formal instruction is not necessary for the development of that knowledge. Indeed, it might well be thought that because an understanding of the conceptual principles underlying whole-number arithmetic is assured, the primary objective of instruction in whole-number arithmetic in children's first years of schooling is just to familiarize children with conventional symbol systems and computational procedures. From the same perspective, instruction is crucial for acquiring knowledge about rational numbers, which do not fit well with the ideas about numbers that children are likely to derive from innate counting structures and so are bound to be difficult. An implication of the view that there is a conceptual discontinuity between counting numbers and fractions is that early instruction in whole-number arithmetic can do little to facilitate later fraction learning. Instead, instructional recommendations have focused on the need for extensive practice (Geary, 1995) and on the use of general information-processing principles to develop effective instructional approaches (e.g., English & Halford, 1995; Geary & Hamson, 2005).

The comparison-of-quantities position has very different implications for mathematics instruction—both in the first years of schooling and later on. This view underscores the interdependence between children's early learning about whole numbers and their later learning about rational numbers, because both involve understanding how units are used to generate and interpret numerical representations. Even instruction in whole-number arithmetic is far from trivial, because it requires introducing children to the concept of unit and the different ways in which units are used in representing whole-number quantities and relations among those quantities. Moreover, the establishment of a strong understanding of units early in instruction is a critical foundation for later fraction learning. In underscoring the interconnectedness of the mathematics material about which children are instructed across the elementary and middle school grades, the comparison-of-quantities perspective indicates the importance of bringing a long-term perspective to the design of mathematics instruction from the very first years of schooling.

Although instructional decisions are seldom explicitly based on the counting-first perspective or the comparison-of-quantities perspective, current instructional practices are clearly much more closely aligned with the counting-first position. That alignment can be seen (a) in the emphasis on counting and small-number addition and subtraction in preschool and beginning elementary school mathematics instruction, (b) in the teaching of multiplication as a kind of addition, and (c) in the lack of attention to issues of unit size, even in the teaching of fractions. In earlier chapters of this book, I argued that a number of the difficulties students experience in mathematics learning derive from these instructional practices. The goal of this concluding chapter is to articulate the instructional ramifications of the alternative comparison-of-quantities perspective.

In the service of that goal, I will no longer be juxtaposing the comparison-of-quantities perspective with the counting-first perspective. In part, this is because the counting-first position actually has very little to say about how instruction should proceed. Instructional practices consonant with this position are for the most part extrapolations of the premise, "Mathematical knowledge begins with counting," rather than implementations of specific instructional recommendations derived from the tenets of the counting-first position. The comparison-of-quantities perspective, in contrast, although not widely represented in current instructional practices, in fact offers considerable insight into fundamental instructional issues. In the next three sections of this chapter, implications of the comparison-of-quantities perspective for three such issues are addressed: (a) the formulation of coherent conceptual goals for mathematics instruction; (b) the integration of conceptual and computational knowledge in instruction; and (c) the conceptual integration of arithmetic instruction with instruction with other important aspects of mathematics, especially measurement, geometry, and data analysis. The instructional ramifications of this discussion are then summarized in the form of three broad instructional recommendations: (a) that the design of mathematics instruction should be guided by a long-term perspective; (b) that instruction in arithmetic should be grounded in an understanding of mathematical units; and (c) that mathematics instruction should aim from the outset for generality in students' understanding of mathematical concepts and principles.

CONCEPTUAL GOALS FOR MATHEMATICS INSTRUCTION

Among the most fundamental issues facing mathematics educators is that of specifying the goals of mathematics instruction. The need for clarity about instructional goals is critical as well for current efforts to promote "evidence-based" instructional practices (Kersting, 2003). Empirical evaluations of the effectiveness of alternative instructional approaches require the construction or selection of assessment instruments, and advocates of different instructional approaches are likely to favor different assessment instruments, corresponding to their differing instructional goals. Thus, Schoenfeld (2006) notes that, in general, the assessment data available for traditional curricula are not as broad in scope as those collected in evaluations of "reform"curricula, making comparisons between the two kinds of curricula difficult. The collection of multiple outcome measures would improve comparability, but the problem of deciding how to weigh different measures would remain insofar as different curricula show different patterns of strengths and weaknesses across the measures.

Nowhere has the need for clarity and consensus about instructional goals emerged more clearly than in the fierce "Math Wars" that were precipitated by concerns that recent reforms in mathematics education were leading to a neglect of computational "basics" (Schoenfeld, 2004; 2006). Although both advocates and critics of the reform recognize that computational skill and conceptual knowledge are complementary rather than antithetical objectives (e.g., Ball et al., 2005; Schoenfeld, 2004; Wu, 1999), the perception that the reform movement has derailed instruction in computational skills continues to engender criticism of it (e.g., Budd et al., 2005; Hoff, 2003).

Although the goal of fostering computational fluency appears to be unambiguous, the formulation of clear conceptual goals is less straightforward. Thompson and Saldanha (2003) point out, with respect to instruction in rational numbers, that it is not realistic to expect preuniversity students to reach the kind of understanding of rational numbers that mathematicians have, an understanding that has a rich and complex history. But if the mathematician's understanding of rational knowledge is not what we expect students to attain, it is crucial for educators to be clear about just what conceptual knowledge they do want students to acquire. Otherwise, instruction in rational numbers is not likely to have much conceptual coherence, no matter how much recognition is given to the importance of conceptual as well as computational learning.

An extension of Thompson and Saldanha's (2003) concern with conceptual coherence is the relation between the conceptual goals of mathematics instruction at different grade levels. Broad conceptual coherence requires that the conceptual goals we set for the first years of mathematics education be consistent with those we set for later years. In particular, early instruction

must anticipate the conceptual knowledge that will be important in later instruction and establish an appropriate foundation for it.

Coherence in Numerical Concepts Across Grade Levels

The comparison-of-quantities perspective offers a clear account of the conceptual relations across grade levels in the numerical concepts and operations that children are expected to learn. Specifically, the conceptual basis
for the whole spectrum of arithmetic instruction from basic whole-number
addition and subtraction through the multiplicative operations and rational numbers is an understanding of the different ways in which units are
used to represent relations between quantities.

The most basic objective in a curriculum that gives an understanding of
units a central place is to understand that any numerical representation is
relative to the unit used. Experience representing the same quantity using
different units can help even very young children to recognize not only that
the numerical value depends on the unit used but that the relation is an inverse one. In the experimental curriculum that Sophian (2004) developed
for Head Start children (predominantly 3- and 4-year-olds), instructional
activities using related geometric shapes, such as an equilateral triangle and
a rhombus equivalent in area to two adjoining triangles, were used to give
children the opportunity to explore the relation between unit size and
number. For example, children filled in geometric patterns with different
shapes and observed how the number of pieces needed to complete the
pattern varied with the size of those pieces.

Similarly, both the curriculum developed by Davydov and his colleagues
in Russia (cf. Davydov, 1975b) and the related Measure Up curriculum
(Dougherty, 2003; Dougherty et al., 2005) use measurement activities to
help first-grade children recognize the importance of the unit used in assigning a numerical value to a quantity. Children learn to assign numerical
values to line segments drawn on graph paper by determining the number
of times a specified unit, which may be the length of a single square on the
graph paper or of several squares, must be iterated to span the whole line
segment, and they learn to represent the relation between the unit and the
line segment with a notation that explicitly identifies the unit as well as the
numerical relation between it and the line segment. Specifically, both the
unit and the total quantity are labeled with letters (e.g., A and B—the labels
are arbitrary). An arrow is then used to connect the two, marked with a numeral indicating the number of iterations of the unit in the quantity, for
example:

$$A \xrightarrow{6} B$$

Children learn likewise to enumerate collections of discrete objects in relation to a unit, which may consist of several separate objects rather than a single one. For instance, if the unit is considered to be "+ +" then the array

$$+ + + + + +$$

consists of three units, but if the unit is "+ + +" then the same array consists of just two units. Children instructed in this way quickly learn to ask, "What is the unit?" when asked a question about numerical values.

Clearly, that is not all there is to understanding units. The construction of composite units and fractional ones and the coordination of different types of units in place value notation, in multiplication and division, and in understanding equivalent fractions, all entail more complex reasoning about units than simply understanding that an enumeration of a given quantity based on smaller units will result in a larger numerical value than an enumeration of the same quantity based on larger units. The confusions that students in the later elementary years and beyond often have about these topics—discussed in chapters 5 and 6—are consistent with the idea that a full understanding of units develops very slowly. As noted in chapter 7, however, in the absence of evidence from children who receive much more explicit instruction in units than is the prevailing practice today, it is impossible to know to what extent this protracted course of development is attributable to the inherent complexity of the material and to what extent it is a result of the way we teach children mathematics. However protracted the process may be, I believe that helping students to understand that all numerical representations depend on the identification of a unit is a crucial starting point. Given that foundation, instruction in multiplication, division, and fractions can made conceptually coherent by articulating the ways in which units are used in each case.

Abstraction as an Instructional Goal Across Grade Levels

In advancing the concept of unit as a key focus of mathematics instruction from the first years of elementary school, the comparison-of-quantities perspective diverges from the commonly held view that instruction should begin with concrete skills and only later endeavor to convey to children the abstract concepts that underlie them. Davydov (1975a) explicitly criticized the practice of avoiding abstraction in the early grades in an argument building upon the principle that long-term instructional goals should inform the design of early instruction.

Beginning with the observation that abstraction is a fundamental characteristic of mathematical thought, Davydov (1975a) argued that the relationship between particular and abstract knowledge is not unidirectional: "The general not only follows from the particular ... but also changes and restructures the whole appearance and arrangement of the particular knowledge which has given rise to it" (p. 98). The implication of this idea is that early instruction that focuses on particulars and eschews abstraction may result in ways of thinking about the particulars that are not congenial to the abstractions to be studied later. Accordingly, Davydov advocated that children should be shown the abstractness of mathematical material from the beginning of instruction, and they should be taught in a way that will develop their capacity for abstraction.

The curriculum that Davydov and his colleagues developed (cf. Davydov, 1975b) reflects this thinking in that it begins with instruction in basic quantitative relations rather than in numerical skills. Through the first half year of first grade, children are encouraged to identify and represent the relations of "equal," "less than," and "greater than" as they characterize pairs of continuous quantities of various kinds (lengths, areas, masses, and volumes) as well as pairs of numerosities. The emphasis on presenting mathematical concepts in their most general form is maintained throughout the curriculum, which extends through the secondary school years. For example, instruction in place value in the second grade incorporates a consideration of a variety of base systems, not just base 10.

An intriguing extension of this approach is incorporated in the Measure Up curriculum (Dougherty, 2003; Dougherty, Okazaki, & Zenigami, 2006), which builds on Davydov's (1975b) work. In Grade 4, base systems are used to introduce students to fractions. For instance, children learn to think of a rectangle partitioned into eight equal parts as a unit in base 8. The equal parts can then be understood as reflecting an initial level of segmentation in base 8, so that each is represented numerically as .1 base 8 (where the symbol "." is the base-8 counterpart of a decimal point so that digits immediately to the right of it represent eighths just as digits immediately to the right of the decimal point in base-10 notation represent tenths). This way of introducing fractions contrasts with other methods of fraction instruction in that it establishes the conceptual unity of place-value-based fraction representations and common fractions from the very beginning of fraction instruction. Moreover, instruction in decimal fractions, like instruction in whole-number place value representations of numbers, is grounded in an understanding of the more general principles underlying the use of any numerical base.

INTEGRATING CONCEPTS AND COMPUTATIONAL SKILLS

Among academics, there is a strong consensus that both computational skill and conceptual understanding are important goals of mathematics learning and instruction, and indeed that they are interdependent (e.g., Kilpatrick, Swafford, & Findell, 2001; Rittle-Johnson, Siegler, & Alibali, 2001; Silver, 1986; Wu, 1999). Three ways in which educators have endeavored to integrate the two are: (a) through the use of manipulatives to link symbolic computations with students' understanding of physical quantities; (b) through the consideration of alternative solution methods for a given problem; and (c) through discussion of the rationales for proposed solution methods, often motivated by the effort to convince others of their validity. From a comparison-of-quantities perspective, an understanding of dimensions of quantity and of the role of units in enumerating quantities is a vital element in using each of these approaches effectively.

Instruction With Manipulatives

A widespread assumption is that the use of physical manipulatives to represent symbolic operations will enable students to grasp the conceptual basis for those operations. Thus, in multidigit addition and subtraction, to take just one example, in order to help students understand the computational process of regrouping, they are taught to perform physical counterparts of those processes with base-10 blocks, trading a single "ten-block" for 10 "one-blocks" or vice versa (e.g., Fuson & Briars, 1990). The expectation is that the physical properties of the material, specifically the fact that the ten-block is identical in size and shape to a row of 10 one-blocks, will help children grasp the equivalence between the two, and then that understanding can be mapped into the procedures of regrouping in written addition and subtraction (Schoenfeld, 1986). Provided that children understand the manipulatives as intended, this instructional strategy makes sense as an application of the principle that instruction should build on what students already know (Dewey, 1990).

The empirical evidence on the effectiveness of manipulatives, however, is uneven at best (Resnick & Omanson, 1987; Uttal, Scudder, & DeLoache, 1997). It cannot be taken for granted that students understand physical activities using manipulatives in the way that educators intend, nor that they understand the connection between that activity and the symbolic procedure.

Uttal et al. (1997), noting that manipulatives are themselves symbols, posit that a part of the problem students face in learning from manipulatives stems from an inadequate appreciation of the fact that the manipulatives are meant to stand for or represent a concept or written symbol. Schoenfeld (1986) points out a number of additional difficulties with the use of isomorphisms between operations with manipulatives and operations with written symbols to promote greater mathematical understanding. In many ways, it seems that the isomorphisms between them are helpful only when you already understand their mathematical meaning.

Viewed naively, the very properties of manipulatives that make them good representations (e.g., the fact that, in working with base-10 blocks, 10 one-blocks can be arranged to look just like a single ten-block) may make it difficult to appreciate the correspondence between operations with them and operations with written symbols. In addition, the isomorphisms only go so far. For instance, in adding 24 + 47 with base-ten blocks, there is no inherent reason why 6 ten-blocks and 11 one-blocks is an unsatisfactory answer. It is the constraints of the place value system that preclude recording the sum that way in doing written arithmetic. Given this nonisomorphism, working with base-10 blocks cannot help children understand why 611 is an unsatisfactory result for 24 + 47.

The comparison-of-quantities perspective suggests a related set of concerns about instruction via manipulatives. One important issue to consider is what quantitative properties and relations students focus on as they carry out operations with manipulatives. Consider, for example, the use of base-10 blocks as a foundation for teaching regrouping. The equivalence of a single "ten-block" and 10 "one-blocks" that is presupposed by the instructor is not necessarily transparent to the student despite the fact that the one-blocks can be arranged to form the same shape as the ten-block. Although the two quantities are equivalent in aggregate amount, they clearly are not in number! In itself the ten block is just a single block, not 10 of anything. Moreover, similarities in shape and aggregate amount often have nothing to do with equivalence in real-life exchanges, such as trading two nickels for a dime, or a quarter for a newspaper. The upshot is that the base-10 blocks model may be far less transparent for students than teachers assume.

Perhaps the most fundamental difficulty with manipulatives is that the ways they are used often perpetuate the conflation of physical and mathematical characteristics that Gal'perin and Georgiev (1969) criticized in relation to young children's equating of units with discrete objects. In teaching students that a small cube is "one" and that a bar 10 times as long as that is a "tens" unit, we reify the concept of unit in much the same way as we do in focusing on discrete objects as the unit of counting. This limitation might be overcome by introducing alternate units, such as a pair of small cubes glued together, and asking children questions such as, "If this is one, then how many ones are equivalent to the bar (the piece usually called a ten-block)?" Depending upon how it was developed, this approach could lead to an exploration of numerical bases other than 10.

Alternative Solution Methods

Many mathematical problems can be solved in more than one way. Encouraging students to identify alternative solution methods has the virtue of shifting the focus from "getting the answer" to understanding the mathematical relations involved. Furthermore, consideration of how different solutions are related can increase students' understanding of why the procedures work.

From a comparison-of-quantities perspective, a general way of thinking about the relation between alternative solutions to arithmetic problems is to analyze the ways in which they use units to represent the quantities involved. Consider, for example, two approaches to the subtraction problem 72 – 57: one involving borrowing and the other successive approximation. In the borrowing method, 1 "ten" is converted to 10 "ones" to avoid having to subtract a larger number of ones from a smaller number of them. Thus, the number "72" is interpreted as 7 tens and 2 ones, which is then converted to 6 tens and 12 ones so that the 7 ones within "57" can be subtracted from the 12, leaving 5 ones. Subtracting the 5 tens of "57" from the 6 tens remaining after regrouping the "72" leaves 1 ten. Putting the ones and tens results together, one gets a final result of 15. Successive approximation is a method often observed among unschooled children working in markets and similar settings (e.g., Carraher et al., 1985). The subtraction 72 – 57 might be calculated through reasoning along these lines: "If I subtracted 60 from the 72, 12 would be left, but I have to give back 3 since I am only subtracting 57, so that makes it 15." Here the unit remains "one" throughout the solution process; a multiple of 10 is subtracted first to simplify the computation, but it is not conceptualized as a number of tens.

The relation between the "partitioning" and "ratio" solutions to sharing problems observed by Empson (1999) can likewise be understood in terms of the adoption of different types of units. In partitioning, children determine the numerical relation between the individual shares to be formed and the units used in the problems to specify the quantity to be shared. Once the numerical relation between these two kinds of units has been calculated, it can be used in further calculations to convert information about the number of additional shares needed to a numerical value based on the units specified in the problem statement. Thus, in an example reported by Empson (1999), several children figured out that if a table of 4 children got three pancakes to share, each child at that table got $\frac{3}{4}$ of a pancake. They then multiplied that figure by 12 to determine the number of pancakes needed for a table of 12 children if each child at that table was to get the same amount to eat as the children at the table of four. In ratio solutions, in contrast, children never determine an individual share. Instead they treat groups of 4 children as a unit, each of which is associated with three pancakes. They determine the number of units of 4 children at the table of 12, and multiply that value (3) by the number of pancakes needed for each of those units.

The method Lampert (1986) used to teach children multidigit multiplication likewise differs from the traditional long-division algorithm in the kinds of composite units that are used. Whereas the traditional algorithm treats both multiplier and multiplicand as composed of hierarchically related units corresponding to the powers of 10, Lampert's (1986) approach was to use units corresponding to the value of the multiplicand as the primary unit, and to construct higher order units based on composites of 10 (or a higher power of 10) of those units. Thus, in one example, her students solved the problem 28×65 by reasoning about glasses containing 65 drops each and jugs containing the equivalent of 10 glasses, or 650 drops. Different students in Lampert's classroom combined these units in different ways to solve the multiplication problem. One summed two jugs plus 8 glasses, computing $(2 \times 650) + (8 \times 65)$, whereas another proposed thinking of the 28 glasses as 2 glasses short of three jugs, leading to the computation $(3 \times 650) - (2 \times 65)$.

Justifications

Perhaps the most profound shift in thinking associated with the reform mathematics movements is the degree of attention given to students' ability, not just to generate mathematical solutions, but to articulate mathematical arguments. An emphasis on justification powerfully conveys to students that procedures are not arbitrary but derive from the shared understanding of quantitative relations achieved by a community of thinkers (Hamm & Perry, 2002). When teachers present themselves as the only person in the classroom who can decree the validity or lack of validity of mathematical ideas, students are likely to conclude that there is no need to make sense of the ideas for themselves.

Twenty years ago, most educators and psychologists would likely have agreed that it is not within students' capabilities, at least in early grades, to articulate why a procedure is or is not mathematically sound (although they might have credited children with intuitions about the matter that are not accessible to verbalization). Contemporary standards for mathematics education in the United States, however, identify the ability to "monitor and reflect on the process of mathematical problem solving" and to "develop and evaluate mathematical arguments" as important expectations for students across the full range of schooling from prekindergarten through Grade 12 (National Council of Teachers of Mathematics, 2000). That position is consistent with Lehrer and Lesh's (2003) developmental analysis which, while underscoring the importance of classroom practices and norms for the development of students' argumentation skills, traces the origins of those skills to basic patterns of everyday narrative discourse. Dialogues from classrooms in which students are actively engaged in the evaluation of mathematical ideas provide a strong existence proof that even students in the early grades of elementary school are quite capable of expressing and justifying their mathematical ideas (e.g., Cobb, Wood, Yackel, & McNeal, 1992; Peterson, 1994).

Often, students' articulation of mathematical arguments is closely inter-twined with the consideration of alternative solution methods because in proposing a solution method, the student is likely to give some explanation for proceeding in the manner he or she indicates. Thus, the student in Lampert's (1986) classroom who proposed thinking of 28 glasses as 2 glasses short of three jugs containing 10 glasses each was not only indicating an alternate computational procedure but also articulating the relations among quantities that make that procedure valid. Likewise, in Cobb et al.'s (1992) observations of second graders determining sums of collections of base-10 blocks, students' mathematical arguments are tightly interwoven with their proposed solutions. Consider, for example, the following ex-cerpt: "... you know there are 2 ten bars that make 20 and then you count [the small cubes] ... Because there's 11 ... then take 10 and that makes 30. And then you put that extra one for 11 and you get 31." On the surface, this appears to be just a step-by-step account of how the student obtained the sum of 2 ten bars and 11 small cubes. But in articulating what she was doing, the student implicitly asserted that the 11 cubes can be decomposed into ten plus one, and relatedly that the decomposition $20 + 11$, which corre-sponds to the way the problem is presented using ten bars and small cubes, is equivalent to the decomposition $30 + 1$, which she constructed in the course of solving the problem.

As these examples illustrate, the mathematical reasoning behind stu-dent-generated solution methods often derives from their construal of how mathematical symbols map onto quantities. Correspondingly, both stu-dents' ability to generate alternative solution methods and their ability to articulate the rationale behind them are likely to depend on instruction that clearly grounds symbol-manipulation procedures in an understanding of how numerical representations of quantities are obtained. This, of course, is a central theme in instruction based on the comparison of quantities, in which children learn to understand all numerical representations as repre-sentations of the relation between a chosen unit and the total quantity being represented.

The Primacy of Concepts in Instruction

An important implication of the preceding discussions of different ap-proaches to linking procedural and conceptual learning is that conceptual goals must drive instruction in computational procedures and not vice versa. Certainly, conceptual and procedural learning are mutually reinforc-ing in that understanding may be advanced through the learning of proce-dures that build on those concepts, and procedural learning may be advanced through the illumination of the conceptual foundations for the procedures. But in the design of instruction, concepts should be used to constrain computational procedures rather than the other way around.

This is because the conceptual impact of any discussion of arithmetic procedures depends upon students' understanding of how the procedures correspond to relations among quantities. For example, the practice of mirroring symbolic procedures with actions on manipulatives becomes just a matter of learning another procedure (i.e., what to do with the manipulatives) unless students understand which quantitative properties of the manipulatives are the focus and how those quantitative properties relate to the symbolic procedures that the manipulatives are intended to illuminate. Likewise, both the ability to generate meaningful alternative solution procedures for arithmetic problems and the ability to explain those solution procedures to others rest on students' understanding of how the symbols that enter into a solution process and the procedural steps carried out with those symbols correspond to quantities and relationships between quantities.

BEYOND ARITHMETIC

Current standards for mathematics education encompass much more than knowledge about numbers and arithmetic operations (National Council of Teachers of Mathematics, 2000). Algebra, geometry, measurement, and data analysis and probability are also recognized as important content areas that should be incorporated in mathematics instruction from prekindergarten through Grade 12. However, a comprehensive conception of how the different content areas identified in the standards interconnect is not offered, despite the recognition given in the standards to the importance of helping children to identify interconnections among mathematical ideas. In practice, arithmetic, geometry, and measurement are very often taught as separate instructional units, with little or no effort to illuminate the connections between them.

Through its emphasis on the role of units in all numerical representations of quantities, the comparison-of-quantities perspective underscores the close interrelation between number and measurement. It also has implications for the integration of algebra and geometry in early instruction.

Measurement

A common instructional practice is to introduce children to measurement by having them iterate some type of unit against a quantity to be measured, and then count the units (cf. Clements, 1999). For instance, one might line up a series of pennies along the edge of a strip of paper and thereby determine that the paper is, say, 16 pennies long. This practice, which treats measurement as an application of counting, can provide insight into the significance of measurement units if the results of using different units are explored and the relations between them examined. But what is seldom noted is that exactly the same relationships arise in counting sets of discrete objects: The adoption of different counting units results in different numerical outcomes. The measurement of continuous quantities and the counting of discrete quantities, then, are intimately linked from a comparison-of-quantities perspective. Both are instantiations of the idea of representing a total quantity by specifying its multiplicative relation to a chosen unit.

Algebra

The relationship between the size of a unit and the results of measurement operations based on that unit is an intrinsically algebraic one in that it is not dependent on the particular quantities being measured or indeed on the particular units being used to measure them. Because the relationship between units and measurement results is so general—independent of the particular units being considered and the particular quantities—the examination of that relationship, which is fundamental to an understanding of both number and measurement, also provides an entry point into the study of algebra. In its most general form, it can be expressed in the algebraic statement:

$$M_{Q,U} / M_{Q,V} = V / U,$$

where U and V designate the size of alternative units (expressed in a common unit) and $M_{Q,U}$ and $M_{Q,V}$ are measures of quantity Q based on those units. This statement expresses the inverse relationship between unit size and measured result in a general way.

Other algebraic relations emerge from students' reasoning about arithmetic operations on familiar quantities. Instantiations of the distributive law, for instance, often arise in informal reasoning about multiplication, in particular from the use of decomposition to determine the product of two large numbers. For instance, consider the reasoning used by a youngster in a Brazilian market to determine the cost of ten coconuts selling for 35 *cruzeiros* each (Carraher et al., 1985). The youngster thought of the total due as the cost of three coconuts, which he knew would come to 105 *cruzeiros*, and then three more coconuts, and three more, and another one. Thus, by summing 105 + 105 + 105 + 35, he arrived at the correct total, 350 *cruzeiros*. His reasoning was based on his understanding of the transaction of selling: The amount to be paid does not depend on whether the coconuts are bought altogether or a few at a time, hence the one large sale can be treated as the sum of a series of smaller ones. The idea that one of the numbers to be multiplied can be decomposed and each of its parts multiplied with the other number in turn, however, is by no means restricted to this situation. In its most general form, it expresses a relation that mathematicians refer to as the distributivity of multiplication over addition or simply the distributive law, a relation that can be expressed algebraically as:

$$(a + b) \times c = (a \times c) + (b \times c).$$

The inverse relation between units and measured results and the distributive law are just two of many algebraic relations that students might discover in the course of reasoning about relations between quantities and arithmetic operations on quantities. Among others, the laws of commutativity of addition and multiplication, the associative laws for each, and the inverse relations between addition and subtraction, on one hand, and multiplication and division, on the other, likewise capture relations that students can readily experience in working with specific quantities and then learn to generalize into algebraic relations. Regardless of the specific relations considered, the important point is that students can be introduced to the abstractness of algebra by exploring the generality of relations that are readily experienced in thinking about specific and readily understood quantities. By encouraging a consideration of the generality of regularities initially identified in a very concrete form, teachers can introduce students to the abstractness of algebraic thinking without dissociating that thinking from the knowledge about quantities that helps students to make sense of prealgebraic mathematics.

Geometry

The concept of *equality* is as fundamental to geometry as it is to the idea of unit that underlies number and measurement. The geometric concepts of *congruence*, *symmetry*, and *similarity* all capture equalities among certain aspects of geometric forms, and the identification of the equalities between pairs of angles or pairs of line segments is a basic element of geometric proof. Thus, in establishing a solid concept of equality as a foundation for instruction in number and measurement, one also lays a foundation for geometry.

Additionally, because the geometric properties of polygons make them well suited for the exploration of the relations between units and numerical representations of quantities that underlie measurement and arithmetic, there is considerable opportunity for synergy between number and geometry in instruction on units. Exercises such as the one depicted in Figure 3.2, where the areas of different shapes are compared by finding a common unit that can be applied to both, illustrate both the potential usefulness of geometric materials in developing the ideas about units and the opportunities, within a curriculum in which units play a central role, for fostering knowledge about geometry as well as about number. Sophian's (2004) experimental Head Start curriculum familiarized children with geometric terms such as *rhombus* and *trapezoid,* and with relations among geometric shapes in the context of a series of activities that also served to illustrate that a variety of units could be used in quantifying a given quantity and to give children the opportunity to observe how the size of the unit used affects the numerical result. In particular, geometric shapes were used to exemplify the notion of *decomposition of units.* Children were shown, for instance, that two adjoining equilateral triangles formed a rhombus, and three of them formed a trapezoid, and then they determined how many of each shape it took to completely fill in a large outlined figure. They constructed simple graphs of their results and then discussed the patterns they saw in the graphs.

INSTRUCTIONAL RECOMMENDATIONS

Three broad instructional recommendations can be derived from the implications of the comparison-of-quantities perspective discussed in earlier sections of this chapter. The first and most general of these recommendations is that the formulation of conceptual objectives for mathematics instruction should be guided by a long-term perspective. This very general recommendation is instantiated in two more specific recommendations: first, that instruction in arithmetic should be grounded in quantity comparisons and specifically in an understanding of numerical representations as representations of the relation between a unit and a total quantity, and second, that mathematics instruction should aim from the outset for generality in students' understanding of mathematical concepts and principles.

The Need for a Long-Term Perspective

The comparison-of-quantities perspective underscores the need for a long-term perspective in the formulation of instructional objectives because it highlights ways in which the difficulties students experience with relatively advanced topics such as fractions may derive from an inadequate grasp of much more basic concepts. Because more advanced topics require conceptual knowledge that may or may not be established in the course of teaching earlier topics, it is not enough that instruction in the early grades familiarize children with the specific topics designated for those grade levels. Early instruction must also establish an appropriate conceptual foundation for material that students will be expected to learn in the future. Thus, early instruction must be designed with a mindfulness of the relationships between the material being taught to young children and the mathematics that students will encounter in later years. Only by identifying the conceptual interrelations among the mathematical material students will encounter across the entire elementary and middle school curriculum can we ensure that the conceptual content of early instruction supports later conceptual objectives.

A Focus on Units

From a comparison-of-quantities perspective, the concept of unit arises and originates as a tool for comparing quantities. Through the use of units, we can not only distinguish inequality from equality relations but also distinguish among different degrees of inequality. We do so by using units to obtain numerical values for the quantities, either obtaining a numerical value for a difference quantity that reflects how much greater one quantity is than another in the original units used to measure those quantities, or else using one as a unit against which we measure the other so as to obtain a numerical value that represents the multiplicative relation between the two.

The comparison-of-quantities perspective thus makes it clear that numbers indicate the magnitude of a quantity only in terms of its relation to a reference unit. Two important elaborations of this basic idea are the use of composite units in place value representations and in understanding multiplicative relations, and the construction of fractional units through partitioning. Because the concept of unit underlies such seemingly distinct topics as counting, measurement, place value, additive relations, multiplicative relations, and fractions, the recommendation that the design of mathematics instruction be informed by a long-term perspective leads naturally to the more specific recommendation that the concept of unit be introduced early and developed as a conceptual bridge illuminating the relations between basic numerical concepts and procedures and more advanced ones.

Teaching for Generality

The idea that mathematics is about the identification of general relationships is by no means unique to the comparison-of-quantities perspective. Where there is a divergence of views is on the question of how, and how early, students should be introduced to this idea. On one hand, the view that young children are not yet capable of highly abstract thinking supports the widespread practice of keeping the focus in the first years of mathematics instruction on very concrete activities. On the other hand, eschewing mathematical abstraction in the early years introduces a risk that children will form a misconception about the nature of mathematical inquiry that may be difficult to overcome (cf. Schoenfeld, 1988).

Although the idea that young children do not think abstractly featured prominently in Piaget's (1969) theory, there is now evidence that even preschool children form a number of abstract concepts, among them the concept of *essences* and the concept of *mental states* (S. A. Gelman & Wellman, 1991; Wellman & Phillips, 2001). Even so, it seems unlikely that young children will be able to grasp instruction in abstract mathematical concepts unless it is grounded in ideas and relations that are meaningful to them. The comparison-of-quantities perspective suggests both that concepts of *quantity* and *relative amount* are likely to be meaningful even to very young children and also that they provide a rich foundation for the exploration and development of general mathematical ideas. What is being proposed is not that abstract concepts should replace concrete activities and observations but rather they should be developed out of those activities and observations. The starting point for any general mathematical statement is the observation of relationships in a concrete context, or across a number of such contexts. The path from those observations to mathematical abstraction is simply inquiry into the generality of the observed relationships: Is that always true? How can we be sure?

Implementing the Recommendations: The El'konin-Davydov Curriculum and Beyond

Davydov (1975a), working with a group of colleagues in Russia in the 1960s, brought developmental-psychological, mathematical, and pedagogical considerations together in designing a curriculum for elementary and secondary school mathematics. All three of the recommendations drawn here—(a) that instructional design be guided by a long-term perspective, (b) that the concept of unit be a central focus, and (c) that instruction aim for establishing general relationships through inquiry about concrete observations—converge with the ideas of Davydov and his colleagues. The curriculum they developed, known today as the El'konin-Davydov curriculum, thus serves as a demonstration of the feasibility of implementing these recommendations in regular classroom instruction.

Although much of the research Davydov and his colleagues had done was lost when their work was disrupted by political turmoil in Russia in the late 1960s, the curriculum they developed is still in use today at over 100 schools in Russia. However, although they share historical roots and a common theoretical orientation, the groups at different schools are for the most part not working in close coordination with each other. As a result, the curriculum is not entirely homogeneous, although there is much in common across schools.

A 1999 assessment of the El'konin-Davydov curriculum in Russia tested the mathematics performance of 2,300 students who had received that curriculum at the end of third grade (the end of elementary school in the Russian system of education). Reporting the results of the testing, Vorontsov (n.d.) concluded "pupils learning in [this] educational system completely fulfill the requirements of the existing state standard" (p. 7). The percentages of students who succeeded on "tasks corresponding to the 'standard' level of elementary school" ranged from 86 to 96%, with the exception of a task that involved dividing multidigit numbers, on which 76% of the pupils tested were successful. In a comment reminiscent of the debate surrounding reform mathematics in the United States, Vorontsov goes on to state, "The results obtained dispel the myth, current in pedagogical circles, of the poor results of mastery of subject matter among children in [these] programs" (p. 7).

Although the El'konin-Davydov curriculum continues to attract the interest of researchers and educators outside of as well as within Russia (e.g., Dougherty, 2003; Steffe, 1975), the lack of homogeneity across contemporary implementations of the curriculum, together with the limited availability of historical records, make it difficult to simply adopt the curriculum and implement it as is in the United States or elsewhere. In addition, inevitable differences in sociocultural and historical contexts make it unclear whether this would be a desirable course of action even if it could be done. Many of the instructional methods introduced within it nevertheless do warrant further study and perhaps emulation. These include the practice of beginning mathematics instruction with a general treatment of the quantitative relations "equal to," "less than," and "greater than"; the practice of introducing numbers as representations of the relation between a unit and a total quantity; and the encouragement of classroom dialogue in which students are active participants in the construction of mathematical generalizations, explanations, and arguments.

The Measure Up curriculum currently in development in Hawaii (Dougherty, 2003) is a promising example of contemporary instructional work that follows the Elkonin-Davydov curriculum closely. A systematic evaluation of the impact of the Measure Up curriculum on student learning is not yet available. However, both theoretically and on the basis of classroom observations, it shows a great deal of promise.

A FRESH LOOK AT MATHEMATICS INSTRUCTION

Instructionally as well as developmentally (cf. chap. 7), there is not enough evidence at present to empirically evaluate the merits of the comparison-of-quantities perspective. At present, its primary value for mathematics instruction is as an invitation to reevaluate long-held assumptions and practices. One reason it is difficult to change the way mathematics is taught is because the expectations of parents and teachers alike are strongly shaped by cultural norms that dictate what children of a particular age should know about numbers. These norms create a sense of consensus that may disguise the fact that they are based more on social conventions than on any principled analysis of instructional objectives and how they can best be met.

In today's climate of concern with empirical outcomes, it is important to remember that the informativeness of outcome data is limited not only by the outcomes we choose to measure but also by the range of instructional approaches we include in our comparisons. Just as a scientist cannot evaluate an hypothesis she or he has never formulated, research on instructional outcomes cannot determine how existing approaches compare with possible ones that have not yet been developed. Therefore, unless we are confident that we have sampled the full range of potentially effective approaches, it is premature to conclude that the most successful within the approaches that have been tried is the best, or even a satisfactory approximation to the best, approach that can be developed.

An important contribution of the comparison-of-quantities perspective, then, is that it illuminates just how limited the range of instructional approaches that have been evaluated to date is. This is especially true for the first several years of mathematics instruction, whether because they have been seen as relatively unproblematic or simply because expectations about what students should be learning in the early grades are so strong and so widely shared. Whatever the reason, insofar as the kinds of instruction children receive in the first grades of school have strong ramifications for their later learning, the limited range of innovation in early instructional programs means that we also do not know a great deal as yet about the possible merits of alternative approaches to mathematics education as a whole. In short, because the comparison-of-quantities perspective and its instructional implications represent a very different and largely untested way of thinking about mathematics instruction than most contemporary practices are based on, they constitute a much-needed reminder of how much we do not yet know about how best to educate students in mathematics.

Naturally, the exploration of alternative instructional approaches should not be a trial-and-error one. In order to steer new instructional efforts in a productive direction, we need to draw upon the best knowledge we have. Davydov's (1975a) strategy was to draw upon mathematical, developmental-psychological, and pedagogical analyses to formulate a conceptually cohesive mathematics curriculum. In today's environment of specialization, developmental psychologists and mathematics educators pursue largely independent inquiries into children's mathematical thinking and learning. It is my view, however, that both perspectives remain essential to any comprehensive analysis of mathematics education. Correspondingly, in this book, I have undertaken to articulate the comparison-of-quantities perspective in relation to both developmental and instructional issues. In doing so, it is my hope to have encouraged greater recognition and appreciation of the complementarity and interdependence of work in developmental psychology and in mathematics education and also to have offered a fresh perspective on existing knowledge in both fields and on the important problem of how best to teach mathematics to children.

References

Anderson, N. H., & Cuneo, D. O. (1978). The height + width rule in children's judgment of quantity. *Journal of Experimental Psychology: General, 107*, 335–378.

Arcavi, A. (1995). Teaching and learning algebra: Past, present, and future. *Journal of Mathematical Behavior, 14*, 145–162.

Baillargeon, R., Kotovsky, L., & Needham, A. (1995). The acquisition of physical knowledge in infancy. In D. Sperber, D. Premack, & A. J. Premack (Eds.), *Causal cognition* (pp. 79–116). Oxford, England: Clarendon Press.

Ball, D. L., Ferrini-Mundy, J., Kilpatrick, J., Milgram, R. J., Schmid, W., & Schaar, R. (2005). Reaching for common ground in K–12 mathematics education. Retrieved from http://www.maa.org/common-ground/cg-report2005.html

Baroody, A. J. (1984). More precisely defining and measuring the order-irrelevance principle. *Journal of Experimental Child Psychology, 38*, 33–41.

Baroody, A. J. (1999). The roles of estimation and the commutativity principle in the development of third graders' mental multiplication. *Journal of Experimental Child Psychology, 74*, 157–193.

Baroody, A. J., & Gannon, K. E. (1984). The development of the commutativity principle and economical addition strategies. *Cognition and Instruction, 1*, 321–339.

Barrett, J. E., & Clements, D. H. (2003). Quantifying path length: Fourth-grade children's developing abstractions for linear measurement. *Cognition and Instruction, 21*, 475–520.

Bausano, M. K., & Jeffrey, W. E. (1975). Dimensional salience and judgments of bigness by three-year-old children. *Child Development, 46*, 988–991.

Behr, M., Harel, G., Post, T., & Lesh, R. (1994). Units of quantity: A conceptual basis common to additive and multiplicative structures. In G. Harel & J. Confrey (Eds.), *The development of multiplicative reasoning in the learning of mathematics* (pp. 121–176). Albany: State University of New York Press.

Behr, M. J., Harel, G., Post, T., & Lesh, R. (1992). Rational number, ratio, and proportion. In D. Grouws (Ed.), *Handbook of research on mathematics teaching and learning* (pp. 296–333). New York: Macmillan.

Behr, M. L., Wachsmuth, I., Post, T. R., & Lesh, R. (1984). Order and equivalence of rational numbers: A clinical teaching experiment. *Journal for Research in Mathematics Education, 15*, 323–341.

Bowers, J., Cobb, P., & McClain, K. (1999). The evolution of mathematical practices: A case study. *Cognition and Instruction, 17*, 25–64.

Brannon, E. M. (2002). The development of ordinal numerical knowledge in infancy. *Cognition, 83*, 223–240.

Brannon, E. M., Abbott, S., & Lutz, D. J. (2004). Number bias for the discrimination of large visual sets in infancy. *Cognition, 93*, B59–B68.

Brannon, E. M., & Van de Walle, G. A. (2001). The development of ordinal numerical competence in young children. *Cognitive Psychology, 43*, 53–81.

Briars, D., & Siegler, R. S. (1984). A featural analysis of preschoolers' counting knowledge. *Developmental Psychology, 20*, 607–618.

Briars, D. J., & Larkin, J. H. (1984). An integrated model of skill in solving elementary word problems. *Cognition and Instruction, 11*, 245–296.

Brown, J. S., & van Lehn, K. (1982). Towards a generative theory of "bugs." In T. P. Carpenter, J. M. Moser, & T. A. Romberg (Eds.), *Addition and subtraction: A cognitive perspective* (pp. 117–135). Hillsdale, NJ: Lawrence Erlbaum Associates.

Bryant, P., Christie, C., & Rendu, A. (1999). Children's understanding of the relation between addition and subtraction: Inversion, identity, and decomposition. *Journal of Experimental Child Psychology, 74*, 194–212.

Bryant, P. E. (1972). The understanding of invariance by very young children. *Canadian Journal of Psychology, 26*, 78–96.

Bryant, P. E. (1982). The role of conflict and of agreement between intellectual strategies in children's ideas about measurement. *British Journal of Psychology, 73*, 242–251.

Bryant, P. E., & Kopytynska, H. (1976). Spontaneous measurement by young children. *Nature, 260*, 773.

Budd, K., Carson, E., Garelick, B., Klein, D., Milgram, R. J., Ramimi, R. A., Schwartz, M., Stotsky, S., Williams, V., & Wilson, W. S. (2005). *Ten myths about mathematics education and why you shouldn't believe them*. http://www.nychold.com/myths-050504.html

Butterworth, B. (1999). *The mathematical brain*. New York: Macmillan.

Byrnes, J. P., & Wasik, B. A. (1991). Role of conceptual knowledge in mathematical and procedural learning. *Developmental Psychology, 27*, 777–786.

Calsyn, C., Gonzales, P., & Frase, M. (1999). *Highlights from TIMSS: Overview and key findings across grade levels*. Washington, DC: National Council for Education Statistics. (ERIC Document Reproduction Service No. ED422190)

Canobi, K. H., Reeve, R. A., & Pattison, P. E. (2003). Patterns of knowledge in children's addition. *Developmental Psychology, 39*, 521–534.

Carey, S. (2001). Cognitive foundations of arithmetic: Evolution and ontogenesis. *Mind & Language, 16*, 37–55.

Carpenter, T. P., Ansell, E., Franke, M. L., Fennema, E., & Weisbeck, L. (1993). Models of problem-solving: A study of kindergarten children's problem-solving processes. *Journal for Research in Mathematics Education, 24*, 428–441.

Carpenter, T. P., Hiebert, J., & Moser J. M. (1981). Problem structure and first-grade children's initial solution processes for simple addition and subtraction problems. *Journal for Research in Mathematics Education, 12*, 27–39.

Carraher, T. N., Carraher, D. W., & Schliemann, A. D. (1985). Mathematics in the streets and in schools. *British Journal of Developmental Psychology, 3*, 21–29.

Carraher, T. N., Carraher, D. W., & Schliemann, A. D. (1987). Written and oral mathematics. *Journal for Research in Mathematics Education, 18*, 83–97.

Case, R., Kurland, M., & Goldberg, J. (1982). Operational efficiency and the growth of short term memory. *Journal of Experimental Child Psychology, 33*, 386–404.

Charman, T., & Baron-Cohen, S. (1995). Understanding photos, models, and beliefs: A test of the modularity thesis of theory of mind. *Cognitive Development, 10*, 287–298.

Chomsky, N. (1959). A review of B. F. Skinner's *Verbal Behavior. Language, 35*, 26–58.

Clearfield, M. W., & Mix, K. S. (1999). Number versus contour length in infants' discrimination of small visual sets. *Psychological Science, 10*, 408–411.

Clearfield, M. W., & Mix, K. S. (2001). Amount versus number: Infants' use of area and contour length to discriminate small sets. *Journal of Cognition and Development, 2*, 243–260.

Clearfield, M. W., & Westfahl, S. M.–C. (2006). Familiarization in infants' perception of addition problems. *Journal of Cognition and Development, 7*, 27–43.

Clements, D. (1999). Teaching length measurement: Research challenges. *School Science and Mathematics, 99*, 5–11.

Cobb, P., Wood, T., Yackel, E., & McNeal, B. (1992). Characteristics of classroom mathematics traditions: An interactional analysis. *American Educational Research Journal, 29*, 573–604.

Cohen, L. B., & Marks, K. S. (2002). How infants process addition and subtraction events. *Developmental Science, 5*, 186–212.

Cole, M. (1992). Culture in development. In M. E. Lamb (Ed.), *Developmental psychology: An advanced textbook* (pp. 731–784). Hillsdale, NJ: Lawrence Erlbaum Associates.

Coley, J. D., & Gelman, S. A. (1989). The effects of object orientation and object type on children's interpretation of the word *big. Child Development, 69*, 372–380.

Confrey, J. (1994). Splitting, similarity, and rate of change: A new approach to multiplication and exponential functions. In G. Harel & J. Confrey (Eds.), *The development of multiplicative reasoning in the learning of mathematics* (pp. 291–330). Albany: State University of New York Press.

Cooper, R. G., Jr. (1984). Early number development: Discovering number space with addition and subtraction. In C. Sophian (Ed.), *Origins of cognitive skills* (pp. 157–192). Hillsdale, NJ: Lawrence Erlbaum Associates.

Correa, J., Nunes, T., & Bryant, P. (1998). Young children's understanding of division: The relationship between division terms in a noncomputational task. *Journal of Educational Psychology, 90*, 321–329.

Cowan, R. (1987). Assessing children's understanding of one-to-one correspondence. *British Journal of Developmental Psychology, 5*, 149–153.

Cowan, R., Dowker, A., Christakis, A., & Bailey, S. (1996). Even more precisely assessing children's understanding of the order-irrelevance principle. *Journal of Experimental Child Psychology, 62*, 84–101.

Cramer, K., & Post, T. (1995). Facilitating children's development of rational number knowledge. In D. Owens, M. Reed, and G. Millsaps (Eds.), *Proceedings of the Seventeenth Annual Meeting of PME-NA.* (pp. 377–382). Columbus, OH: Psychology of Mathematics Education.

Cramer, K. A., Post, T. R., & del Mas, R. C. (2002). Initial fraction learning by fourth- and fifth-grade students: A comparison of the effects of using commercial curricula with the effects of using the Rational Number Project Curriculum. *Journal for Research in Mathematics Education, 33*, 111–144.

Cummins, D. D. (1988). The role of understanding in solving word problems. *Cognitive Psychology, 20*, 405–438.

Cummins, D. D. (1991). Children's interpretations of arithmetic word problems. *Cognition and Instruction, 8*, 261–289.

Davydov, V. V. (1975a). Logical and psychological problems of elementary mathematics as an academic subject. In L. P. Steffe (Ed.), *Children's capacity for learning mathematics. Soviet studies in the psychology of learning and teaching mathematics* (Vol. 7, pp. 55–107). Chicago: University of Chicago Press.

Davydov, V. V. (1975b). The psychological characteristics of the "prenumerical" period of mathematics instruction. In L. P. Steffe (Ed.), *Children's capacity for learning mathematics. Soviet studies in the psychology of learning and teaching mathematics* (Vol. 7, pp. 109–205). Chicago: University of Chicago Press.

Davydov, V. V., & Tsvetkovich, Z. H. (1991). The object sources of the concept of fractions. In L. P. Steffe (Ed.), *Soviet studies in mathematics education: Psychological abilities of primary children in learning mathematics* (Vol. 6, pp. 86–147). Reston, VA: National Council of Teachers of Mathematics.

Dean, A. L., & Malik, M. M. (1986). Representing and solving arithmetic word problems: A study of developmental interaction. *Cognition and Instruction, 3*, 211–227.

De Corte, E., & Verschaffel, L. (1987). Using retelling data to study young children's word-problem-solving. In J. A. Sloboda & D. Rogers (Eds.), *Cognitive processes in mathematics* (pp. 42–59). Oxford, England: Clarendon Press.

De Corte, E., Verschaffel, L., & De Win, L. (1985). Influence of rewording verbal problems on children's problem representations and solutions. *Journal of Educational Psychology, 77*, 460–470.

Dehaene, S. (1992). Varieties of numerical abilities. *Cognition, 44*, 1–42.

Dehaene, S. (1997). *The number sense: How the mind creates mathematics*. Oxford University Press.

Dehaene, S. (2002). Author's response: Is number sense a patchwork? *Mind & Language, 16*, 89–100.

Dehaene, S., & Cohen, L. (1991). Two mental calculation systems: A case study of severe acalculia with preserved approximation. *Neuropsychologia, 29*, 1045–1074.

Dehaene, S., Spelke, E. S., Pinel, P., Stanescu, R., & Tsivkin, S. (1999). Sources of mathematical thinking: Behavioral and brain-imaging evidence. *Science, 284*, 970–974.

Dewey, J. (1990). *The child and the curriculum*. Chicago: University of Chicago Press. (Original work published 1956)

Dougherty, B. (2003, July). *Measure up*. Plenary address at the meetings of the International Group for the Psychology of Mathematics Education, Honolulu, HI.

Dougherty, B., Okazaki, C., Zenigami, F., & Venenciano, L. (2005). *Measure Up grade 1, 4th draft. Teacher notes & masters and student materials*. Honolulu, HI: Curriculum Research and Development Group.

Dougherty, B., Okazaki, C., & Zenigami, F. (2006). *Measure Up grade 4, draft. Teacher notes & masters and student materials*. Honolulu, HI: Curriculum Research and Development Group.

Durkin, K., Shire, B., Riem, R., Crowther, R. D., & Rutter, D. R. (1986). The social and linguistic context of early number word use. *British Journal of Developmental Psychology, 4*, 269–288.

Empson, S. B. (1999). Equal sharing and shared meaning: The development of fraction concepts in a first-grade classroom. *Cognition and Instruction, 17*, 283–342.

English, L. D., & Halford, G. S. (1995). *Mathematics education: Models and processes*. Mahwah, NJ: Lawrence Erlbaum Associates.

Fantz, R. L. (1958). Pattern vision in young infants. *Psychological Review, 8*, 43–47.

Fantz, R. L. (1964). Visual experience in infants: Decreased attention to familiar patterns relative to novel ones. *Science, 146*, 668–670.

Feigenson, L. (2005). A double-dissociation in infants' representations of object arrays. *Cognition, 95*, B37–B48.

Feigenson, L., Carey, S., & Spelke, E. (2002). Infants' discrimination of number vs. continuous extent. *Cognitive Psychology, 44*, 33–66.

Fodor, J. (1983). *The modularity of mind*. Cambridge, MA: MIT Press.

Frydman, O., & Bryant, P. (1988). Sharing and the understanding of number equivalence by young children. *Cognitive Development, 3*, 323–339.

Frye, D., Braisby, N., Love, J., Maroudas, C., & Nicholls, J. (1989). Young children's understanding of counting and cardinality. *Child Development, 60*, 1158–1171.

Fuson, K. C. (1988). *Children's counting and concepts of number*. New York: Springer-Verlag.

Fuson, K. C., & Briars, D. (1990). Using a base-ten blocks learning/teaching approach for first- and second-grade place-value and multidigit addition and subtraction. *Journal for Research in Mathematics Education, 21*, 180–206.

Fuson, K. C., Pergament, G. G., Lyons, B. G., & Hall, J. W. (1985). Children's conformity to the cardinality rule as a function of set size and counting accuracy. *Child Development, 56*, 1429–1436.

Gallistel, C. R., & Gelman, R. (1992). Preverbal and verbal counting and computation. *Cognition, 44*, 43–74.

Gal'perin, P., & Georgiev, L. S. (1969). The formation of elementary mathematical notions. In J. Kilpatrick & I. Wirszup (Eds.), *Soviet studies in the psychology of learning and teaching mathematics: The learning of mathematical concepts* (Vol. 1, pp. 189–216). Chicago: University of Chicago Press.

Gao, F., Levine, S. C., & Huttenlocher, J. (2000). What do infants know about continuous quantity? *Journal of Experimental Child Psychology, 77*, 20–29.

Gathercole, V. C. (1985). More and more and more about more. *Journal of Experimental Child Psychology, 40*, 73–104.

Geary, D. C. (1995). Reflections of evolution and culture in children's cognition: Implications for mathematical development and instruction. *American Psychologist, 50*, 24–37.

Geary, D. C., & Hamson, C. O. (2005). *Improving the mathematics and science achievement of American children: Psychology's role*. Retrieved December 30, 2005, from http://www.apa.org/ed/geary.html

Gelman, R. (1982). Accessing one-to-one correspondence: Still another paper about conservation. *British Journal of Psychology, 73*, 209–220.

Gelman, R. (1991). Epigenetic foundations of knowledge structures: Initial and transcendent constructions. In S. Carey & R. Gelman (Eds.), *The epigenesis of mind: Essays on biology and cognition* (pp. 293–322). Hillsdale, NJ: Lawrence Erlbaum Associates.

Gelman, R. (1993). A rational-constructivist account of early learning about numbers and objects. In D. Medin (Ed.), *Learning and motivation* (pp. 61–96). New York: Academic Press.

Gelman, R. (1998). Domain specificity in cognitive development: Universals and nonuniversals. In M. Sabourin, F. Craik, & M. Roberts (Eds.), *Advances in psychological science: Biological and cognitive aspects* (Vol. 2, pp. 557–579). East Sussex, England: Psychology Press.

Gelman, R., & Gallistel, C. R. (1978). *The child's understanding of number*. Cambridge, MA: Harvard University Press.

Gelman, R., & Meck, E. (1983). Preschoolers' counting: Principles before skill. *Cognition, 13*, 343–359.

Gelman, S. A., & Wellman, H. M. (1991). Insides and essences: Early understandings of the non-obvious. *Cognition, 38*, 213–244.

Gopnik, A., & Wellman, H. M. (1994). The theory theory. In L. A. Hirschfeld & S. A. Gelman (Eds.), *Mapping the mind: Domain specificity in cognition and culture* (pp. 257–293). New York: Cambridge University Press.

Greer, B. (1992). Multiplication and division as models of situations. In D. Grouws (Ed.), *Handbook of research on mathematics teaching and learning* (pp. 276–295). New York: Macmillan.

Groen, G., & Resnick, L. B. (1977). Can preschool children invent addition algorithms? *Journal of Educational Psychology, 69,* 645–652.

Haith, M. M. (1998). Who put the cog in infant cognition? *Infant Behavior & Development, 21,* 167–179.

Hamm, J. V., & Perry, M. (2002). Learning mathematics in first-grade classrooms: On whose authority? *Journal of Educational Psychology, 94,* 126–137.

Hecht, S. A., Close, L., & Santisi, M. (2003). Sources of individual differences in fraction skills. *Journal of Experimental Child Psychology, 86,* 277–302.

Hiebert, J. (1982). The position of the unknown set and children's solutions of verbal arithmetic problems. *Journal for Research in Mathematics Education, 13,* 341–349.

Hiebert, J. (1984a). Children's mathematics learning: The struggle to link form and understanding. *The Elementary School Journal, 84,* 497–513.

Hiebert, J. (1984b, March). Why do some children have trouble learning measurement concepts? *Arithmetic Teacher,* 19–24.

Hiebert, J., & Wearne, D. (1985). A model of students' decimal computation procedures. *Cognition and Instruction, 2,* 175–205.

Hiebert, J., & Wearne, D. (1992). Links between teaching and learning place value with understanding in first grade. *Journal for Research in Mathematics Education, 23,* 98–122.

Hirschfeld, L., & Gelman, S. (Eds.). (1994). *Mapping the mind: Domain specificity in cognition and culture.* Cambridge, England: Cambridge University Press.

Hobbs, M., & Bacharach, V. R. (1990). Children's understanding of big buildings and big cars. *Child Study Journal, 20,* 1–18.

Hoff, D. J. (2003, Feb. 19). Adding it all up. *Education Week,* 22(23). Retrieved November 15, 2004, from http://www.edweek.org/ew/ewstory.cfm?slug=23research.h22

Hudson, T. (1983). Correspondences and numerical differences between disjoint sets. *Child Development, 54,* 84–90.

Hunting, R. P., & Davis, G. E. (1991a). Dimensions of young children's conceptions of the fraction one half. In R. P. Hunting & G. E. Davis (Eds.), *Early fraction learning* (pp. 27–53). New York: Springer-Verlag.

Hunting, R. P., & Davis, G. E. (Eds.). (1991b). *Early fraction learning.* New York: Springer-Verlag.

Huttenlocher, J., Newcombe, N., & Sandberg, E. H. (1994). The coding of spatial location in young children. *Cognitive Psychology, 27,* 115–147.

Ibarra, C. G., & Lindvall, C. M. (1982). Factors associated with the ability of kindergarten children to solve simple arithmetic story problems. *Journal of Educational Research, 75,* 149–155.

Inhelder, B., & Piaget, J. (1958). *The growth of logical thinking from childhood to adolescence.* New York: Basic Books.

Inhelder, B., & Piaget, J. (1964). *The early growth of logic in the child: Classification and seriation.* New York: Harper & Row.

Inhelder, B., Sinclair, H., & Bovet, M. (1974). *Learning and the development of cognition.* Cambridge, MA: Harvard University Press.

Johnston, T. D., & Edwards, L. (2002). Genes, interactions, and the development of behavior. *Psychological Review, 109,* 26–34.

Kahneman, D., Treisman, A., & Gibbs, B. (1992). The reviewing of object files: Object specific integration of information. *Cognitive Psychology, 24,* 175–219.

Kail, R. V. (2004). Cognitive development includes global and domain-specific processes. *Merrill-Palmer Quarterly, 50*, 445–455.

Kamii, C., & Clark, F. B. (1995). Equivalent fractions: Their difficulty and educational implications. *Journal of Mathematical Behavior,* 365–378.

Kamii, C. K. (1985). *Young children reinvent arithmetic.* New York: Teachers College Press.

Kersting, K. (2003). Bolstering evidence-based education. *APA Monitor, 34*, 56.

Kieren, T. (1988). Personal knowledge of rational numbers: Its intuitive and formal development. In J. Hiebert & M. Behr (Eds.), *Number concepts and operations in the middle grades* (pp. 53–92). Reston, VA: National Council of Teachers of Mathematics.

Kilpatrick, J., Swafford, J., & Findell, B. (2001). *Adding it up: Helping children learn mathematics.* Washington, DC: National Academy Press.

Kintsch, W., & Greeno, J. G. (1985). Understanding and solving arithmetic word problems. *Psychological Review, 9*, 109–129.

Klahr, D., & Wallace, J. G. (1976). *Cognitive development: An information-processing view.* Hillsdale, NJ: Lawrence Erlbaum Associates.

Koechlin, E., Dehaene, S., & Mehler, J. (1997). Numerical transformations in five-month-old human infants. *Mathematical Cognition, 3*, 89–104.

Kornilaki, E., & Nunes, T. (2005). Generalizing principles in spite of procedural differences: Children's understanding of division. *Cognitive Development, 20*, 388–406.

Kouba, V. (1989). Children's solution strategies for equivalent set multiplication and division word problems. *Journal for Research in Mathematics Education, 20*, 147–158.

Kribs-Zaleta, C. M., & Bradshaw, D. (2003). A case of units. *Teaching Children Mathematics, 9*, 397–399.

Lamon, S. J. (1993). Ratio and proportion: Connecting content and children's thinking. *Journal for Research in Mathematics Education, 24*, 41–61.

Lampert, M. (1986). Knowing, doing, and teaching multiplication. *Cognition and Instruction, 3*, 305–342.

Lawton, C. A. (1993). Contextual factors affecting errors in proportional reasoning. *Journal for Research in Mathematics Education, 24*, 460–466.

Laxon, V. J. (1981). On the problems of being more or less the same. *Journal of Experimental Child Psychology, 31*, 531–543.

Le Corre, M., Van de Walle, G., Brannon, E. M., & Carey, S. (2006). Re-visiting the competence/performance debate in the acquisition of the counting principles. *Cognitive Psychology, 52*, 136–169.

Lehrer, R., & Lesh, R. (2003). Mathematical learning. In W. Reynolds & G. Miller (Eds.), *Comprehensive handbook of psychology* (Vol. 7, pp. 357–391). New York: Wiley.

Leslie, A. M. (1994). ToMM, ToBy, and agency: Core architecture and domain specificity. In L. Hirschfeld & S. Gelman (Eds.), *Mapping the mind: Domain specificity in cognition and culture* (pp. 119–148). Cambridge, England: Cambridge University Press.

Lickliter, R., & Honeycutt, H. (2003). Developmental dynamics: Toward a biologically plausible evolutionary psychology. *Psychological Bulletin, 129*, 819–838.

Light, P. H., Buckingham, N., & Robbins, A. H. (1979). The conservation task as an interactional setting. *British Journal of Educational Psychology, 49*, 304–310.

Lipton, J. S., & Spelke, E. S. (2003). Origins of number sense: Large-number discrimination in human infants. *Psychological Science, 14*, 396–401.

Lipton, J. S., & Spelke, E. S. (2004). Discrimination of large and small numerosities by human infants. *Infancy, 5*, 271–290.

Locke, J. (1894). *An essay concerning human understanding* (Vol. 1). New York: Dover.

Mack, N. K. (1995). Confounding whole-number and fraction concepts when building on informal knowledge. *Journal for Research in Mathematics Education, 26*, 422–441.

Mandler, G., & Shebo, B. J. (1982). Subitizing: An analysis of its component processes. *Journal of Experimental Psychology: General, 11*, 1–22.

Markman, E. M. (1979). Classes and collections: Conceptual organization and numerical abilities. *Cognitive Psychology, 11*, 395–411.

Markman, E. M. (1990). Constraints children place on word meanings. *Cognitive Science, 14*, 57–77.

McCrink, R., & Wynn, K. (2004). Large-number addition and subtraction by 9-month-old infants. *Psychological Science, 15*, 776–781.

McGarrigle, J., & Donaldson, M. (1975). Conservation accidents. *Cognition, 3*, 341–350.

McGarrigle, J., Grieve, R., & Hughes, M. (1978). Interpreting inclusion: A contribution to the study of the child's cognitive and linguistic development. *Journal of Experimental Child Psychology, 26*, 528–550.

Meck, W., & Church, R. M. (1983). A mode-control model of counting and timing processes. *Journal of Experimental Psychology: Animal Behavior Processes, 9*, 320–334.

Michie, S. (1984). Why preschoolers are reluctant to count spontaneously. *British Journal of Developmental Psychology, 2*, 347–358.

Miller, K. F. (1984). Child as the measurer of all things: Measurement procedures and the development of quantitative concepts. In C. Sophian (Ed.), *Origins of cognitive skills* (pp. 193–228). Hillsdale, NJ: Lawrence Erlbaum Associates.

Miller, K. F. (1989). Measurement as a tool for thought: The role of measuring procedures in children's understanding of quantitative invariance. *Developmental Psychology, 25*, 589–600.

Miller, K. F., & Baillargeon, R. (1990). Length and distance: Do preschoolers think that occlusion brings things together? *Developmental Psychology, 26*, 103–114.

Miller, K. F., Smith, C. M., Zhu, J., & Zhang, H. (1995). Preschool origins of cross-national differences in mathematical competence: The role of number-naming systems. *Psychological Science, 6*, 56–60.

Miller, S. A. (1976). Nonverbal assessment of Piagetian concepts. *Psychological Bulletin, 83*, 405–430.

Miura, I. T., Okamoto, Y., Kim, C. C., Chang, C.–M., Steere, M., & Fayol, M. (1994). Comparisons of children's cognitive representation of number: China, France, Japan, Korea, Sweden and the United States. *International Journal of Behavioural Development, 17*, 401–411.

Miura, I. T., Okamoto, Y., Vlahovic-Stetic, V., Kim, C. C., & Han, J. H. (1999). Language supports for children's understanding of numerical fractions: Cross-national comparisons. *Journal of Experimental Child Psychology, 74*, 356–365.

Mix, K. S., Huttenlocher, J., & Levine, S. C. (2002). Multiple cues for quantification in infancy: Is number one of them? *Psychological Review, 128*, 278–294.

Mix, K. S., Levine, S. C., & Huttenlocher, J. (1997). Numerical abstraction in infants: Another look. *Developmental Psychology, 33*, 423–428.

Moore, C., & Frye, D. (1986). Context, conservation and the meanings of *more*. *British Journal of Developmental Psychology, 4*, 169–178.

Moore, C. F., Dixon, J. A., & Haines, B. A. (1991). Components of understanding in proportional reasoning: A fuzzy set representation of developmental progressions. *Child Development, 62*, 441–459.

Moore, D., Benenson, J., Reznick, J. S., Peterson, M., & Kagan, J. (1987). Effect of auditory numerical information on infants' looking behavior: Contradictory evidence. *Developmental Psychology, 23*, 665–670.

Moss, J. (2002). Percents and proportion at the center: Altering the teaching sequence for rational number. In B. Litwiller & G. Bright (Eds.), *Making sense of fractions, ratios, and proportions* (pp. 109–120). Reston, VA: National Council of Teachers of Mathematics.

Moss, J., & Case, R. (1999). Developing children's understanding of the rational numbers: A new model and an experimental curriculum. *Journal for Research in Mathematics Education, 30*, 122–147.

National Council of Teachers of Mathematics (2000). *Principles & standards for school mathematics*. Retrieved November 25, 2005, from http://standards.nctm.org/document/appendix/process.htm#bp2

Neilson, I., Dockrell, J., & McKechnie, J. (1983). Does repetition of the question influence children's performance in conservation tasks? *British Journal of Developmental Psychology, 1*, 163–174.

Nesher, P., Greeno, J. G., & Riley, M. S. (1982). The development of semantic categories for addition and subtraction. *Educational Studies in Mathematics, 13*, 373–394.

Neufeldt, V., & Guralnik, D. B. (Eds.). (1994). *Webster's new world dictionary, 3rd college edition*. New York: Simon & Schuster.

Ni, Y. (2001). Semantic domains of rational numbers and the acquisition of fraction equivalence. *Contemporary Educational Psychology, 26*, 400–417.

Nunes, T., & Bryant, P. (1995). Do problem situations influence children's understanding of the commutativity of multiplication? *Mathematical Cognition, 1*, 245–260.

Nunes, T., & Bryant, P. (1996). *Children doing mathematics*. Oxford, England: Blackwell.

Nunes, T., Light, P., & Mason, J. (1993). Tools for thought: The measurement of length and area. *Learning and Instruction, 3*, 39–54.

Ohlsson, S. (1991). Knowledge requirements for teaching: The case of fractions. In P. Goodyear (Ed.), *Teaching knowledge and intelligent tutoring* (pp. 25–59). Norwood, NJ: Ablex.

Park, J. –H., & Nunes, T. (2001). The development of the concept of multiplication. *Cognitive Development, 16*, 763–773.

Peterson, P. L. (1994). Knowledge transforming: Teachers, students, and researchers as learners in a community. In J. Mangieri & C. C. Block (Eds.), *Creating powerful thinking in teachers and students: Diverse perspectives* (pp. 51–79). New York: Holt, Rinehart & Winston.

Piaget, J. (1952). *The child's conception of number*. New York: Norton.

Piaget, J. (1969). *The psychology of the child*. New York: Basic Books.

Piaget, J. (1970). Piaget's theory. In P. H. Mussen (Ed.), *Carmichael's manual of child psychology* (Vol. 1, pp. 703–732). New York: Wiley.

Piaget, J., & Inhelder, B. (1975). *The origin of the idea of chance in children*. New York: Norton.

Piaget, J., Inhelder, B., & Szeminska, A. (1960). *The child's conception of geometry*. New York: Harper.

Pinker, S. (1995). *The language instinct*. New York: HarperCollins.

Rasmussen, C., Ho, E., & Bisanz, J. (2003). Use of the mathematical principle of inversion in young children. *Journal of Experimental Child Psychology, 85*, 89–102.

Ravn, K. E., & Gelman, S. A. (1984). Rule usage in children's understanding of "Big" and "Little". *Child Development, 55*, 2141–2150.

Resnick, L. B. (1982). Syntax and semantics in learning to subtract. In T. P. Carpenter, J. M. Moser, & T. A. Romberg (Eds.), *Addition and subtraction: A cognitive perspective* (pp. 25–38). Hillsdale, NJ: Lawrence Erlbaum Associates.

Resnick, L. B. (1989). Developing mathematical knowledge. *American Psychologist, 44*, 162–169.

Resnick, L. B. (1992). From protoquantities to operators: Building mathematical competence on a foundation of everyday knowledge. In G. Leinhardt, R. Putnam, & R. A. Hattrup (Eds.), *Analysis of arithmetic for mathematics teaching* (pp. 373–429). Hillsdale, NJ: Lawrence Erlbaum Associates.

Resnick, L. B. (1994). Situated rationalism: Biological and social preparation for learning. In L. Hirschfeld & S. Gelman (Eds.), *Mapping the mind: Domain specificity in cognition and culture* (pp. 474–493). Cambridge, England: Cambridge University Press.

Resnick, L. B., & Omanson, S. F. (1987). Learning to understand arithmetic. In R. Glaser (Ed.), *Advances in instructional psychology* (Vol. 3, pp. 41–95). Hillsdale, NJ: Lawrence Erlbaum Associates.

Resnick, L .B., & Singer, J. A. (1993). Protoquantitative origins of ratio reasoning. In: T. Carpenter, E. Fennema, & T. Romberg (Eds.), *Rational numbers: An integration of research* (pp. 107–130). Hillsdale, NJ: Lawrence Erlbaum Associates.

Riley, M. S., Greeno, J. G., & Heller, J. I. (1983). Development of children's problem-solving ability in arithmetic. In H. P. Ginsburg (Ed.), *The development of mathematical thinking* (pp. 153–196). New York: Academic Press.

Rittle-Johnson, B., Siegler, R. S., & Alibali, M. W. (2001). Developing conceptual understanding and procedural skill in mathematics: An iterative process. *Journal of Educational Psychology, 93*, 346–362.

Robinson, K. M., & Ninowski, J. E. (2003). Adults' understanding of inversion concepts: How does performance on addition and subtraction inversion problems compare to performance on multiplication and division inversion problems? *Canadian Journal of Experimental Psychology, 57*, 321–330.

Sackur-Grisvard, C., & Leonard, F. (1985). Intermediate cognitive organizations in the process of learning a mathematical concept: The order of positive decimal numbers. *Cognition and Instruction, 2*, 157–174.

Saxe, G. B. (1977). A developmental analysis of notational counting. *Child Development, 48*, 1512–1520.

Saxe, G. B. (1979). Children's counting: The early formation of numerical symbols. *New Directions for Child Development, 3*, 73–84.

Saxe, G. B., & Moylan, T. (1982). The development of measurement operations among the Oksapmin of Papua New Guinea. *Child Development, 53*, 1242–1248.

Schaeffer, B., Eggleston, V. H., & Scott, J. L. (1974). Number development in young children. *Cognitive Psychology, 6*, 357–379.

Schliemann, A. D., & Carraher, D. W. (2002). The evolution of mathematical reasoning: Everyday versus idealized understandings. *Developmental Review, 22*, 242–266.

Schoenfeld, A. (1985). *Mathematical problem solving*. New York: Academic Press.

Schoeneld, A. H. (1986). On having and using geometric knowledge. In J. Hiebert (Ed.), *Conceptual and procedural knowledge: The case of mathematics* (pp. 225–264). Hillsdale, NJ: Lawrence Erlbaum Associates.

Schoenfeld, A. H. (1988). When good teaching leads to bad results: The disasters of "well-taught" mathematics courses. *Educational Psychology, 23*, 145–166.

Schoenfeld, A. H. (2004). The math wars. *Educational Policy, 18*, 253–286.

Schoenfeld, A. H. (2006). What doesn't work: The challenge and failure of the What Works Clearinghouse to conduct meaningful reviews of studies of mathematics curricula. *Educational Researcher, 35*, 13–21.

Sera, M., & Smith, L. B. (1987). *Big* and *Little*: "Nominal" and relative uses. *Cognitive Development, 2*, 89–111.

Sherman, T. (1985). Categorization skills in infants. *Child Development, 56*, 1561–1573.

Shipley, E. F., & Shepperson, B. (1990). Countable entities: Developmental changes. *Cognition, 34*, 109–136.

Siegler, R. S. (1979). What young children do know. *Contemporary Psychology, 24*, 613–615.

Siegler, R. S. (1987). The perils of averaging data over strategies: An example from children's addition. *Journal of Experimental Psychology: General, 116*, 250–264.

Siegler, R. S. (1988). Strategy choice procedures and the development of multiplication skill. *Journal of Experimental Psychology: General, 117*, 258–275.

Siegler, R. S. (1995). How does change occur: A microgenetic study of number conservation. *Cognitive Psychology, 28*, 225–273.

Silver, E. A. (1986). Using conceptual and procedural knowledge: A focus on relationships. In J. Hiebert (Ed.), *Conceptual and procedural knowledge: The case of mathematics* (pp. 181–198). Hillsdale, NJ: Lawrence Erlbaum Associates.

Simon, T. (1997). Reconceptualizing the origins of number knowledge: A "non-numerical" account. *Cognitive Development, 12*, 349–372.

Simon, T. J., Hespos, S. J., & Rochat, P. (1995). Do infants understand simple arithmetic? A replication of Wynn (1992). *Cognitive Development, 10*, 253–269.

Singer, J. A., Kohn, A. S., & Resnick, L. B. (1997). Knowing about proportions in different contexts. In T. Nunes & P. Bryant (Eds.), *Learning and teaching mathematics* (pp. 115–132). East Sussex, England: Psychology Press.

Smith, C. L., Solomon, G. E. A., & Carey, S. (2005). Never getting to zero: Elementary school students' understanding of the infinite divisibility of number and matter. *Cognitive Psychology, 51*, 101–140.

Sophian, C. (1987). Early developments in children's use of counting to solve quantitative problems. *Cognition and Instruction, 4*, 61–90.

Sophian, C. (1988). Limitations on children's knowledge about counting: Using counting to compare two sets. *Developmental Psychology, 24*, 634–640.

Sophian, C. (1997). Beyond competence: The significance of performance for conceptual development. *Cognitive Development, 12*, 281–303.

Sophian, C. (2000a). From objects to quantities: Developments in preschool childrens' judgments about aggregate amount. *Developmental Psychology, 36*, 724–730.

Sophian, C. (2000b). Perceptions of proportionality in young children: Matching spatial ratios. *Cognition, 75*, 145–170.

Sophian, C. (2002). Learning about what fits: Preschool children's reasoning about effects of object size. *Journal for Research in Mathematics Education, 33*, 290–302.

Sophian, C. (2004). Mathematics for the future: Developing a Head Start curriculum to support mathematics learning. *Early Childhood Research Quarterly, 19*, 59–81.

Sophian, C., Garyantes, D., & Chang, C. (1997). When three is less than two: Early developments in children's understanding of fractional quantities. *Developmental Psychology, 33*, 731–744.

Sophian, C., Harley, H., & Martin, C. S. (1995). Relational and representational aspects of early number development. *Cognition and Instruction, 13*, 253–268.

Sophian, C., & Kailihiwa, C. (1998). Units of counting: Developmental changes. *Cognitive Development, 13*, 561–585.

Sophian, C., & Madrid, S. (2003). Young children's reasoning about many-to-one correspondences. *Child Development, 74*, 1418–1432.

Sophian, C., & Madrid, S. (2004, August). *The importance of units in preparing children for fractions*. Paper presented at the International Congress of Psychology, Beijing.

Sophian, C., & McCorgray, P. (1994). Part–whole knowledge and early arithmetic problem solving. *Cognition and Instruction, 12*, 3–33.

Sophian, C., & Vong, K. I. (1995). The parts and wholes of arithmetic story problems: Developing knowledge in the preschool years. *Cognition and Instruction, 13*, 469–477.

Sophian, C., Wood, A., & Vong, K. I. (1995). Making numbers count: The early development of numerical inferences. *Developmental Psychology, 31*, 263–273.

Spelke, E. S., Breinlinger, K., Macomber, J., & Jacobson, K. (1992). Origins of knowledge. *Psychological Review, 99*, 605–632.

Spelke, E. S., & Tsivkin, S. (2001). Initial knowledge and conceptual change: Space and number. In M. Bowerman & S. Levinson (Eds.), *Language acquisition and conceptual development* (pp. 70–97). Cambridge, England: Cambridge University Press.

Spinillo, A. G., & Bryant, P. E. (1991). Children's proportional judgments: The importance of "half". *Child Development, 62*, 427–440.

Spinillo, A. G., & Bryant, P. E. (1999). Proportional reasoning in young children: Part–part comparisons about continuous and discontinuous quantity. *Mathematical Cognition, 5*, 181–197.

Stafylidou, S., & Vosniadou, S. (2004). The development of students' understanding of the numerical value of fractions. *Learning and Instruction, 14*, 503–518.

Starkey, P., & Cooper, R. G., Jr. (1980). Perception of numbers by human infants. *Science, 210*, 1033–1035.

Starkey, P., Spelke, E. S., & Gelman, R. (1990). Numerical abstraction by human infants. *Cognition, 36*, 97–127.

Steffe, L. P. (Ed.). (1975). *Children's capacity for learning mathematics. Soviet Studies in the Psychology of Learning and Teaching Mathematics* (Vol. 7). Chicago: University of Chicago.

Steffe, L. P. (2002). A new hypothesis concerning children's fractional knowledge. *Journal of Mathematical Behavior, 20*, 267–307.

Steffe, L. P., Cobb, P., & von Glasersfeld, E. (1988). *Construction of arithmetical meanings and strategies*. New York: Springer-Verlag.

Stigler, J. W., Fuson, K. C., Ham, M., & Kim, M. S. (1986). An analysis of addition and subtraction word problems in American and Soviet elementary mathematics textbooks. *Cognition and Instruction, 3*, 153–171.

Strauss, M. S. (1979). Abstraction of prototypical information by adults and 10-month-old infants. *Journal of Experimental Psychology: Human Learning and Memory, 5*, 618–632.

Strauss, M. S., & Curtis, L. E. (1981). Infant perception of numerosity. *Child Development, 52*, 1146–1152.

Thompson, P. W., & Saldanha, L. A. (2003). Fractions and multiplicative reasoning. In J. Kilpatrick, G. Martin, & D. Schifter (Eds.), *Research companion to the Principles and Standards for School Mathematics* (pp. 95–114). Reston, VA: National Council of Teachers of Mathematics.

Tomasello, M. (1999). *The cultural origins of human cognition*. Cambridge, MA: Harvard University Press.

Trick, L., & Pylyshyn, Z. (1994). Why are small and large numbers enumerated differently? A limited-capacity preattentive stage in vision. *Psychological Review, 101*, 80–102.

Uller, C., Carey, S., Huntley-Fenner, G., & Klatt, L. (1999). What representations might underlie infant numerical knowledge? *Cognitive Development, 14*, 1–36.

Uttal, D. H., Scudder, K. V., & DeLoache, J. S. (1997). Manipulatives as symbols: A new perspective on the use of concrete objects to teach mathematics. *Journal of Applied Developmental Psychology, 18*, 37–54.

Vamvakoussi, X., & Vosniadou, S. (2004). Understanding the structure of rational numbers: a conceptual change approach. *Learning and Instruction, 14*, 453–467.

Verge, C. G., & Bogartz, R. S. (1978). Functional measurement analysis of the development of dimensional coordination in children. *Journal of Experimental Child Psychology, 25*, 337–353.

Vergnaud, G. (1982). A classification of cognitive tasks and operations of thought involved in addition and subtraction problems. In T. P. Carpenter, J. M. Moser, & T. A. Romberg (Eds.), *Addition and subtraction: A cognitive perspective* (pp. 39–59). Hillsdale, NJ: Lawrence Erlbaum Associates.

Vergnaud, G. (1983). Multiplicative structures. In R. Lesh & M. Landau (Eds.), *Acquisition of mathematical concepts and processes* (pp. 127–174). New York: Academic Press.

Vorontsov, A. B. (n.d.). *The results of testing the quality of education at the time of finishing elementary school.* Moscow: International Association "Developmental Learning."

Vygotsky, L. S. (1978). *Mind in society.* Cambridge, MA: Harvard University Press.

Wagner, S. H., & Walters, J. (1982). A longitudinal analysis of early number concepts: From numbers to number. In G. E. Forman (Ed.), *Action and thought* (pp. 137–161). New York: Academic Press.

Wellman, H. M., & Phillips, A. T. (2001). Developing intentional understandings. In B. Malle, L. Moses, & D. Baldwin (Eds.), *Intentions and intentionality: Foundations of social cognition* (pp. 125–148). Cambridge, MA: MIT Press.

Wilkening, F. (1979). Combining stimulus dimensions in children's and adults' judgments of area: An information integration analysis. *Developmental Psychology, 15*, 25–33.

Wilkinson, A. C. (1976). Counting strategies and semantic analysis as applied to class inclusion. *Cognitive Psychology, 8*, 64–85.

Wolf, Y. (1995). Estimation of Euclidean quantity by 5- and 6-year-old children: Facilitating a multiplication rule. *Journal of Experimental Child Psychology, 59*, 49–75.

Wood, J. N., & Spelke, E. S. (2005a). Chronometric studies of numerical cognition in five-month-old infants. *Cognition, 97*, 23–39.

Wood, J. N., & Spelke, E. S. (2005b) Infants' enumeration of actions: Numerical discrimination and its signature limits. *Developmental Science, 8*, 173–181.

Wu, H. (1999, Fall). Basic skills versus conceptual understanding: A bogus dichotomy in mathematics education. *American Educator*, 1–7.

Wynn, K. (1990). Children's understanding of counting. *Cognition, 36*. 155–193.

Wynn, K. (1992a). Addition and subtraction by human infants. *Nature, 358*, 749–750.

Wynn, K. (1992b). Children's acquisition of the number words and the counting system. *Cognitive Psychology, 20*, 220–251.

Wynn, K. (1992c). Evidence against empiricist accounts of the origins of numerical knowledge. *Mind & Language, 7*, 315–332.

Wynn, K. (1995). Origins of numerical knowledge. *Mathematical Cognition, 1*, 35–60.

Wynn, K. (1996). Infants' individuation and enumeration of actions. *Psychological Science, 7,* 164–169.

Wynn, K., Bloom, P., & Chiang, W.–C. (2002). Enumeration of collective entities by 5-month-old infants. *Cognition, 83,* B55-B62.

Xu, F. (2003). Numerosity discrimination in infants: Evidence for two systems of representation. *Cognition, 89,* B15-B25.

Xu, F., & Spelke, E. S. (2000). Large-number discrimination in 6-month-old infants. *Cognition, 74,* B1-B11.

Xu, F., Spelke, E. S., & Goddard, S. (2005). Number sense in human infants. *Developmental Science, 8,* 88–101.

Yuzawa, M., Bart, W. M., & Yuzawa, M. (2000). Development of the ability to judge relative areas: Role of the procedure of placing one object on another. *Cognitive Development, 15,* 135–152.

Author Index

Subject Index

Definitions appear on pages in bold.